RETHINKING VIRTUAL PLACES

THE SPATIAL HUMANITIES

David J. Bodenhamer, John Corrigan, and
Trevor M. Harris, editors

RETHINKING VIRTUAL PLACES

ERIK MALCOLM CHAMPION

INDIANA UNIVERSITY PRESS

This book is a publication of

Indiana University Press
Office of Scholarly Publishing
Herman B Wells Library 350
1320 East 10th Street
Bloomington, Indiana 47405 USA

iupress.org

Manufactured in the United States of America

First printing 2021

Library of Congress Cataloging-in-Publication Data

Names: Champion, Erik, author.
Title: Rethinking virtual places / Erik M. Champion.
Description: Bloomington, Indiana : Indiana University Press, [2021] |
   Series: The spatial humanities | Includes bibliographical references and
   index.
Identifiers: LCCN 2021022473 (print) | LCCN 2021022474 (ebook) | ISBN
   9780253058348 (hardback) | ISBN 9780253058355 (paperback) | ISBN
   9780253058362 (ebook)
Subjects: LCSH: Human-computer interaction. | Virtual reality—Philosophy. |
   Environmental psychology. | Cyberspace. | Computer games—Design.
Classification: LCC QA76.9.H85 C4243 2021 (print) | LCC QA76.9.H85 (ebook) | DDC
   004.01/9—dc23
LC record available at https://lccn.loc.gov/2021022473
LC ebook record available at https://lccn.loc.gov/2021022474

CONTENTS

FOREWORD

I WROTE MY FIRST COMPUTER GAMES (ONE WAS A TEXT-BASED SPORTS GAME based on simple physics; the other, a single-player Dungeons & Dragons–type game, was inspired by the Stephen Jackson interactive books) around 1982. They were on a programmable calculator with a huge one-and-a-half-kilobyte memory and a twenty-digit display, so graphics were an impossible dream; the operations had to do all the work. I had to use mathematic commands to extract ten different values from a single number to create a large number of rooms, treasures, and monsters. They were both very popular with my high school classmates, but I had no idea why they "worked."

I discovered virtual reality (VR) around the end of 1990 while I was working in Japan building roads. During a brief break, a friend and I found a VR system (CyberGlove and headgear) running in the back of a furniture shop in a giant downtown building. In 2004, I had the opportunity to revisit Japan and attend VSMM2004 in Gifu, where Professor Bob Stone recounted a history of VR and its usability and decried that very system for its chunkiness and user unfriendliness. And yet even now I can remember the shock of putting my hand under a running virtual tap and feeling the water.

My encounter with this VR system was a kind of personal Ragnarök. I had just finished a master's project in three-dimensional computer-aided design and stage design, and it struck me with some dread that this crude VR system could do away with professional spatial designers. In the last three decades, my fears do not seem to have been realized, and I am very interested as to why this is so. Game design and online worlds have destroyed virtual reality modeling language (VRML) and the other would-be contenders, technical wonders have appeared and disappeared overnight, and the ongoing debate over presence versus immersion is still being fought. The graphics technology has leaped ahead, and yet what we are doing inside these games and virtual worlds, and how these worlds are being presented to us, is still flat and caricatured. And what we learn from these experiences is not sensorially evocative or personalized and spatially shared but rather projected onto the flat box of a computer screen.

As members of the general public, do we truly get the opportunity to interact with digital media in a thematically appropriate and meaningful way? Is there a way in which we can dissolve the screen? Can we create experiences that aren't entered and modified by typing on an electric keyboard? Can the content itself be imaginatively reschematized so that it physically or virtually molds the user experience without destroying individual feelings of exploring, contributing, and sharing? How does this data come alive?

I am also very interested in what salient details, features, and triggers help immerse people and to what extent the rich detail from their immersive experience can be shared with others inside a "world" or communicated to spectators outside that world. How can virtual creations involving huge changes in scale and perspective over space and time be presented to people in such a way that they are not dwarfed by the experience but can fluidly explore and reposition these changes in dimension, scale, and perspective?

ACKNOWLEDGMENTS

I AM GRATEFUL TO THE TEAM FROM INDIANA UNIVERSITY PRESS FOR THEIR work on this publication. I would especially like to thank Jennika Baines for her guidance and support in developing this book as well as the series editors for their support. Many anonymous reviewers and experts assessed this book for its applicability and impact to academia, industry, and the public sector; I thank them and those who graciously allowed me to include their images. Your support and feedback have been greatly appreciated. I would like to thank Dr. Jakub Majewska and Dr. Jeffrey Jacobson for their suggestions and feedback on some of the ideas outlined in this book.

RETHINKING VIRTUAL PLACES

INTRODUCTION
Rethinking Virtual Places

Why Design Virtual Places?

Why should we design virtual places? For distant places hard to reach, discarded, incomplete, or contested, constraints and affordances can be added that reveal some of the potential experiences they offer with none or little of the risk of physically going to them. While it is possible that one day, the development of overpowering virtual sensations and vivid imagery may compel us to lose interest in the real world, or become manipulated by other, "unreal" ones (a favorite theme of Hollywood writers), such days are far in the future. Of more immediate concern are the risks to social skills, health, and our ability to concentrate and pay attention for long periods of time.

This book was originally planned to be titled *Designing the 'Place' of Virtual Space*, but *Rethinking Virtual Places: Dwelling, Culture, Care* is more appropriate. Rather than providing a guide or even a mantra for designing (and developing) virtual places, this book is a collection of essays that tries to push the writing and practice of place philosophy and place design toward a more directly useful and testable set of hypotheses and heuristics. The aim is to provide something to chew on for those of you who wish to design virtual places in answer to theories of the real world or critique virtual places as a not entirely new field that has both more and less in common with real-world place design than many have suspected.

I will also investigate why so many virtual places are sterile, dead, or lifeless and why, despite all the criticism of virtual museums and other simulations, we keep building them and hosting them on the web or as standalone virtual environments. Each chapter aims to focus on a central argument and cover a central term and its related definition or theoretical premise, prove or disprove at least one previous understanding or proposal, or critically examine at least one case study.

Why a Book if So Many Virtual Places and Virtual Worlds Have Failed?

Despite the many architects talking about virtual environments in the early 1990s (Novak 2002, 2015; Packer and Jordan 2002; Wiltshire 2014), there is relatively little publicly accessible research on making, experiencing, and critiquing virtual places, and what is available is scattered among conference papers, book chapters, and edited collections (Champion 2011). The most relevant research literature is more likely to be found in the computational sciences and is not often or easily accessed by humanities scholars. As for the projects these papers discuss, they, too, are difficult to find (a point explored further in chapter 10).

I have an overall purpose here: to communicate with humanities scholars the importance of understanding how digital and virtual places are designed, experienced, and critiqued. I suggest that technology is *not* the fundamental problem in designing virtual places. Are there specific needs or requirements of real places that prevent us from relying on digital media and "online world" experts? Or is it not so much that the new tools are currently too cumbersome or unreliable but that our conventional understanding of place design and place-related knowledge and information needs to change?

Arguably, the subject areas of the humanities have traditionally been dominated by, or have exclusively been in, two dimensions. I suggest the terms *place*, *cultural presence*, *game*, and *world* are critically significant, especially from an interactively platial rather than merely spatial perspective. Clearer definitions would enrich the understanding and use of these terms and reveal the importance of real-world place design *and* virtual world design in terms of interaction, immersion, and meaning. Simpler and clearer terms may help us cut across artificial and opaque disciplinary boundaries.

Admittedly, various disciplines will be tempted to claim they have solved their problems. Virtual reality developers, presence researchers, and human-computer interaction evaluators can point to decades of experiments; architects can claim interactive places are merely a subdomain of architecture; computer-aided design developers may declare their tools are sufficiently sophisticated; and game designers may argue (and indeed have argued) that games are interactive places par excellence. Although I will borrow from the aforementioned fields, I will question all these premises.

These problems are of complex, interwoven, and multidisciplinary importance, but for clarity's sake, I have ordered my answers into chapters that are grouped around four primary issues.

How can we work across the divides of place design and place philosophy? The chapters on virtual museums, dead and dying online worlds, architecture, and virtual place theory revolve around this issue.

Why is interaction design in virtual places so difficult? I also look at how we can improve prototyping and how mechanics are so often underappreciated. Do they help separate virtual places from worlds, realms, environments, and realities? This issue is also touched on in the chapter on culture. Virtual cultural places are extremely difficult to design, and I try to explain here why and what we can do about it.

How do we learn from "place"? Interactive places and our use of our mental and physical capabilities are both tied into this central question. The body is both our center and our interface, but the early design of place as a screen has not helped contextual immersivity (as opposed to system immersivity). A related issue is a lack of cultural significance in virtual places, where culture and physical embodiment are often separated. I question this simple division.

How can we integrate the virtual place experience with design, evaluation, and learning from that experience? The final chapters on evaluation and platforms address this question as well as how we can move from technical solutions to community-supporting and community-supported places.

I am not convinced we fully understand the design and experience of real places, so I have focused on virtual places that are inspired by elements and themes of the real, not parasitically, but also not in terms of pure virtuality. Only if I felt confident that I understood how virtual places best relate to real places, would I then examine how to best explore the concept of virtuality.

References

Champion, Erik. 2011. *Playing with the Past*. London: Springer.

Novak, Marcos. 2002. "Liquid Architectures in Cyberspace (1991)." In *Multimedia: From Wagner to Virtual Reality*, edited by Randall Packer and Ken Jordan, 272. New York: W. W. Norton.

———. 2015. "Transmitting Architecture: The Transphysical City (1996)." C Theory. Last modified May 3, 2016. Accessed August 2, 2017. hhttp://journals.uvic.ca/index.php /ctheory/article/view/14653/5520.

Packer, Randall, and Ken Jordan, eds. 2002. *Multimedia: From Wagner to Virtual Reality*. New York: W. W. Norton.

Wiltshire, Alex. 2014. "Virtual Reality: The 1990s Technology Set to Change the World of Design." *de zeen* Magazine. Last modified May 3, 2016. Accessed August 2, 2017. http:// www.dezeen.com/2014/03/30/oculus-rift-virtual-reality-new-dimension-design.

chapter one

A POTTED HISTORY OF VIRTUAL REALITY

IN THIS CHAPTER, I WILL FOLLOW FOUR THREADS: SCIENCE FICTION, THE emphasis of virtual reality (VR) on vision, the misleading charms of realism, and the ludic corruption (through developments in in-game content and related interfaces) that home entertainment systems and related interactive devices have had on a sense of place. I will attempt to relay not a comprehensive history or explanation of VR but an overview of the development of VR and its relation to how we design and experience virtual places.

Historical Highlights of VR

The forerunner to VR may be considered the 1838 stereoscope (Virtual Reality Society 2018), with its twin mirrors combining to project a single image, which "eventually developed into the View-Master, patented in 1939 and [is] still produced today." Nineteenth-century panorama technology blurred the distinction between two-dimensional and three-dimensional space, as did, for example, the Vitarama, an eleven projector–based system that was invented for the 1939 New York World's Fair by Fred Waller and Ralph Walker (*Encyclopaedia Britannica* 2014; Science Museum Group n.d.). Waller and Walker also developed, using a synchronized three-projector system, the Cinerama widescreen film format, the first film for which was presented in 1952 (Lowood 2015). It did not require special recording equipment (Cook and Sklar 2019), but despite the initial audience reaction at the 1952 premiere (Mullen 1952/1998), it soon proved too expensive to keep the new technology commercially viable (Horak 2016). However, there are Cinerama theaters in operation today, including one in Seattle, all currently closed due to the coronavirus. (See fig. 1.1.)

Morton Heilig's 1957 Sensorama Simulator (patented in 1962) allowed people to view mostly passive three-dimensional films (Brockwell 2016). For his 1962 doctoral thesis research, Ivan Sutherland was inspired to invent the Sketchpad,

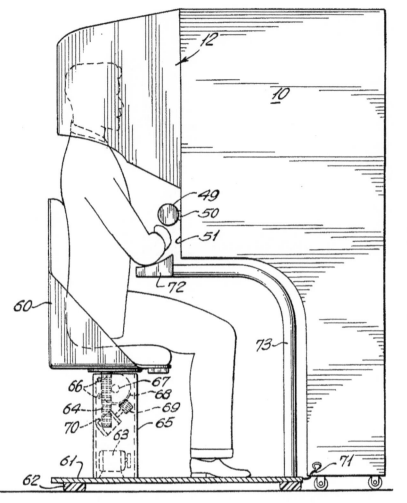

Figure 1.1 Sensorama by Morton Leonard Heilig. https://en.wikipedia.org/wiki/Sensorama. Heilig M. (1962). US Patent #3,050,870, October 1, 1961, Public Domain, uploaded February 26, 2008.

the forerunner to computer-aided design (CAD) systems today, by Memex from "As We May Think" by Vannevar Bush (1945). Sutherland also invented the Ultimate Display (1965) (Sterling 2009) and the world's first head-mounted display (HMD), nicknamed the "Sword of Damocles" (Lowood 2015). Not only did these machines exist and work, but you can also buy one today. You, too, could be the proud owner of the 1962 version of the Sensorama Machine (see USC School of Cinematic Arts 2021). (See fig. 1.2.)

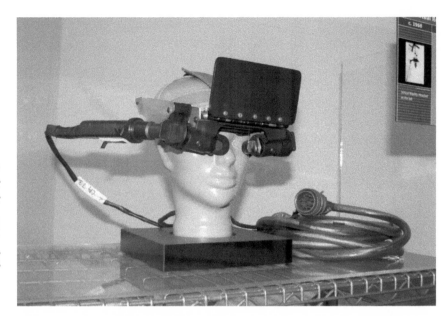

Figure 1.2 Sword of Damocles. Copyright Pargon, Flickr. https://www.flickr.com/photos/pargon /2444155973. April 26, 2008, CC BY 2.0.

In 1968, Douglas Engelbart and his team (at the Augmentation Research Center, Stanford Research Institute) presented, for the first time in the world, a ninety-minute public multimedia demonstration of a networked computer system. The system included a computer mouse and a two-dimensional display with editing capability, hypermedia, multiple windows, and video teleconferencing. As a young man, Engelbart had "dreamed of 'flying' through a variety of information spaces." (See fig. 1.3.)

The term *virtual environment* was allegedly coined at the Massachusetts Institute of Technology (MIT) around 1978, when a team there designed the Aspen Movie Map project (Evenden 2016). The three-dimensional building models had facades generated by texture-mapped photos, and their two-dimensional screen coordinates were collated into a database of buildings so that data could be hyperlinked to more data sources.

Intuitive and thematic entertainment interfaces and devices took a while to appear (table 1.1). One example was Mattel's 1989 Power Glove, which was the "first video game controller that allow[ed] players to operate Nintendo games with intuitive hand gestures" but also was a commercial failure and a disappointing device for game play ("Power Glove" n.d.). However, it has been resurrected recently for hobbyists.

Definitions

Just as with definitions of *presence* and *immersion*, definitions of VR seem to concentrate on experiential or technical explanations. As John Steuer (1992) has remarked,

Figure 1.3 MIT Aspen Movie Map, 1980. Credit: MIT Architecture Machine Group. Photo by Robert Mohl. The image is also at https://medium.com/facebook-design-business-tools /enterprise-software-design-a-call-to-arms-dd420d33850b.

Table 1.1. VR Inventions

Year	Invention	Significance
1838	The stereoscope (Charles Wheatstone)	A pioneering device that although simple in construction, levered human binocular vision to create what seemed to be a real three-dimensional object.
1849	The lenticular stereoscope (David Brewster)	The addition of lenses meant the stereoscope could be small enough to be handheld.
1935	Pygmalion Spectacles (Stanley G. Weinbaum)	Goggles that provided movie sight and sound, with characters that interacted with the wearer: a fictional device that foreshadowed virtual reality.
1937	Vitarama (Frederic Waller, 1937 New York Fair)	Eleven-projector system that led to the development of Cinerama (a synchronized three-projector system).
1938	*Virtual reality* coined by Antonin Artaud: *Le Théâtre et son double*	Earliest published date of "virtual reality" (la réalité virtuelle").

(*Continued*)

Table 1.1. *Continued*

Year	Invention	Significance
1939	The View-Master (William Gruber)	Leveraging recent developments in color photography, featuring seven stereoscopic three-dimensional pairs of transparent but high-quality color photos, suitable for tourism.
1943	First computer: ENIAC (electronic numerical integrator and computer)	At the University of Pennsylvania, the first large-scale electronic computer.
1962	Sensorama (derived from an earlier "Experience Theatre" prototype)	Considered one of the earliest VR systems.
1968	Virtual Reality Headset Prototype (Ivan Sutherland and Bob Sproull)	Nicknamed the Sword of Damocles, it was the forerunner of head-mounted displays (HMDs), connecting to a computer, not a camera.
1968– 69	Networked computers	The 1969 ARPANET foreshadowed the internet and was demonstrated in public in 1968.
1968	Mouse demo	Douglas Engelbart gave a demonstration of the first computer mouse (Tweney 2010).
1970s	Videoplace	Projectors, video cameras, special-purpose hardware, and on-screen user silhouettes placed users within an interactive environment.
1978	First multi-user dungeon (MUD)	Multi-user dungeon, text-based, one of the first virtual worlds (Roy Trubshaw, Richard Bartle). Inspired by *Zork* (1977), which was created by MIT students who, in turn, were inspired by the 1975 game *Adventure*).
1978	Aspen Movie Map	Pioneering three-dimensional hypermedia system gave an impression of a virtual tour through Aspen Colorado. Methods foreshadowed Google Maps.
1991	Ubiquitous computing	In his article "The Computer for the 21st Century," Mark Weiser (1999) introduced the concept of ubiquitous computing.

Table 1.1. *Continued*

Year	Invention	Significance
1992	University of Illinois at Chicago presented the first Cave Automatic Virtual Environment (CAVE)	CAVE was a VR theater, a cube with ten-square-foot walls onto which images were projected so that users were surrounded by sights and sounds. One or more people wearing lightweight stereoscopic glasses walked freely in the room, their head and eye movements tracked to adjust the imagery, and they interacted with three-dimensional virtual objects by manipulating a wand-like device with three buttons.
1997	Virtual reality modeling language (VRML) version 2.0	VRML became an ISO standard (a test version was released in 1994). Its creators intended it to be a "platform-independent way to send 3D worlds across the Internet" (Couch n.d.).
2016	Oculus VR (Kickstarted in 2012, bought by Facebook in 2014)	With two development kits, a low price point, and comfort but also acceptable viewing, the Oculus Rift brought VR to the consumer; required cables (tethered).
2016	Microsoft HoloLens 1 released for preorder sales	Pro-consumer-priced MR (see-through) "smartglasses"; stand-alone device; untethered; version 2 was released in 2019.
2016	HTC Vive	Consumer-level VR via a HMD connected to a powerful computer; tethered.
2016	PlayStation VR	Consumer-level VR with HMD connected to PlayStation IV game console (PS VR); tethered.
2017	Magic Leap (stand-alone MR device)	Well-marketed yet until recently a rather mysterious stand-alone AR device at the pro-consumer level; untethered.
2019	The Oculus Quest	Cheap, easy to configure, without the need for an external PC or wires, and with free hand tracking available, it could be the VR headset that finally makes VR accessible and affordable for the general public.

Figure 1.4 CAVE: A user in the CAVE™. Photo by Roberta Dupuis-Devlin, Electronic Visualization Laboratory, the University of Illinois at Chicago, USA. Copyright EVL with permission.

popular media has tended to base VR on notions of technology rather than experience. Interestingly, these definitions are vision based but don't clearly state that for a full VR experience, the head of the participant should be fully tracked (when you turn your head, the VR space automatically adjusts so that your eyes convince you that you are moving in real, actual space), and 360-degree video is often confused with full VR (Smith 2015; Goldman and Falcone 2016). (See fig. 1.4.)

Jack Loomis (2016) argues that definitions of VR have blurred and that thanks to HMDs and improved phone cameras, 360-degree panoramas count as VR. For him, the compelling distinction is presence: "the experience of being within a compellingly realistic 3D world."

However, early devices and projects provided an experience that was not, as far as I know, called virtual reality. Although the term was used much earlier in French theater, as an explicitly computational term, *virtual reality* has been attributed to computer scientist Jaron Lanier in 1987 (Virtual Reality Society n.d.). Even today, thirty years later, definitions vary.

Bruce Damer and Randy Hinrichs (2014, 17), in *The Oxford Handbook of Virtual Reality*, quote Michael Heim's 1992 definition: "Virtual reality is a technology that convinces the participant that he or she is actually in another place by substituting the primary sensory input with data received produced by a computer . . . when the virtual world becomes a workspace and the user identifies with the virtual body and feels a sense of belonging to a virtual community."

This definition relies more on persuasion and identity. Interestingly, although Damer and Hinrichs (2014, 19) declared that virtual worlds need to be virtual places, they never defined *place* (which is only in *The Oxford Handbook of Virtuality* index once, under *virtual places*) despite the fact that "place" is also part of Heim's definition of virtual place. Place does not seem to be a concern for the forty-three chapters of *The Oxford Handbook of Virtuality* (Grimshaw 2013), except, perhaps, for my chapter. Some of the authors do not contrast VR with the real world. For example, Brian Massumi (2014, 55–79) argues that virtuality is a dimension of reality. Another possible reason *place* is not fully defined or addressed in that volume is that careful use of terms in this field is infrequent: for example, Heim (2014) notes the terms *virtual reality* and *cyberspace* have been used loosely.

The online *Oxford English Dictionary* (*English Oxford Living Dictionaries* n.d.) defines *virtual reality* clearly: "the computer-generated simulation of a three-dimensional image or environment that can be interacted with in a seemingly real or physical way by a person using special electronic equipment, such as a helmet with a screen inside or gloves fitted with sensors."

For the *Encyclopedia Britannica*, Henry E. Lowood (2018b) defined VR in terms of display glasses and other pieces of equipment, not as a successful experience of a place that one is not physically present in: "the use of computer modeling and simulation that enables a person to interact with an artificial three-dimensional (3-D) visual or other sensory environment. VR applications immerse the user in a computer-generated environment that simulates reality through the use of interactive devices, which send and receive information and are worn as goggles, headsets, gloves, or body suits."

The *Online Cambridge Dictionary* (n.d.) differs markedly: "[Virtual reality is] a set of images and sounds, produced by a computer, that seem to represent a place or a situation that a person can take part in." The *Merriam-Webster* (n.d.) definition differs as well: "an artificial environment which is experienced through sensory stimuli (such as sights and sounds) provided by a computer and in which one's actions partially determine what happens in the environment; also: the technology used to create or access a virtual reality."

Ishbel Duncan, Alan Miller, and Shangyi Jiang (2012, 950) defined *virtual worlds* as follows: "A Virtual World can be defined as visual environments that have been developed further from three-dimensional (3-D) web-based technologies to form multi-user virtual environments (MUVEs) such as Second Life."

So far, virtual worlds are not usually VR environments but rather online, multiplayer, three-dimensional digital environments. According to John Wann and Mark Mon-Williams (1996, 833), "A Virtual Environment (VE) is a representation that 'capitalizes upon natural aspects of human perception by extending visual information in three spatial dimensions.' The typical image of a person in goggles, pawing at the air as they experience a VE/VW [Virtual World] is a common misconception of what VR is, but this interface of VR is one which is highly immersive for the user."

And according to Brian Jackson (2015), "Virtual Reality (VR) is the use of computer technology to create a simulated environment. Unlike traditional user interfaces, VR places the user inside an experience. Instead of viewing a screen in front of them, users are immersed and able to interact with 3D worlds. By simulating as many senses as possible, such as vision, hearing, touch, even smell, the computer is transformed into a gatekeeper to this artificial world. The only limits to near-real VR experiences are the availability of content and cheap computing power."

Before moving on, I need to qualify that if definitions rely on subjective factors, then the definition does depend on the participant, be it their sense of engagement, their stereovision, their attention, or their discomfort. Jackson's definition seems to rely on a premise that VR will automatically create "an experience," fully interactive and completely immersive, but this is an ambitious guarantee.

Furthermore, VR is *not* just the use of computer technology to create a simulated environment, because it does not exclude traditional computer display–based three-dimensional simulations. Researchers also seem to use the phrases *digital environments* and *virtual environments* interchangeably. While we might distinguish them by saying that digital environments do not have to be three-dimensional and virtual environments do, in practice I don't hear people talking about two-dimensional virtual (or digital) environments, nor do they reserve virtual environments for only fully head-tracked digital three-dimensional environments.

Differences between Virtual Reality and Augmented Reality

Brian Jackson (2015) explains VR and augmented reality (AR) as follows:

> Virtual Reality and Augmented Reality are two sides of the same coin. You could think of Augmented Reality as VR with one foot in the real world: Augmented Reality simulates artificial objects in the real environment; Virtual Reality creates an artificial environment to inhabit.
>
> In Augmented Reality, the computer uses sensors and algorithms to determine the position and orientation of a camera. AR technology then renders the 3D graphics as they would appear from the viewpoint of the camera, superimposing the computer-generated images over a user's view of the real world.
>
> In Virtual Reality, the computer uses similar sensors and math. However, rather than locating a real camera within a physical environment, the position of the user's eyes are located within the simulated environment. If the user's head turns, the graphics react accordingly. Rather than compositing virtual objects and a real scene, VR technology creates a convincing, interactive world for the user.

This is a clear, if not ideal, definition, as few VR projects are truly inhabitable, and it does help us distinguish VR from AR. AR generally places computer-rendered objects in the real world via a screen (or glasses or visor), and that object's three-dimensional coordinates are supposed to be precisely calibrated within the real world (although this definition is dissipating); however, typically the participant is only roughly located in relation to the augmented objects, which tend to float, hover, or otherwise obstruct the physical space.

The Cognitive Load of AR

AR is a little harder to define in practice. I suggest that AR calculates real-world data to superimpose a digital simulation onto a camera, screen, or see-through display to show the real world or provide nonvisual data to the participant based on their view or position relative to the real world. Unfortunately, many phone applications say they provide AR when they merely retrieve the user's latitude and longitude and let a digital object or text hover approximately over a spot on the viewfinder of the phone's camera. I'd prefer to call that type of rough-and-ready proto-AR a layered or collaged reality.

An exacting three-dimensional-calibrated definition of the term *augmented* implies the digitally generated additional content not only supplements but also improves the real world (Azuma 2004). Further, many earlier uses and descriptions of AR in projects and publications assumed AR had to be vision based; however, I suggest nonsighted people also experience reality.

Additionally, AR implies the physical content is most important and the digital is a smaller improvement to the underlying reality; however, I assert that the digital content mixed with the real-world content could actually create an experience of a totally different reality, world, or place. Therefore, I prefer the term *mixed reality* (MR), although it has traditionally been defined more vaguely (fig. 1.5) as "the merging of real and virtual worlds somewhere along the 'virtuality continuum' which connects completely real environments to completely virtual ones." In other words, MR is a digitally provided experience somewhere between AR and VR (Milgram and Kishino 1994).

In their book, Tobias Hollerer and Dieter Schmalstieg (2016) argue that AR has a problem. The computer-generated imagery of the film world creates its own world, but AR must relate to what people are interested in in the real world, creating more cognitive loading for people: they have to operate in a real world and an AR-altered real world.

Mixed Reality

AR/MR is predicted to take precedence over VR, but it is still early days. AR/MR also faces conceptual challenges: it is overly vision focused; people are confused by the distinction between the two terms; people have different ideas about the term *reality*; and there is confusion between equipmental system immersivity and a subjective sense of presence (who decides it is successful: the test scores, the technical specifications, or the participant's subjective experience?). Is AR necessarily a transparent experience, a form of invisible computing, where the digital interface and other digital augmentations disappear and there is no connection between the real and the virtual?

Figure 1.5 Milgram Spectrum (Milgram, Takemura, Utsumi, and Kishino), https://en.wikipedia.org/wiki/Reality%E2%80%93virtuality_continuum#/media/File:Virtuality_Continuum_2.jpg. Public Domain, uploaded November 22, 2007.

The context of *place* is missing from VR. While VR is subjective, it is too often seen as only objective, as if technology provides a consistent immersive experience for everyone. By definition, VR has been locked in place with technological parameters, not subjective ones, with a strong focus on visual parameters. The concept of *reality* in VR has been seldom discussed, let alone the process for how people can communicate to each other about their virtual experiences or the idea of whether their virtual experiences should be incorporated into the virtual world itself. For a virtual place, this feedback cycle is not simply nice to have; it is essential.

In addition to this technical straitjacket, VR lacks rich, engaging content and meaningful connections to a real-world context. On the other hand, implementation is quicker now, leading to more idea-based development than before. VR now overlaps with games, and AR is increasingly dominating market share. Designing and deploying these applications for the general public is accelerating, with the trend moving away from corporate showcases and research labs and toward garage-level development.

Place-Confounding Issues

From Science Fiction to Science Fact

Despite being promoted through advanced equipment with elevated values of scale, speed, performance, lightness, and ubiquity, VR has no clear logical development, because it is heavily dependent on individuals and market forces. A short history of VR will be highly subjective, and it won't fully explain why some inventions and concepts have succeeded while others failed or what the forerunners in the future will be; however, by detailing it, I can point out some general threads.

Notably, and somewhat predictably, the notion of VR entered the zeitgeist via science fiction, with Stanley G. Weinbaum's 1935 short story "Pygmalion's Spectacles." This vision of VR told of a goggle-based contraption that offered users a holistic holographic experience that went as far as to include touch and olfactory elements.

Robots came into being in 1961 on a car factory floor (Laumond 2012), but the idea behind robots and physical incarnations of them have been highly influenced by science fiction, especially the 1950 book *I, Robot* (and the related theory, the three laws of robotics, developed in 1942) by the writer Isaac Asimov; however, his robot science fiction series, consisting of thirty-eight short stories and three novels, started in 1939 or 1940.

The influence of science fiction reached past the development of flying cars, robots, and stories of virtual places. The Sega VR (1991), arguably the first consumer VR headset (Dormehl 2017), may have been influenced by *RoboCop* and *The Day the Earth Stood Still*, "with a sleek black plastic design that concealed LCDs, stereo headphones, and internal 'inertial sensors' for tracking head movement," and in a talk entitled "A Sense of Place" (CES 2006), Google's chief technology advocate Michael T. Jones (Bisson 2008) apparently "admitted that Google Maps on the iPhone was his first attempt at creating a [Star Trek] tricorder."

Science fiction's influence also extended to VR-related programming. Former SGI employee Brian McCloskey revealed *Snow Crash* was the inspiration for Cosmo Software: "The original notion was that we would all be donning our 3D 'avatars,' virtual representations of ourselves, as we headed into the vast virtual worlds of cyberspace to meet and greet each other. If you've read the book 'Snow Crash,' you know what I mean. (When I worked for SGI's Cosmo Software, developer of the leading VRML player, it was mandatory reading.)"

Milner (2012) defined dystopia as "an imaginary world deliberately conceived as being worse than our own; a utopian one conceived as better." While VR is synonymous with precision and accuracy and the promise of the future, it has been strongly influenced by science fiction and, therefore, has reveled in dystopic scenescapes that one does not interact with, let alone modify.

VR Has Been Vision Focused

The dystopic scenescapes of VR have been overwhelmingly visual, but not interactive. John Steuer (1992) noted that popular media has tended to base VR around notions of technology rather than experience. Many dictionary definitions are technology based rather than experience based, although they often include the unclear criterion that VR needs to seem "real." For example, I noted earlier that the online *Oxford English Dictionary* (*English Oxford Living Dictionaries* n.d.) defines *virtual reality* as "requiring interaction in a seemingly real or physical way."

Although most VR examples emphasize vision, not "[an]other sensory environment," there is huge market potential to involve more of the senses. Lowood further said VR requires a computer-generated environment "simulating reality" through the use of interactive devices ("goggles, headsets, gloves, or bodysuits"), but he also declared VR involves the "'illusion of being there' (telepresence) [which] is effected by motion sensors that pick up the user's movements and adjust the view on the screen accordingly, usually in real time."

This is a conventional definition of VR (Pan and Hamilton 2018), based on the fundament of head tracking. For example, walking may seem trivial, but walking in VR is not. Many computer scientists would argue that VR requires head tracking along with a digital simulation of a three-dimensional environment that surrounds the participant and appears to be, and preferably is, interactive (for more information and a more demanding definition, see Jackson [2015]). The entire environment needs to dynamically update convincingly fast whether one moves one's head or one's feet. This is both technically and experientially challenging. The definition implies two conditions: a digitally simulated "reality" or environment that changes according to the participant's location and orientation *and* a participant's belief that the digital simulation is their primary environment.

The provision of precise, quick, and stable head-tracking equipment is not always sufficient for many people. Head-tracking the dynamic (free) viewpoint of a human in a three-dimensional digitally projected or displayed space does not necessitate that the human participant believes or acts in that "virtual reality." A comprehensive definition should be based on the creative synergy of hardware, software, and beliefs (or observable actions and reactions)—in other words, both the technology and the *subjective experience* of being immersed in a digital environment.

Early Games Were Not Places

What is arguably considered the first game was created by a physicist in 1958 (Tretkoff 2008; Guins 2017; BNL n.d.). The history is complicated and contentious, though, for in 1952, for his PhD thesis at the University of Cambridge, A. S. Douglas created a graphical computer game version of tic-tac-toe (Winter 2018a). It was programmed on an EDSAC vacuum-tube computer, which had a cathode ray tube. Because of EDSAC's uniqueness, no one could play the game outside of the University of Cambridge.

David Winter (2018b) credits Ralph H. Baer as "inventor of the video game" for developing video games in the 1960s, especially *Chase* (1967) (from an idea he had in 1951), which Winter differentiates from a cathode ray tube "shooting game" proposal by Thomas T. Goldsmith Jr. and Estle Ray Mann (Walker 2016) because their 1948 patent did not rely on generating and sending video signals. Yet, arguably, the first well-known and widely played game intended for the computer was *SpaceWar!* invented by Steve Russell at MIT on an MIT PDP-1 mainframe computer (Bellis 2018).

Doom was released by id in 1993; it followed 1992's *Wolfenstein 3D* by Apogee but included technical improvements, the concept of a "death match," and the ability for non-id authors to add levels. Henry E. Lowood (2018a) described 1993's *Doom* by id as the "first-person shooter electronic game released in December 1993 that changed the direction of almost every aspect of personal computer (PC) games, from graphics and networking technology to styles of play, notions of authorship, and public scrutiny of game content." (See table 1.2.)

Computer games have relied heavily on more twitch-based games (testing player reactions) and visuals, but far less on sound and smell, while touch

Table 1.2. Game Inventions

Year	Invention	Significance	Inventor
1948	"Cathode Ray Tube Amusement Device" patent	Arguably first computer game patent (but not necessarily a video game?)	Goldsmith & Mann
1950	*Bertie the Brain*	Earliest known publicly demonstrated electronic game. Bertie the Brain was an arcade game version of tic-tac-toe, but it used lights, not a video screen.	Josef Kates
1952	*Tic-Tac-Toe*	First graphical computer game.	A. S. Douglas
1958	*Tennis for Two*	First video game (disputably). *Tennis for Two* was created on a Brookhaven National Laboratory oscilloscope and played by the public (analog and hardwired, but could not be programmed).	William Higinbotham
1962	*SpaceWar!*	The first well-known and widely played game intended for computers.	Steve Russell, MIT
1967	*Chase* (and "Brown Box" console video system)	Arguably the first commercial video game console invented.	Ralph Baer
1971	*Computer Space* (based on Baer's table tennis game)	The first arcade game (disputably).	Nolan Bushnell, Atari
1972	*Pong* (based on Baer's table tennis game)	Well-known early video game (tennis simulator).	Nolan Bushnell, Atari
1972	*The Odyssey*	First commercial home video game console.	Magnavox
1975	*Colossal Cave Adventure* (1975–76)	Prototype for text-based computer games and interactive fiction. Inspired *Zork* (1977), *MUD* (1978).	Will Crowther
1976	Fairchild Video Entertainment System (later Channel)	The first programmable home video game console, it used a new microchip.	Fairchild
1991–97	*Neverwinter Nights* (not the same as the game series a decade later)	"The first graphical MMORPG" (massively multiplayer online role-playing game) (Barton 2008; Anon 2019).	Stormfront Studios
1993	*DOOM*	Known as the first first-person shooter and established competitive multiplayer gaming as the leading-edge category of games on personal computers, defining a game genre.	DOOM: id Software

Figure 1.6 Microsoft HoloLens Version 1. Erik Champion.

interfaces have been difficult to research or to market. The development of VR technology in terms of what it presents has not gone hand in hand with interaction experience; the latter has been taken up by game design, but in recent years, the two fields have begun to converge again. This is not completely true, however; for example, the mixed-reality Microsoft HoloLens started life as a developer-led product for the home consumer entertainment market, but its repurposing for a large project for the US Army has seen a great deal of its second version purchased directly by the military. Consumers had to wait. (See fig. 1.6.)

However, overall, I think my observation stands: VR has not focused on what people do *in* place but what people can view *of* place. This is also partly due to technical problems, for example, experiencing the sensation of walking when one is virtually present in a place rather than physically present.

Place Has "Between-ness"

There are few between-place experiences in VR. Reasons for this include their development having a military focus, built environment (as in architectural models) focus, reaction-speed focus, and living-room chair theme (i.e., walking in place is difficult). Where is the *encounter* of space? Creating avatars or other virtual representations of people so that they can *meet* other people has been difficult. The early chat rooms did not know how to leverage their limited three-dimensional spaces for communication and so developed ancillary voice-chat and video-chat applications. Moving back to more traditional means of communication has solved the more practical issues of communicating with friends or strangers, but it has also taken away the incentive to develop new forms of virtual person-to-person communication, as relayed or modified via platial interaction.

How do people interact via spaces? This question is discussed in chapters 6 and 7, but here I would just add that because virtual places have typically been static backgrounds, there has not been a shared framework of taking away or adding to places. Even the multiplayer-networked computer games based around shooting each other typically don't change the place; projectile damage on walls or dead bodies strewn around scenes of battle are often fleetingly shown on each other's screens, but they are erased after a few seconds. This also means that a feedback system of how participants experienced, interacted with, and modified a space is not evident to others.

Although some of the early games previously mentioned were multiplayer (or, at least, two player), very few were collaborative spaces. And seated VR often relies on a sweet spot for a single person. This is clear in stereo walls that are CAVE-like or curved; some seated positions are better and more immersive than others, and furthermore, you don't know exactly where the other person is looking. Luckily, MR has the ability to overlay or insert images, videos, or three-dimensional models into the historical place, and they are improving to the point where you can gain an idea of where the participant is looking and what they are responding to (fig. 1.7).

VR: Less about Realism, More about Imaginative Destination

In 1838, Charles Wheatstone's research demonstrated that the brain processes the different two-dimensional images from each eye into a single object of three dimensions. Viewing two side-by-side stereoscopic images or photos through a stereoscope gave the user a sense of depth and immersion. The later development of the popular View-Master stereoscope (patented 1939) was used for "virtual tourism." The design principles of the stereoscope are used today in the popular Google Cardboard and low-budget VR HMDs for mobile phones.

Tourism is about places, but it is more than just visiting a place; it is also about traveling to a place to experience it. The logistics of traveling to wonderful and popular places are often considerable. Many cannot visit due to costs, the time required, or other personal factors. Sometimes these places are closed, inaccessible, or suffering from, ironically, too many tourists.

Smartphones can deliver site-related panoramas and stereo movies, so organizations do not need to pay for interface devices. Customers and visitors have their own and typically know how to use them, and smartphones are increasingly

Figure 1.7 Collaborative Mixed Reality. Mafkereseb Bekele, Erik Champion, Hafizur Rahaman.

powerful portable computers with headphone connections, gyroscopes and accelerometers, GPS, typically two cameras, physical and virtual buttons, and quality screens. They can allow for personalization (through taking videos or photos of the experience) or sharing with other people just by handing over the device or posting to social media.

However, smartphones are generalists; they heat up and can lose battery power very quickly when running graphics and AR applications. Using a phone while navigating through a real space can also be disconcerting and distracting. They are also, of course, so small that no matter the resolution, one always feels one is looking at a tiny postcard through a screen; they, therefore, do not convey a sense of spatial immersion very effectively. And people don't like downloading more applications (Damala et al. 2013; Bennett and Budka 2018).

And yet virtual tourism's potential market is huge. When I commenced a PhD via the University of Melbourne to work with Lonely Planet in 2001 on a three-dimensional internet tourism research project, Lonely Planet told me of its surprising discovery: it had an audience of virtual tourists, people who would buy its travel books but never travel to the subject matter (Champion 2019). Now it and other companies have become very interested in digitally mediated virtual tourism both on this planet (Butler 2016) and, thanks to NASA, on others (Foxe 2018).

There is an exploding range of consumer HMDs that can cover many of these situations (fig. 1.8). Even film companies like Weta, Disney, and Lucasfilm are developing their own VR and AR tools and showcases, including coloring books (Cox 2015). VR films are now being developed by tourism and travel companies as Mark Zuckerberg (Butler 2016) predicted: "just as we take photos and videos and post them on our social media platforms, eventually people will be able to capture 3D scenes that others will be able to see."

I noted earlier that AR typically means a computer-generated visualization that augments (adds to rather than dominates) our sense of the real world around us. In contrast, MR, lying between AR and VR, merges the real and virtual rather than augments the former with the latter (Billinghurst 2017). Today even smartphone cameras that overlay a floating picture on the screen are called AR technology, but the traditional definition typically requires the computer augmentation to appear to be spatially located in the real world. AR and MR examples are usually vision based, but they don't have to be; there is audio AR (Robertson 2018) and even olfactory AR: as you walk over the Belgian field where the Battle of Waterloo took place, an Arduino microcontroller, triggered by GPS coordinates, wafts simulated smells of the buried musket balls' gunpowder toward your face (Eve 2015).

Given the expense, complexity, and sedentary nature of most VR systems, and that digitally simulated smell is particularly difficult (Matthews 2017; Ruppenthal 2018), AR and MR seem to have more potential for virtual tourism than providing or loaning suitable devices. Wi-Fi is commonplace in and around tourist places, many people have their own powerful smartphones and tablets, they

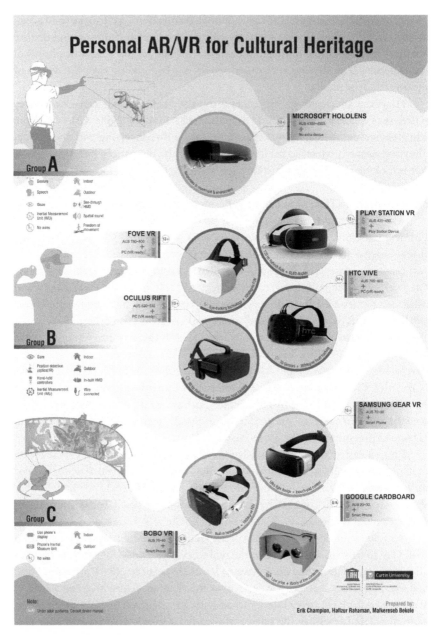

Figure 1.8 Types of Head-Mounted Displays. Hafizur Rahaman, Erik Champion.

are less likely to damage their own device than one provided by a business or museum, and they know how to use it. However, content needs to be tailored to specific devices (fig. 1.8), installed, checked, and maintained; smartphones can overheat; tablets can get in the way of the experience; any consumer device powerful enough to host rich and immersive experiences risks perceived obsolescence and planned obsolescence (Spinks 2015) within two years and sometimes within one year (Spence 2015).

If we are to move past one-hit AR wonders like Pokémon Go (Humphery-Jenner 2016) toward scalable yet engaging content and stable tools, then appropriate evaluation research—and long-term and robust infrastructure—would be very nice to have. Formats like OpenXR and WebXR show promise for bringing content across desktops and HMDs (without having to download plugins), but we still face a particular nontechnological challenge: our preconceptions about virtual reality.

Summary

What is the predicted growth for VR domestic and global markets? Market intelligence firm International Data Corporation predicted that "spending on AR and VR products and services will be up 69% next year [in 2019]" (Sinclair 2018). According to Marcus Torchia and Michael Shirer (2018), forecasts predict spending on augmented and virtual reality to surpass US$20 billion by the end of 2019, compared to US$12 billion in 2018. The numbers look impressive and might compel us to assume the development of VR was smooth and steady, but its history has been a wild and oscillating ride.

Not surprisingly, then, the terms used for virtual environments, VR, cyberspace, presence, and immersion are all contentious, and their usage varies. For example, while an environment in the real world is typically a place, virtual environments are seldom complete environments. Few people seem to *completely* agree on a definition (see *The Oxford Handbook of Virtuality* [Grimshaw 2013] for evidence).

Despite or perhaps because of this conceptual muddle, the number of exciting technological showcases is rivaled by the number of failed and broken equipment and deserted VR centers. Whichever year we are in is the year that AR/VR/MR/XR will breakthrough, perhaps even prove to be a "paradigm shift" (Carter 2019), and yet any VR software and hardware currently full of promise seems to get old very quickly.

Virtual environments were historically designed for single uses and single users, with a massive focus on the visual. The related tools are likewise designed to look for singular interaction; two-dimensional processes and the "surround" screens do not create a sense of place.

Historically, VR has depicted images of place, but it does not transport us to or allow us to inhabit space. Our memories of a place include the effort expended to get there, the place's relationship to other places (places within places); the time and wear of inhabitation; the activities the place engages and triggers; the sense of embodiment the place evokes; the paths and souvenirs from other places the place garners and modifies; the manner in which the place separates movement and activity from rest, repose, and reflection; and the identity the place captures.

VR is not just equipment, but neither is place merely a collection of objects and their relationships in space. Places are not just spaces around singular objects; they do not provide for only single usage or for one person at a time. Place is the experiencing *of* experience. Places are experientially enriching spaces, and VR, as we shall see, is a technology to not merely visualize other forms of reality but also experience them. In the next chapter, I will examine one type of virtual environment claiming to be a virtual place, the virtual museum, to see why examples of this type of virtual environment do not exploit the features and opportunities of place or leverage the fascinating new potential of *virtual* places.

References

Azuma, R. 2004. "Overview of Augmented Reality." Paper presented at the ACM SIGGRAPH 2004 Course Notes, Los Angeles, CA. Accessed June 16, 2021. http://doi .acm.org/10.1145/1103900.1103926.

Bellis, Mary. 2018. "The History of Computer and Video Games." ThoughtCo. Updated August 23, 2019. Accessed March 4, 2021. https://www.thoughtco.com/history-of -computer-and-video-games-4066246.

Bennett, Matthew Robert, and Marcin Budka. 2018. "Augmented Reality Promises to Rescue Dying Museums—So Why Don't Visitors Want to Use It?" The Conversation. Last Modified November 29, 2018. Accessed January 23, 2021. https://theconversation.com /augmented-reality-promises-to-rescue-dying-museums-so-why-dont-visitors-want-to -use-it-107845.

Billinghurst, Mark. 2017. "What Is Mixed Reality?" Medium. Last Modified March 31, 2017. Accessed March 22, 2021. https://medium.com/@marknb00/what-is-mixed-reality -60e5cc284330.

Bisson, Simon. 2008. "Science Fiction's Influence on Technology: Ideas Made Real." ITPro. Last Modified January 26, 2008. Accessed March 4, 2019. https://www.itpro.co.uk /159879/science-fictions-influence-on-technology-ideas-made-real.

BNL (Brookhaven National Library). n.d. "The First Video Game?" BNL: About Brookhaven. Accessed March 4, 2021. https://www.bnl.gov/about/history/firstvideo .php.

Brockwell, H. 2016. "Forgotten Genius: The Man Who Made a Working VR Machine in 1957." *techradar* (wearables). Accessed June 16, 2021. https://www.techradar.com/au /news/wearables/forgotten-genius-the-man-who-made-a-working-vr-machine-in-1957 -1318253.

Bush, Vannevar. 1945. "As We May Think." *Atlantic*, July 1945. Accessed January 30, 2020. https://www.theatlantic.com/magazine/archive/1945/07/as-we-may-think/303881/.

Butler, Alex. 2016. "Virtual Reality and New Technologies Increasingly a Part of the Travel Industry." Lonely Planet: Travel News. Last Modified April 11, 2016. Accessed March 21, 2019. https://www.lonelyplanet.com/news/2016/04/11/travel-tourism-virtual -reality/.

Cambridge Dictionary. n.d. "Virtual reality." Accessed March 3, 2019. http://dictionary
.cambridge.org/dictionary/english/virtual-reality.

Carter, Jeremy Story. 2019. "The 'Paradigm Shift' of Virtual Reality Tourism." *Blueprint for
Living.* Last Modified April 12, 2016. Accessed January 22, 2020. https://www.abc.net
.au/radionational/programs/blueprintforliving/virtual-reality-technologies-and
-tourism/7312152.

Champion, Erik. 2019. "Virtual Reality Adds to Tourism through Touch, Smell and Real
People's Experiences." *The Conversation.* Last Modified March 21, 2019. Accessed
January 30, 2020. https://theconversation.com/virtual-reality-adds-to-tourism
-through-touch-smell-and-real-peoples-experiences-101528.

Cook, David A., and Robert Sklar. 2019. "History of the Motion Picture." *Encyclopædia
Britannica.* Encyclopædia Britannica.

Cox, Jamieson. 2015. "Disney Is Using Augmented Reality to Bring Coloring Books to Life."
The Verge. Last Modified October 5, 2015. Accessed March 21, 2019. https://www
.theverge.com/2015/10/5/9453703/disney-research-augmented-reality-coloring-books.

Damala, Areti, Tobias Schuchert, Isabel Rodriguez, Jorge Moragues, Kiel Gilleade, and
Nenad Stojanovic. 2013. "Exploring the Affective Museum Visiting Experience:
Adaptive Augmented Reality (A2R) and Cultural Heritage." *International Journal of
Heritage in the Digital Era* 2 (1): 117–42.

Damer, Bruce, and Randy Hinrichs. 2014. "The Oxford Handbook of Virtual Reality." In
The Oxford Handbook of Virtuality, edited by Mark Grimshaw, 17–41. Oxford: Oxford
University Press.

Dormehl, Luke. 2017. "8 Virtual Reality Milestones That Took It from Sci-Fi to Your Living
Room." Yahoo. Last Modified November 14, 2017. Accessed March 3, 2021. https://
finance.yahoo.com/news/8-virtual-reality-milestones-took-221651381.html.

Duncan, Ishbel, Alan Miller, and Shangyi Jiang. 2012. "A Taxonomy of Virtual Worlds Usage
in Education." *British Journal of Educational Technology* 43 (6): 949–64.

Encyclopaedia Britannica. 2014. "Cinerama." Last Modified December 8, 2014. https://www
.britannica.com/topic/Cinerama.

English Oxford Living Dictionaries. n.d. "Virtual reality." Accessed July 27, 2017. https://en
.oxforddictionaries.com/definition/virtual_reality.

Eve, Stuart. 2015. "Finding Out What the Past Smelled Like." *Atlantic.* Last Modified March
11, 2015. Accessed March 21, 2021.

Evenden, Ian. 2016. "The History of Virtual Reality: Step Back in Time to See How Art Fused
with Cutting-Edge VR Technology to Create Entire Worlds. . . ." *Science Focus: The
Online Home of BBC Focus Magazine* (blog), November 6, 2016. Accessed June 16, 2021.
https://www.sciencefocus.com/future-technology/the-history-of-virtual-reality/.

Foxe, Ken. 2018. "Become a Virtual Space Tourist with NASA's Exoplanet Travel Bureau."
Lonely Planet: Travel News. Last Modified June 25, 2018. Accessed January 30, 2020.
https://www.lonelyplanet.com/news/2018/06/25/virtual-space-tourist-nasa-exoplanet/.

Goldman, Josh, and John Falcone. 2016. "Virtual Reality Doesn't' Mean What You Think It
Means." CNET. Last Modified March 10, 2016. Accessed July 30, 2017. https://www
.cnet.com/au/news/virtual-reality-terminology-vr-vs-ar-vs-360-video/.

Grimshaw, Mark, ed. 2013. *The Oxford Handbook of Virtuality.* Oxford: Oxford University
Press.

Guins, Raiford. 2017. "Following the Bouncing Ball: Tennis for Two . . . at the Strong!" *Play
Stuff* (blog). The Strong: National Museum of Play. Last Modified March 4, 2019.
Accessed January 30, 2020. https://www.museumofplay.org/blog/chegheads/2017/01
/following-the-bouncing-ball-tennis-for-two-at-the-strong.

Heim, Michael. 2014. "The Paradox of Virtuality." In *The Oxford Handbook of Virtuality*, edited by Mark Grimshaw, 111–23. Oxford: Oxford University Press.

Hollerer, Tobias, and Dieter Schmalstieg. 2016. "Introduction to Augmented Reality." In *Augmented Reality: Principles and Practice*, 1–32. Los Angeles, CA: UCLA.

Horak, Jan-Christopher. 2016. "This Is Cinerama." UCLA Library, Film & Television Archive. Last Modified January 8, 2016. Accessed June 11, 2021. https://www.cinema.ucla.edu/blogs/archival-spaces/2015/01/08/cinerama.

Humphery-Jenner, Mark 2016. "What Went Wrong with Pokémon Go? Three Lessons from Its Plummeting Player Numbers." The Conversation. Last Modified October 19, 2016. Accessed March 21, 2019. https://theconversation.com/what-went-wrong-with-pokemon-go-three-lessons-from-its-plummeting-player-numbers-67135.

Jackson, Brian. 2015. "What Is Virtual Reality? [Definition and Examples]." *AR Blog: Augmented Reality Marketing Resources, Trends, Videos and Case Studies*, June 24, 2015. Marxent: 3D Commerce. http://www.marxentlabs.com/what-is-virtual-reality-definition-and-examples/.

Laumond, Jean-Paul. 2012. "Robotics: Hephaestus Does It Again." Translated by Liz Libbrecht. Inaugural Lecture, January 19, 2012. Collège de France. OpenEdition Books. Last Modified March 3, 2019. Accessed January 30, 2020. https://books.openedition.org/cdf/540?lang=en.

Loomis, Jack M. 2016. "Presence in Virtual Reality and Everyday Life: Immersion within a World of Representation." *PRESENCE: Teleoperators and Virtual Environments* 25 (2): 169–74.

Lowood, Henry E. 2015. "Virtual reality." *Encyclopædia Britannica*. Last Modified May 14, 2015. Accessed July 30, 2020. https://www.britannica.com/technology/virtual-reality.

———. 2018a. "Doom." *Encyclopædia Britannica*. Last Modified March 4, 2019. Accessed January 30, 2020. https://www.britannica.com/topic/Doom.

———. 2018b. "Virtual reality." *Encyclopædia Britannic*. Last Modified November 16, 2018. Accessed November 20, 2020. https://www.britannica.com/technology/virtual-reality.

Massumi, Brian. 2014. "Envisioning the Virtual." In *Oxford Handbook of Virtuality*, edited by Mark Grimshaw, 55–70. Oxford: Oxford University Press.

Matthews, David. 2017. "Why Smells Are So Difficult to Simulate for Virtual Reality." Upload. Last Modified March 9, 2017. Accessed March 21, 2019. https://uploadvr.com/why-smell-is-so-difficult-to-simulate-in-vr/.

Merriam-Webster. 2on.d. "Virtual reality." Last Modified July 4, 2017. Accessed June 16, 2021. https://www.merriam-webster.com/dictionary/virtual%20reality.

Milgram, Paul, and Fumio Kishino. 1994. "A Taxonomy of Mixed Reality Visual Displays." *IEICE TRANSACTIONS on Information and Systems* 77 (12): 1321–29.

Milner, Andrew. 2012. "Science Fiction and Dystopia: What's the Connection?" The Conversation. Last Modified March 3, 2019. Accessed January 30, 2020. https://theconversation.com/science-fiction-and-dystopia-whats-the-connection-8586.

Mullen, David. 1998 (1952). "And Now . . . CINERAMA." Transcribed and edited by American WideScreen Museum. The American WideScreen Museum. Last Modified March 4, 2019. Accessed March 4, 2021. http://www.widescreenmuseum.com/widescreen/ac-cinerama.htm.

Pan, Xueni, and Antonia F. de C. Hamilton. 2018. "Understanding Dual Realities and More in VR." *British Journal of Psychology* 109 (3): 437–41. https://doi.org/doi:10.1111/bjop.12315.

"The Power Glove." n.d. Website. Accessed March 4, 2021. http://thepowerofglove.com/.

Robertson, Adi. 2018. "Bose's Augmented Reality Glasses Use Sound Instead of Sight." The Verge. Last Modified March 12, 2018. Accessed March 21, 2019. https://www.theverge .com/2018/3/12/17106688/bose-ar-audio-augmented-reality-glasses-demo-sxsw-2018.

Ruppenthal, Alex. 2018. "Sniff Test: Study Incorporates Smell into Virtual Reality." WTTW. Accessed March 5, 2018. https://news.wttw.com/2018/03/05/sniff-test-study -incorporates-smell-virtual-reality.

Science Museum Group. n.d. "Vitarama Corporation." Science Museum Group. Accessed January 30, 2020. http://collection.sciencemuseum.org.uk/people/ap27788/vitarama -corporation.

Sinclair, Brendan. 2018. "AR/VR Spending to Jump 69% in 2019—IDC." gamesindustrybiz. Last Modified December 6, 2018. Accessed March 22, 2021. https://www .gamesindustry.biz/articles/2018-12-06-ar-vr-spending-to-jump-69-percent-in-2019 -idc.

Smith, Will. 2015. "Stop Calling Google Cardboard's 360-Degree Videos 'VR.'" WIRED. Last Modified July 4, 2017. Accessed January 30, 2020. https://www.wired.com/2015/11/360 -video-isnt-virtual-reality/.

Spence, Ewan. 2015. "Your Smartphone Will Be Obsolete in Two Years." Forbes. Last Modified April 2, 2015. Accessed March 21, 2019. https://www.forbes.com/sites /ewanspence/2015/04/02/smartphone-obsolescence-android-iphone/#1ac94a2e2fc8.

Spinks, Rosie. 2015. "We're All Losers to a Gadget Industry Built on Planned Obsolescence." The Guardian. Last Modified March 23, 2015. Accessed March 21, 2019. https://www .theguardian.com/sustainable-business/2015/mar/23/were-are-all-losers-to-gadget -industry-built-on-planned-obsolescence.

Sterling, Brian. 2009. "Augmented Reality: 'The Ultimate Display' by Ivan Sutherland, 1965." WIRED, September 20, 2009. Accessed June 1, 2021. https://www.wired.com/2009/09 /augmented-reality-the-ultimate-display-by-ivan-sutherland-1965/.

Steuer, Jonathan. 1992. "Defining Virtual Reality: Dimensions Determining Telepresence." Journal of Communication 42 (4): 73–93.

Torchia, Marcus, and Michael Shirer. 2018. "Worldwide Spending on Augmented and Virtual Reality Expected to Surpass $20 Billion in 2019, According to IDC." IDC. Last Modified December 6, 2018. Accessed March 22, 2021. https://www.businesswire.com /news/home/20181206005037/en/Worldwide-Spending-on-Augmented-and-Virtual -Reality-Expected-to-Surpass-20-Billion-in-2019-According-to-IDC.

Tretkoff, Ernie. 2008. "This Month in Physics History: October 1958; Physicist Invents First Video Game." APS News 17 (9). Last Modified March 3, 2019. Accessed January 30, 2020. https://www.aps.org/publications/apsnews/200810/physicshistory.cfm.

USC School of Cinematic Arts. 2021. "Morton Heilig: The Father of Virtual Reality." Accessed June 16, 2021. https://www.uschefnerarchive.com/mortonheilig/.

Virtual Reality Society. 2018. "What Is Virtual Reality?" The Franklin Institute. Last Modified 2017. Accessed July 4, 2017. https://www.vrs.org.uk/virtual-reality/what-is -virtual-reality.html.

———. n.d. "When Was Virtual Reality Invented?" Virtual Reality Society. Last Modified 2017. Accessed January 30, 2020. https://www.vrs.org.uk/virtual-reality/invention .html.

Walker, Akex. 2016. "The First Video Game Might Have Been Invented in 1947." Kotaku. Last Modified March 30, 2016. Accessed March 4, 2019. https://www.kotaku.com.au/2016 /03/the-first-video-game-might-have-been-invented-in-1947/ https://www.kotaku .com.au/2016/03/the-first-video-game-might-have-been-invented-in-1947/.

Wann, John, and Mark Mon-Williams. 1996. "What Does Virtual Reality NEED?: Human Factors Issues in the Design of Three-Dimensional Computer Environments." *International Journal of Human-Computer Studies* 44 (6): 829–47.

Winter, David. 2018a. "Noughts and Crosses: The Oldest Graphical Computer Game." pong -story.com. Last Modified 2018. Accessed June 11, 2021. http://www.pong-story.com /1952.htm.

———. 2018b. "Welcome to Pong-Story." pong-story.com. Last Modified 2018. Accessed June 11, 2021. http://www.pong-story.com/intro.htm.

chapter two

DEAD, DYING, FAILED WORLDS

Given the speed, range, and proliferation of virtual reality (VR) technology and commercial application development, virtual world designers are especially at risk of duplicating the strategic disasters of earlier technology. Not only is it is nearly impossible to uncover everything that has been done before in this field, but new technology also does not prevent us from revisiting blunders in earlier projects that were conceptual errors of judgment rather than issues with technical limitations.

Early Examples of Spatial Immersion–Based Technology

Apart from the development of head-mounted displays (HMDs) and related technology for games, immersive VR was the main promise of spatial immersion–based technology. The most famous example was probably CAVE (Cave Automatic Virtual Environment) developed at the Electronic Visualization Laboratory at the University of Illinois, Chicago, in 1992. Since then, many game engines (and related real-time rendering engines) have also developed ways to project onto four to six walls simultaneously, track the user's movement and position, and render images onto the walls, which are calibrated with active-shutter three-dimensional goggles (so that each eye sees the correctly calibrated stereo image that flashes on and off in front of their eyes, preferably at 60 frames per eye for a total of 120 frames per second, to avoid a sensation of flickering). CAVEUT, Quest3D, VRUI (virtual reality user interface), Crytek's CryENGINE game engine, and BlenderVR are just some of the technical options.

What has stopped the widespread distribution of VR lab content? The technology is accelerating, but there are few shared formats and standards between the competing VR systems. Because the user typically stands in the middle of the room and the images are calibrated to share their viewpoint, interaction is limited, and their viewing position cannot be easily and accurately shared with others in the same space.

Games, on the other hand, feature shared content, work across the screens of many different home computers, and don't have specific viewing requirements.

Because gaming is a $100 billion industry, it is much easier to hire game programmers and create new and engaging ways of providing thematic feedback to the users. Also, unlike specialist VR centers, game consoles can last for up to ten years, providing continuity and allowing for the sharing of games and game-related content across millions of computers.

Furthermore, commercial games are typically derivatives of well-known cultural genres, which create inspiration for game play, interface, and objectives, while VR systems have provided many of these design elements from scratch. Games are also based on a challenge: for users to find out more about the virtual environment. Task performance evaluation is made possible in computer games, as they are already based on thematic feedback and rewards. We are drawn to competition, challenge, and fantasy. Not being adventure or quest based, virtual reality environments (VREs) seldom provide feedback or reward, and many even lack challenging tasks to complete; they merely show content or allow the user to navigate through the environment. While they do occasionally provide challenges, they seldom provide information or instruction through failure. Games, on the other hand, provide more information and learning opportunities precisely through commonplace failure. Computer games reward attention and variation to strategy, but they penalize inattention and distraction.

Academics build VREs and virtual learning environments (VLEs); game companies build games. One would think that the learning affordances and opportunities of games were also evident in VLEs and VREs, but many early virtual environments were designed to showcase and promote computer vision–related research, not to extend and analyze learning objectives and outcomes of specific content areas.

Because of their relative affordability, many dedicated users, and capacity for user-added modifications (mods), games can create and transfer large amounts of data and digital assets. One may even claim that computer games offer procedural knowledge–based learning rather than the descriptive knowledge–based learning provided by VREs and VLEs.

Multiplayer Worlds

In *Critical Gaming: Interactive History and Virtual Heritage* (Champion 2016a), I suggested three ways to add a sense of "world" to virtual worlds:

1. As designers we could allow for different ways of doing things or perceiving things (virtual environments typically do not have many options for expressive interaction).
2. We could provide more social dimensions, which in the earlier book I called worldliness. For example, in such a world, the player may be able to or be forced to choose between a range of self-identifying livelihoods and positions that make it possible to develop and maintain social skills and status.

3. A virtual world may involve learning how to translate and disseminate, or even modify or create, the language or material value systems of real or digitally simulated inhabitants. In this situation, the gameplay hinges on how well culturally appropriate information can be learned and developed by the player. Ideally, the virtual world, virtual environment, or computer game can store, display, and retrieve information on the encounters of people in places.

I now wonder if such a simple list is helpful. Certainly, virtual worlds may help us practice different activities, define ourselves through social identity, or learn about the world around us (and store contextual knowledge). But one could as easily say learning is part of an activity. Put another way, virtual worlds might allow us to practice, role-play, learn, and store knowledge (design, build, collect, write, perform, or draw). But they could allow us to do these things with dynamic and sometimes chaotic parameters.

A world is also beyond our complete control and our complete cognitive and perceptual grasp. Is the feeling that the world has unknowable *beyondness*, limitless knowledge, endless space, or irresolvable uncertainty a useful emotion? Should virtual worlds have a sense of closure, of narrative finality, or should they be closer to free-range exploration?

I still believe a simple typology of virtual environments based on overall functional needs could be useful. In the last two decades, we could say, virtual environments have evolved into online game worlds (role-playing, text-based interactive fiction worlds or shooter games), social encounter worlds (via text and sometimes personalizable avatars for dating or classroom and language learning), and semi-inhabitable or buildable worlds.

The more successful online worlds tend to have a real-world-related activity, via trade of items or level design (such as *EverQuest*, *Lineage*, or *World of Warcraft*). Such large-scale worlds raise interesting questions about how to design effective and user-friendly navigation (Jiang and Ormeling 2000) and social interaction (Jeffrey and Mark 1998). Even in text-based worlds, there is scope to use spatial patterns to denote speaking mode, activity, privacy, and visibility of the other participants (Lee, Said, and Tan 2016). One limitation of many virtual communities is that text and sound do not often locate the speaker or writer in a useful or thematically meaningful way, although the same may be said of behavior, habit, or activity in the real world; however, virtual communities are generally not as contextual and place related as real-world communities.

Early three-dimensional digital models were ported to three-dimensional technology, such as virtual reality modeling language (VRML), that was difficult for nonprogrammers to learn. It required a great deal of effort to make interactive worlds; anything large or detailed would greatly tax its ability to render and update. Even VRML's inventors admitted that VRML lacked a "killer" application; it never found a distinctive and commercially useful purpose (Walsh and

Figure 2.1 ActiveWorlds Entry World, 2020. Erik Champion, screenshot.

Bourges-Sévenier 2001). Placelessness is commonly found in virtual worlds, early virtual environments, and the virtual worlds of the 1990s, and there are even current examples of worlds lacking place (which I will not name here).

Hybrid virtual world–MMORPGs (Massively Multiplayer Online Role-Playing Games) are dying, failed, or simply vanished, and online social worlds are often lifeless, dead, dying, or failed—lifeless, because they were never very lively (populated, perhaps, but not lively, as interaction was so limited); dead, because so many have been given up or disappeared; and failed, because, once the initial novelty wore off, it became clear that there was nothing of purpose to accomplish in these "worlds." Like VRML, they lacked a "killer app"—an application people just had to have.

For example, 1995 saw the emergence of AlphaWorlds (renamed Active-Worlds in 1996). ActiveWorlds (fig. 2.1) still exists (Activeworlds 2021) but was recently referred to as a "graveyard" (Emerson 2016; Hernandez 2016). While Croquet (a software development kit available in 2007) was renamed Open Cobalt Alpha (but does not appear to be active in 2021, although there may be spinoffs), Project Wonderland ceased when Sun was taken over by Oracle, although there is an Open Wonderland reportedly still accessible but now apparently inactive. Adobe Atmosphere (available from 2002 to 2004) is long gone. Given this, arguably *Second Life* is the most famous current example of a multiplayer world, even if the visitor numbers (especially the returning ones) should be taken with a grain of salt (Saunders et al. 2011).

According to the BBC's Lauren Hansen, *Second Life* was difficult for businesses to maintain interest in or to provide easy-to-use and access facilities, while clients often had trouble with the learning curve required to navigate and design or otherwise modify the "worlds" or ensuring their computers were powerful enough to do so (Hansen 2009). *Second Life* designers had to balance the desire for generic updates across a broad range of machines with the requirements of individual designs, so we shouldn't blame them for taking the road of greater customers even if it affected the complexity and realism of the rendered and streamed environments. And their decision to charge educational institutes to rent land is of course their right; they are/were a commercial enterprise. We can, however, criticize the range of interaction available in *Second Life* and the limited degree to which it allowed people to socialize.

Apart from usability and navigation issues (navigation is a continually underrated challenge in designing and using virtual worlds, a problem we will return to later in the book), *Second Life* is distinct from other prevalent application(s) of social media in at least two important ways: it is immediate (synchronous), and it does not, so far, scale to mobile technology. It has also fallen behind social media competitors. In the first half of 2011, *Second Life* saw nearly a million users log on every month, but Facebook saw roughly five hundred million user logins in the same time frame.

Dan and Chip Heath (2011) on Slate.com complained that *Second Life* failed "the milkshake test." In Clay Christensen's *The Innovator's Solution*, he explains the metaphor of a milkshake: It was designed and sold as a simple alternative to breakfast for busy morning commuters, who required a highly portable food source that could be easily eaten while on the move; any added features only get in the way of this main task. According to Heath and Heath, *Second Life* did not perform an explicit and necessary or desirable "job"; it did have features and promise, but it did not offer the majority of visitors any clear reason to keep using it.

In response, a year later, in 2012, Sarah Lacy wrote that in the view of its founder Philip Rosedale, *Second Life* (or SecondLife, as she liked to describe it) was actually a success: "SecondLife has 1 million active users. . . . The problem— really the only problem, but a big one nonetheless—is they couldn't ever find a way to make those numbers grow. . . . As Rosedale pointed out, VCs invested half a billion dollars in SecondLife competitors, and none of them found a way to get beyond that number either."

Rosedale expressed surprise that so many of the houses built in *Second Life* were similar to real-world houses ("Rosedale said one of the biggest surprises he had building Second Life was how when given total creative license, most of the houses just looked like ones in Malibu," the article notes, although given its luxurious and internationally famous lifestyle reputation, I can't see how Malibu represents typical suburbs). Perhaps Rosedale thought that *Second Life* was too early, as Lacy's 2012 article suggests.

However, Lacy went further; she equated *Second Life* with the economy and significance of nationhood: "He built something audacious and crazy that one million people still use, something that has three-quarters of a billion dollars coursing through its weird virtual economy every year, something that has had no signs of slowing, even as it doesn't grow. He's basically built a small virtual nation."

In the article "Second Life Turns 10: What It Did Wrong, and Why It May Have Its Own Second Life," James Wagner Au (2013) wrote, "There's little point in creating an innovative product if its innovations are too frustrating and confusing to use." Although he argued that *Second Life* and its open-source alternatives, such as *OpenSims*, may be a great platform for the elderly, those who have disabilities, or those with learning difficulties, these platforms do not seem to have secured large numbers of users.

The anthropologist Tom Boellstorff (2015, 91–92) claimed that there is a notion of place in *Second Life*. He proposed that virtual worlds are dependent on the notion of place, which in turn is dependent on people, and Boellstorff (2015, 182) quoted a "resident" who declared "the people that inhabit this space are what makes it real." Arguably they are "residents": they believe there are certain distinct and separate places, and although there are breaks in attendance, there is a notion of social collaboration and empathy *in place* and certain places are used to meet people.

Philip Rosedale's company High Fidelity promised many new technical advantages over *Second Life*: full three-dimensional audio; facial feature awareness, aided by sensors that could capture gaze, facial expressions, and body language; user-contributed computing power; scriptable application programming interface for users to add their own JavaScript programming; support for the major HMD-based VR systems; and open-source client and server.

Both Rosedale's new company and virtual world product and *Second Life* cofounder and original CTO Cory Ondrejka's three-dimensional world company Cloud Party (which was Facebook-driven) elected to use new technology, but one wonders if the place-making potential of their applications improved. What is their current status? The open-source Linden Lab spin-off version of High Fidelity was announced with some fanfare (Manthorpe 2016) and entered beta testing in April 2016, offering VR talk shows and dance parties. But in 2019, Linden Lab cut a quarter of the High Fidelity staff, blaming insufficient VR headset–using clients (Roettgers 2019), and in 2020, they appear to have shut up shop. Meanwhile, Cloud Party (which ran in a browser without requiring registration) was bought out by Yahoo in 2014 and closed down (Etherington 2014). Linden Lab has now started a new virtual world platform called SANSAR, which runs on PC (Steam) and VR (HTC Vive and Oculus Rift), but in 2019 it went through staff cuts, (Au 2019) and in 2020 Linden Lab sold it.

Computer Games

Computer games have succeeded where virtual worlds have failed. In market terms, they have grown considerably year after year, even if PC-based games are decreasing in proportion to mobile-based ones. In 2019, Ukie (2021) calculated that the UK games industry had a market valuation of £7 billion, while in the United States, the Entertainment Software Association's (ESA) 2017 report declared the game industry made over US$24 billion that year and employed over 220,000 individuals, with the rate of employment increasing at twice the rate of the overall US job market (Siwek 2017). In 2016, Newzoo predicted the games industry was worth US$99.6 billion, and in 2019, it predicted the industry would be worth US$152.1 billion (Wijman 2019).

The success of the entertainment industry is not limited to Western countries. Research firm Newzoo's "2016 Global Games Market Report" (Warman 2016) declared the Asia-Pacific sector made US$46.6 billion in 2016. By 2019, Newzoo declared the five most profitable gaming markets would be the United States, China, Japan, South Korea, and Germany (with China in second only because of its current licensing freeze on new games).

And what of MMORPGs and MMOs (Massively Multiplayer Online games) in general? According to Williams and colleagues (2006, 339–40), "MMOs are of course merely one of several online 'places' in which social interaction might occur, but they are unique in the fact that they collect and mix people pursuing goals in three-dimensional space. This makes them arguably more 'place'-like than a standard text-based chat room. . . . But are MMOs truly like real-world spaces? Any 'place' is governed to some extent by its architecture."

Activision Blizzard's *World of Warcraft* is an interesting hybrid. It is sold as a computer game and played through a browser on a subscription basis. Although in 2015 articles cautioned there had been a more than 40 percent dip in subscriptions, in 2016 the new installment *Legion* sold 3.3 million copies (Frank 2016), allegedly boosting *World of Warcraft* numbers to over 10 million (although Activision Blizzard does not confirm these numbers). The year 2016 also saw a movie released based on the game (but the less said about the movie, the better). As shown on the company's 2017 first quarter business report, Activision Blizzard's profit (and profit margins) is staggering and does not belong in this chapter.

Virtual Museums and Virtual Galleries

It might seem strange to talk about the failings of virtual worlds as places by first considering the use of virtual museums. Virtual museums typically don't provide a clear sense of place, while real-world museums typically do. So, what is the purpose of virtual museums? They are vaguely defined, according to Erkki Huhtamo (2013), so here I will concentrate on websites and projects that claim to be more than simply online collections, implying some form of spatial location or spatial organization.

Virtual museums are too perfect (Baldwin 2017), they lack signs of human inhabitation and imperfection, yet real-world museums are inhabitable spaces, possibility spaces, civic debate arenas, and persuasive capturers of culture, although they have constraints and affordances that demand attention. Despite the hype of early virtual worlds, they, along with virtual museums, have seldom managed to capture and retain worthwhile visitor numbers (Sylaiou et al. 2009). What were the main features and attractions of virtual museums? Why have they gone in and out of fashion and have they been of any benefit to real-world museums?

I view virtual galleries (see, for example, the "Art Galleries of Second Life" page (Bohen.org, n.d.) as more than simple online categories. Real-world galleries

Figure 2.2 The Altes Museum, Berlin. Erik Champion.

differ from museums in general; they are typically businesses attempting to sell art, while museums provide artifacts and art pieces for education, conservation, reflection, and research. Online galleries, I assume, would be more useful if they helped the selling and valuing of artwork. While some famous museums also function as galleries, they typically do more than merely sell art; they provide the time and space to reflect on how art has changed and evolved (or not evolved) through the platial arrangement and juxtaposition of artifact and curated information.

The Altes Museum (1823–30) by Karl Friedrich Schinkel is an exemplar of the physical importance of physical museums (fig. 2.2). Museums have internal vistas and overhead views; they relate to other parts of the urban framework and landscape. The way they spatially (and via ornamentation) divide up collections is the result of care and thought, not merely a repeating line of positioning code. Their physical and environmental constraints help create their perceived sense of character and authenticity.

Virtual museums aim to do what exactly? Mirror a more rewarding real-world experience? Educate the public, reveal hidden collections, explain processes, or offer comparisons? Perhaps virtual museums could stage online works of art in your virtual home. They could offer previsit experiences or allow the public to buy or lease art from an online interface. Virtual museums could also reveal processes beyond curatorship, reveal the development of the museum building as an artifact, or use the virtual online museum building as a container for data flow of real-world visitors.

Galleries may not have all the spatial requirements of museums in terms of providing ways to compare across cultures and collections, but real-world galleries still have some advantages over virtual ones: One can see how fragile art is protected respectfully in a real gallery, and the imperfections of artwork can be viewed up close. One can walk around collections, allowing spatial narratives to affect one's understanding of the collection, and real-world space and scale permits the viewer to choose distance and angle, helping them select their own space. Furthermore, galleries provide vantage points to view other people as kinesthetic sculpture amid the art.

Studies of real-world museums and how they use images on their websites reveal that the aims of visitors include more than to just experience the art collection: they also wish to experience the museum's actual physical space *and* enjoy the presence of others (Somers 2018). For instance, Pat Hadley (2017) and his digital agency *cogapp* (in the United Kingdom) surveyed twenty-four museum websites and found "three strong trends" for images: depictions of the buildings or grounds, the collection and its "treasures," and photos of the visitors (or "how will I feel when I get there?").

Strong branding of museums through their web presence emphasizes their spatial grandeur (and setting), the exploratory nature of the collection experience, and the shared social sense of expectation and atmosphere. One, two, or all three of these powerful communication devices are typically missing from a virtual museum experience.

A considerable amount of art is designed to form a mental gestalt based on the observer's movement around it. As the sculptor Adolf Hildebrand wrote in *The Problem of Form in Painting and Sculpture*, "It is important for the process, and a thing not to be neglected, that the artist should at once conceive and hew out of the stone all that. Further appears to the eye at one time in a consideration's certain plane" (Hildebrand, Meyer, and Ogden 1907).

Some writers promote virtual museums as being free of the limitations of real museums. Klaus Müller (2013, 304) said virtual museums no longer need walls and "virtual museum 'spaces' can take on any shape they want, but they lack the conventional authority and emotion a museum building evokes." In the article "The Uses of Virtual Museums: The French Viewpoint," Roxane Bernier (2002) provided more reasons for virtual museums: newfound freedom from awkward display spaces, freedom from "limitations on objects," and "indefinite storytelling" (although perhaps this phrase means there is more variety in how virtual museums' stories can be told or experienced). She quoted Mokre (1998) and Davallon (1997): "None of the limitations of the physical museum apply to the virtual museum. There are no awkward display spaces, no limitations on the number of objects accessible to the visitor, and indefinite storytelling about those objects from which we can pass on tradition."

If real-world museums pose so many difficulties, it is surprising that millions visit them each year. Some of the most famous tourist destinations in the world

Figure 2.3 The Pantheon, Rome. Erik Champion.

are museums: the Louvre in Paris; El Prado in Madrid; the British Museum in London; the Smithsonian Institution in Washington, DC; the State Hermitage in Saint Petersburg; the Vatican Museums in Rome; the Uffizi Gallery in Florence; and the Rijksmuseum in Amsterdam (Lande and Lande 2012). Even historic monuments like the Pantheon in Rome, the Parthenon (and associated Acropolis Museum) in Athens, and the Taj Mahal in Agra are, though also famous destinations, in a sense museums (fig. 2.3).

Why should we visit these famous real-world museums? According to a list of the "41 incredible museums to visit before you die," compiled by Soo Kim (2011) for the *Telegraph*, the most incredible museums on the list were chosen due to influence, size and wealth of the collection or building, and performances. And many of these museums are visited precisely because of their spatial complexity. Sir John Soane's Museum is not a huge national museum, but it is listed as number eleven on this list and is highly popular *because of* its spatial idiosyncrasies (fig. 2.4). Richard Dorment (2011) reports, "The Oxford Dictionary of Architecture calls Sir John Soane's Museum 'one of the most complex, intricate, and ingenious series of interiors ever conceived.' It is also a delightful rabbit warren of a place, with interlocking rooms on different levels crammed from floor to ceiling with pictures, prints, drawings, plaster casts, antique fragments, books and architectural models."

Museums are designed to protect their contents from direct light and other ravaging effects of time. Museums have an exterior that reflects their surroundings; they are often a firmament in the old city or cultural precinct. By contrast, virtual museums do not have to worry about light or moisture or erosion from human breathing or touch. Virtual museums do not require visitors to travel far or to exhaust themselves in the reaching or completion of the museum experience. Virtual museums do not need to worry about the safe movement and viewing of human bodies.

Not having such factors as necessary for consideration may seem to be virtues. I would argue the converse; the lack of such constraints is typically a hindrance to the design and rich, evocative, and memorable experience of virtual museums. While physical museums have to deal with major challenges in design or in catering to audiences, these "limitations" provide character through resourceful solutions. And despite those who extol their virtues, virtual museums have issues—many of them. The first one is, Why? An online catalog allows for the display of many previously unseen and fragile artworks, but a virtual museum implies a spatial, immersive experience, one that can be spatially navigated, traversed with intent, or wandered through.

Do virtual museums fully convey the three-dimensional nature of spatial art? Real-world museums can fragment, point to or situate art against vistas or spatial progressions (stairs, entryways, above or below or alongside of lifts). Do virtual museums integrate the spatial relationship of a real and situated art object as it contextually relates or replies to its surroundings or to the embodied properties of visitors? Do they leverage the ability of digital media to include interaction, real-time data, and other information concerning the intentions or performance of the visitors?

Unfortunately, interaction is limited, according to Raul S. Wazlawick and colleagues (2001), and where it is possible, it is usually trivial and unexciting. P. Petridis and colleagues (2005) noted, "Usually, interaction is confined to reading labels with little information on the exhibits, shop booklets, and audio guided tours." Virtual museums do not need to offer physical protection from the

Figure 2.4 Sir John Soane's House and Museum, https://commons.wikimedia.org/wiki/File:Sir
_John_Soane%27s_House_and_Museum;_the_hallway_and_stairs_at_Wellcome_V0013538.jpg.

elements, real-life preservation, a procession of set spatial narratives, or adherence to causality and the laws of nature. Virtual artworks could transition into each other based on the physiology of the user, or the way the viewer navigates the work could influence the way the art presents itself.

How would we assess the success of virtual museums? Stella Sylaiou and colleagues (2013) argued that an important criterion of virtual museums is a sense of presence, of being there. They believe presence is a (494): "generic metric assessing the overall experience of the visitor rather than the information retained or the visitor's success in task completion." This suggests we could measure (virtual) presence, but as chapter 9 will explain, presence is itself not a simple, unitary phenomenon, and the lack of genuine spatially immersive virtual museums is a major hindrance to traditional notions of virtual presence.

I do see online virtual museums with useful content, for example, the Smithsonian 3D Digitization online portal. Smaller museums and galleries also use Sketchfab (a self-described three-dimensional and augmented reality platform) to create guided audio tours of three-dimensional interior and exterior models. The Collections in the 3D UK project at the Brighton Museums website are also trying to provide for more feedback and two-way interaction on curation.

Are these online, digital 3D collections equivalent to museums? No, I think they are closer to virtual galleries or online collections with tools. Virtual museums don't have people, much less crowds, but because of this convenience, they are also empty and no longer function as civic spaces or memorable spectacle spaces. Spectators are part of the museum spectacle (Parker and Saker 2020). Not so much a theater in the round as flaneurship in the round, traditional museum visits incorporate observation, serendipity, and judgment. You can add feedback and other media back into online digital collections, but while they are still collections, they are no longer *places*. Human interaction and signs of human interaction and inhabitation may be more formal, distant, and subtle in physical museums than they are in, say, people's homes, but they still exist.

Virtual museums can educate, provide artistic context, and allow people to peruse. They can provide access to art as purchasable (and downloadable) commodities. They can provide previsit information or information on the background or development of artworks and artifacts. They can also, using digital technology, overlay the virtual collection with visualizations of who remotely visited and why. They are still not *places*. Places require mutual spectatorship; spatial, cultural, and urban context; process; embodiment but rewarding ergodic space; material vulnerability; curatorship (opinions and interpretations); and space to debate (civic space) (fig. 2.5).

Virtual Heritage Environments

If a notion of place has a cultural dimension, one might well think that online digital environments showcasing heritage sites would be excellent examples of virtual

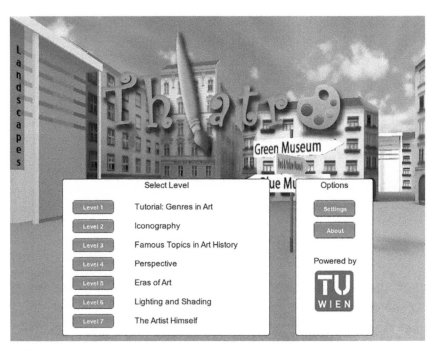

Figure 2.5 ThIATRO. Copyright Josef Wolfartsberger, with permission.

places. Virtual environments designed to convey heritage content are often called virtual heritage environments (VHEs) or three-dimensional digital heritage projects. Virtual heritage has been described as a fusion of VR technology with cultural heritage content (Addison 2000; Addison, Refsland, and Stone 2006), and Robert J. Stone and Takeo Ojika (2000) defined virtual heritage as "the use of computer-based interactive technologies to record, preserve, or recreate artifacts, sites and actors of historic, artistic, religious, and cultural significance and to deliver the results openly to a global audience in such a way as to provide formative educational experiences through electronic manipulations of time and space."

Why do we really need virtual heritage? Galleries, libraries, archives, and museums (GLAM industries) can only display a fraction of the collections that they own and have access to. Museums simply lack the space to display much of their collection (Bradley 1970). Many authors have outlined other problems encountered in preserving cultural heritage in physical museums (Barsanti et al. 2014; CSIRO 2014; Baio 2015; Michaelis, Jung, and Behr 2012), but the issue affects more than just specialized museum collections; digital disruptions of technology affect libraries and even at the scale of the internet, there are serious questions as to what can be preserved (Lepore 2015).

In Australia, the Commonwealth Scientific and Industrial Research Organization of Australia (CSIRO 2014) released a report stating, "Australia's cultural institutions risk losing their relevance if they don't increase their use of digital technologies and services." The Digital Productivity Flagship director, Michael Brünig (2014), stated the Australian GLAM industry is worth AUD$2.5 billion a year, with roughly only a quarter digitized and 629 kilometers' worth of archival material. Brünig warned us that even though there is a shift to open-access models and greater collaboration with the public, we still need to explore new approaches to copyright management that stimulate creativity and support creators.

VHEs can display content in new and more experientially appropriate ways, bridging disparate collections and remote sites with the intangible heritage of shareholders beyond the physical constraints of the real world. So ideally, VHEs help the public

- create, share, and discuss hypothetical or counterfactual places;
- meet virtually in these places with colleagues to discuss them; and
- contextually understand limitations forced on the original inhabitants of the simulated environment.

The technology also promises to help content experts and scholars develop experiential ways to entice a new and extended audience to admire both the content and the methods of their area of research while providing them with feedback mechanisms and community input that does not require physical visitation.

Early VHEs were low resolution and unreliable or required specialist equipment, with limited interaction. Games were and still are far more interactive and arguably the most successful form of virtual environments, so it would seem to be a masterstroke to use new interactive web formats and cutting-edge game engines for virtual heritage (Santos et al. 2014). I have observed that serious games and virtual heritage have not promoted the main message of heritage (Champion 2016b), particularly world heritage, to communicate the local and universal cultural significance of place, tradition, and artifact.

Designers have insufficiently leveraged real-world museums as collaborative places of engagement and reflection or virtual museums as dynamic synthetic portals where the illusions and affordances of digital media can best serve pedagogical objectives (Geser and Niccolucci 2013). Indeed, while virtual heritage models would seem to be a useful and complementary application for virtual museums, examples of combined virtual museum and virtual heritage projects are few and far between.

While the presence of other people through virtual characters may indeed create a sense of excitement, and encourage greater use of virtual environments, this does not mean we must build virtual environments for thousands of people; after all, we can experience some sense of the presence of another culture in an otherwise empty museum. Unlike social presence, which requires other people to appear to be in the same real or virtual environment, we can experience a sense of another cultural perspective without (necessarily) having to meet or hear other people. However, cultural presence does require a feeling of layered history as a situated palimpsest, and it does raise the issue of what sort of interaction would best allow us to understand the mindset of other distant or exotic societies. I will explore this phenomenon more in chapter 8.

There are other more immediate, practical issues. Despite initiatives such as the London Charter (London Charter for the Computer-Based Visualization of Cultural Heritage website 2009) and the Seville Charter (Lopez-Menchero and Grande 2011), shared standardized evaluation data is difficult to find, as there are few publicly accessible models (Barsanti et al. 2014). Scholars have complained about user-experience issues and a scarcity of suitable pedagogical material (Economou and Tost 2008). There are also myriad practical and technical problems, such as how we are to gauge the accuracy of the recording and modeling process from a single three-dimensional mesh or how we are to judge the relative authenticity of the simulated material (Pitzalis et al. 2010; De Reu et al. 2012). Virtual museums can also share this problem as the technology is often hidden, while for commercial games and virtual worlds, companies are often reluctant to provide data to researchers or allow them to run experiments with actual users.

Is Technological Obsolescence Responsible for Faded Virtual Worlds?

Is technology solely to blame for the disappearance of virtual worlds and elaborate digital game spaces? In some places, supposedly obsolete technology has not disappeared. For example, arcade games are still popular in Japan (Ashcraft 2017): arcade game centers are part of the urban landscape, located near major train stations, modifying their services (softer cushions and blankets for older customers) and developing VR capabilities for some of their games. While the number of arcade game centers is decreasing, they are still popular, and their popularity is not predicated primarily on the most recent technology. I suggest the real problem has been developing sufficient engaging content, attracting and keeping visitors, and leveraging the specific advantages of the medium.

Summary

Indubitably there are many examples of failed virtual worlds, virtual museums, and specialist VREs (including virtual heritage projects). I have argued that many of the currently available digital or virtual worlds, museums, and online games have failed in the eyes of not just myself but also many critics, users, and players. But the primary goal of this chapter has been to argue that these digital or virtual immersive environments have not been virtual places and that at least part of their difficulties has arisen from this missing sense of place. What "sense of place" is, however, is still vague and elusive.

Museums imprison our agency; glass boxes protect the artifacts *from us*. They also dictate limited views and juggle space issues and logistic issues. Sadly, virtual museums as metaphors for real-world museums are seldom interesting, because they seldom provide a strong comparison to museums in terms of physical challenges, social interaction, functions and features, spectator spectacle, or institutional history, profile, and respect. Museums often have a fascinating history of power, prestige, and debate, but this is often hidden from the public, and so is the collaborative notice of information finding that happens in real museums. I suggest most virtual museums are no more interactive and institutionally challenging than the majority of art studios.

Part of the problem may have been the level of expectations. The 1999 Guggenheim Virtual Museum (GVM) by architectural firm Asymptote Architecture promised to be completely three dimensional. Interested curators hoped it would be as engaging as the 1998 game *Half-Life* and yet stay easy to use for all (Wired Staff 2000). *Half-Life* is not an easy game that can be absorbed in ten minutes; it was not designed to view traditional art or act as a communication portal between curators.

In a 2017 article, "Learning from the Virtual," one of Asymptote Architecture's codirectors looked back at this 1999 project and declared, "As virtually 'inhabitable' entities, both projects [the GVM and the 1999 Virtual New York Stock Exchange] were unprecedented 'architectural environments'" (Rashid 2017).

Consider *Half-Life* again: it is an absorbing, immersive, and highly commended game, but you don't fully inhabit it. Inhabitation is not such a simple concept as providing a three-dimensional digital model with alien monsters and environmental puzzles to solve. The developers of the Guggenheim Virtual Museum probably did not aim to reach *Half-Life* levels of engagement, but in 2017, they did claim their 1999 projects showed the way forward for inhabitable virtual space: just add HMDs. Yet inhabitation is still more complex than viewing a three-dimensional digital model with an HMD.

Computer games have goals, challenges (often including simulation of life, typically hostile), optional strategies, thematic feedback, and rewards. Virtual museums, virtual galleries, and their related cousins in virtual heritage are lifeless and immutable. Ironically, the problem of place and placelessness seems most prevalent in VHEs, yet heritage is typically (but not always) fixed in place and time.

The computer game industry, by contrast, is booming. Yet even though they offer challenges and rewards, games are not normally virtual worlds. Most virtual worlds are too structured to offer consistently and persistently "engaging" challenges. When they are sandbox worlds (open worlds) they have an information design challenge: to provide their players with just enough information to make sense of where they are and what they will be asked to do without impinging on their sense of agency. As they need to share data and digital assets across many servers, they are not virtual worlds in the sense of user-driven permanence; they offer few opportunities to significantly personalize the virtual world with the actions and consequences of player-led decisions.

If they are history- and heritage-based virtual worlds (and there are a few examples), they typically have trouble balancing historically accurate information and depictions with opportunities for players to "leave their mark," as it were.

How do we augment virtual places with actual place history without *museumizing* the game play experience? How can interaction help players understand how ancient or alien places are perceived and affect others?

Digital media designers can certainly blend experiential journeys with historically accurate stage sets, but I am asking for more: rituals that use, are circumscribed by, and help identify place; transit places between the profane and the sacred, between social classes and states of mind; some way of conveying ergodic feedback through the place; alterity ("sense of other") in embodiment; thematic cultural constraints expressed spatially; place as civic space; and ways of accumulating socially meshed affordances through the landscape. These seven goals may not be communicated now, but I will elaborate on them and provide some possible answers in upcoming chapters.

There is an even more important fundamental issue to creating virtual online environments that are useful, durable, and preserved: why is a three-dimensional model more valuable than traditional media? How are or how can the potential place affordances be better leveraged in three dimensions? Could some of these old virtual environments and online worlds be revitalized, or can we learn from their mistakes to improve the design and use of their successors?

In the following two chapters, I will argue that some of the problems have arisen because these virtual environments were not virtual places; they lacked "a sense of place." The next chapter will examine how architectural theory has not usefully addressed the issue of how to design virtual places, because it has been too keen to concentrate on internal battles between competing essentialist theories and because the history of architectural discourse has not emphasized the importance of interaction.

The fourth chapter will focus on what philosophy has offered the development of virtual place-making. There has been a surprising lack of discussion of virtual places in philosophy, despite much talk of place and placelessness in the real world (Relph 1976).

References

Activeworlds. 2021. "Activeworlds." Accessed April 24, 2021. https://www.activeworlds.com/.

Addison, Alonso C. 2000. "Emerging Trends in Virtual Heritage." *Multimedia, IEEE* 7 (2): 22–25.

Addison, Alonso C., Scott Refsland, and Robert Stone. 2006. "Special Issue: Virtual Heritage Guest Editors' Introduction." *Presence: Teleoperators & Virtual Environments* 15 (3): iii–iv. http://www.mitpressjournals.org/doi/pdf/10.1162/pres.15.3.iii?cookieSet=1.

Ashcraft, Brian. 2017. "Why Arcades Haven't Died in Japan." Kotaku. Last Modified February 16, 2017. Accessed February 16, 2020. https://www.kotaku.com.au/2017/02/why-arcades-havent-died-in-japan/.

Au, Wagner James. 2013. "Second Life Turns 10: What It Did Wrong, and Why It May Have Its Own Second Life." Gigaom. Last Modified June 23, 2013. Accessed May 26, 2019. https://gigaom.com/2013/06/23/second-life-turns-10-what-it-did-wrong-and-why-it-will-have-its-own-second-life/.

———. 2019. "Linden Lab Lays Off over 20 Members of Sansar Team, Confirm Insiders; Social VR Platform to Continue Operating with Skeleton Crew." *New World Notes* (blog), November 4, 2019. Accessed July 19, 2020. https://nwn.blogs.com/nwn/2019/11 /sansar-linden-lab-layoff-social-vr-.html.

Baio, Andy. 2015. "Never Trust a Corporation: As Google Abandons Its Past, Internet Archivists Step In to Save Our Collective Memory." The Message, January 28, 2015. Last Modified August 3, 2017. Accessed August 3, 2017. https://medium.com/message /never-trust-a-corporation-to-do-a-librarys-job-f58db4673351.

Baldwin, Joan. 2017. "Saying What You Mean & Getting Better at What You Do." *Leadership Matters: Thoughts on 21st Century Museum Leadership by Joan Baldwin* (blog), June 12, 2017. Accessed April 24, 2021. https://leadershipmatters1213.wordpress.com/2017/06/12 /saying-what-you-mean-getting-better-at-what-you-do/.

Barsanti, S. Gonizzi, F. Remondino, B. Jiménez Fenández-Palacios, and D. Visintini. 2014. "Critical Factors and Guidelines for 3D Surveying and Modelling in Cultural Heritage." *International Journal of Heritage in the Digital Era* 3 (1): 141–58.

Bernier, Roxane. 2002. "The Uses of Virtual Museums: The French Viewpoint." Paper presented at the Sixth International Conference of Museums and the Web, Boston, MA, April 18–22, 2002.

Boellstorff, Tom. 2015. *Coming of Age in Second Life: An Anthropologist Explores the Virtually Human*. Princeton, NJ: Princeton University Press.

Bohen.org. n.d. "Virtual Museum Guggenheim Museum." Accessed April 25, 2021. http:// bohen.org/project/virtual-museum.

Bradley, Russ V. V. Jr. 1970. "A Critical Analysis of the Writings of Amos Rapoport." *Journal of Architectural Education* 24 (2–3): 16–25.

Brünig, Michael. 2014. "Historic Collections Could Be Lost to 'Digital Dinosaurs.'" The Conversation. Last Modified September 26, 2014. Accessed August 3, 2017. http:// theconversation.com/historic-collections-could-be-lost-to-digital-dinosaurs-31524.

Champion, E. 2016a. *Critical Gaming: Interactive History and Virtual Heritage*. Edited by Marilyn Deegan et al. Digital Research in the Arts and Humanities. Abingdon, UK: Routledge.

———. 2016b. "The Missing Scholarship behind Virtual Heritage Infrastructures." Paper presented at the Eurographics Workshop on Graphics and Cultural Heritage, Genoa, October 5–7, 2016. https://diglib.eg.org/handle/10.2312/gch20161383.

CSIRO (Commonwealth Scientific and Industrial Research Organisation). 2014. "Australian Museums Must Innovate or Risk Becoming 'Digital Dinosaurs.'" News release. Last Modified September 16, 2014. Accessed October 27, 2020. http://www.csiro.au/en /News/News-releases/2014/Australian-museums-risk-becoming-digital-dinosaurs.

Davallon, Jean. 1997. "Une Écriture Éphémère: L'exposition Face Au Multimédia." *Degrés (Bruxelles)* 25 (92–93): h1–h27.

De Reu, Jeroen, Gertjan Plets, Geert Verhoeven, Philippe De Smedt, Machteld Bats, Bart Cherretté, Wouter De Maeyer, et al. 2012. "Towards a Three-Dimensional Cost-Effective Registration of the Archaeological Heritage." *Journal of Archaeological Science* 40 (2): 1108–21. https://doi.org/10.1016/j.jas.2012.08.040.

Dorment, Richard. 2011. "Sir John Soane's Museum: The Museum That Time Forgot." *Telegraph*. Last Modified May 26, 2017. Accessed July 27, 2017. http://www.telegraph .co.uk/culture/art/art-news/8354262/Sir-John-Soanes-Museum-the-museum-that -time-forgot.html.

Economou, Maria, and Laia Pujol Tost. 2008. "Educational Tool or Expensive Toy? Evaluating VR Evaluation and Its Relevance for Virtual Heritage." In *New Heritage:*

New Media and Cultural Heritage, edited by Yehuda Kalay, Thomas Kvan, and Janice Affleck, 242–60. Oxford: Routledge.

Emerson, Sarah. 2016. "Who Is the Last Active Player in This Long-Dead MMO?" Motherboard: Tech by Vice. Last Modified March 30, 2016. Accessed March 21, 2019. https://motherboard.vice.com/en_us/article/8q8qx5/who-is-the-last-active-player-in -this-long-dead-mmo-active-worlds.

Etherington, Darrell. 2014. "Yahoo Acquires Virtual World Gaming Startup Cloud Party, Will Shut It Down." Tech Crunch. Last Modified January 24, 2014. Accessed January 30, 2020. https://techcrunch.com/2014/01/24/yahoo-acquires-will-shut-down -browser-based-virtual-world-gaming-startup-cloud-party/.

Frank, Allegra. 2016. "World of Warcraft Sees Big Numbers Hot Off Legion Launch." Polygon, September 8, 2016. Last Modified May 27, 2017. Accessed August 3, 2017. https://www.polygon.com/2016/9/8/12851794/world-of-warcraft-legion-sales-launch -day-subscribers-record.

Geser, Guntram, and Franco Niccolucci. 2013. "Virtual Museums, Digital Reference Collections and e-Science Environments." *Uncommon Culture* 3 (5/6): 12–37.

Hadley, Pat. 2017. "What Do the Best Museum Websites All Do?" *Cogapp* (blog), June 2, 2017. Accessed April 24, 2021. https://blog.cogapp.com/what-do-the-best-museum-websites -all-do-8d6727504605.

Hansen, Lauren. 2009. "What Happened to Second Life?" BBC News Magazine. Last Modified May 26, 2017. Accessed August 2, 2017. http://news.bbc.co.uk/2/hi/8367957.stm.

Heath, Dan, and Chip Heath. 2011. "Why Second Life Failed: How the 'Milkshake Test' Helps Predict Which Ultrahyped Technology Will Succeed and Which Won't." *Slate*, November 8, 2011. Last Modified March 3, 2017. Accessed August 2, 2017. http://www .slate.com/articles/business/moneybox/2011/11/why_second_life_failed_how_the _milkshake_test_helps_predict_which_ultra_hyped_technology_will_succeed _and_which_won_t_.html.

Hernandez, Patricia. 2016. "YouTuber's Journey into Abandoned MMO Is Creepypasta Material." Kotaku. Last Modified March 29, 2016. Accessed March 21, 2019. https:// www.kotaku.com.au/2016/03/youtubers-journey-into-abandoned-mmo-is -creepypasta-material/.

Hildebrand, Adolf, Max Meyer, and Robert Morris Ogden. 1907. *The Problem of Form in Painting and Sculpture*. New York: G.E. Stechert. Last Modified May 30, 2017. Accessed August 2, 2017. https://archive.org/details/problemofforminpoohild.

Huhtamo, Erkki. 2013. "On the Origins of the Virtual Museum." In *Museums in a Digital Age*, edited by Ross Parry, 121–35. London: Taylor & Francis.

Jeffrey, Phillip, and Gloria Mark. 1998. "Constructing Social Spaces in Virtual Environments: A Study of Navigation and Interaction." Workshop on personalized and social navigation in information space, Stockholm, March 16–17, 1998.

Jiang, Bin, and Ferjan Ormeling. 2000. "Mapping Cyberspace: Visualizing, Analysing and Exploring Virtual Worlds." *Cartographic Journal* 37 (2): 117–22.

Kim, Soo. 2011. "41 Incredible Museums to Visit before You Die." *Telegraph*. Last Modified May 26, 2017. Accessed August 2, 2017. http://www.telegraph.co.uk/travel/lists/worlds -best-museums-to-visit-before-you-die-bucket-list/.

Lande, Nathaniel, and Andrew Lande. 2012. *The 10 Best of Everything: An Ultimate Guide for Travelers*. 3rd ed. National Geographic 10 Best of Everything: An Ultimate Guide. Washington, DC: National Geographic.

Lee, Kean Wah, Noraini Said, and Choon Keong Tan. 2016. "Exploring the Affordances of the Writing Portal (TWP) as an Online Supplementary Writing Platform (For the Special

Issue of GLoCALL 2013 and 2014 Conference Papers)." *Computer Assisted Language Learning* 29 (6): 1116–35. https://doi.org/10.1080/09588221.2016.1172644.

Lepore, Jill. 2015. "The Cobweb: Can the Internet Be Archived?" *The New Yorker: Annals of Technology*. Last Modified January 21, 2015. Accessed August 2, 2017. http://www.newyorker.com/magazine/2015/01/26/cobweb.

London Charter for the Computer-Based Visualization of Cultural Heritage website. Accessed July 20, 2020. http://www.londoncharter.org/.

Lopez-Menchero, Victor Manuel, and Alfredo Grande. "The Principles of the Seville Charter." In *CIPA Symposium Proceedings*, edited by Karel Pavelka, 2-6. Prague, Czech Republic: Czech Technical University in Prague, Faculty of Civil Engineering, 2011.

Manthorpe, Rowland. 2016. "Remember Second Life? Now It's Being Reborn in Virtual Reality." WIRED. Last Modified October 24, 2016. Accessed March 23, 2019. www.wired.co.uk/article/philip-rosedale-high-fidelity.

Michaelis, Nils, Yvonne Jung, and Johannes Behr. 2012. "Virtual Heritage to Go." Proceedings of the Seventeenth International Conference on 3D Web Technology, Los Angeles, CA, August 4–5, 2012.

Mokre, M. 1998. "New Technologies and Established Institutions. How Museum Present Themselves in the World Wide Web." *Technisches Museum Wien*. Austria: Internal Report.

Müller, Klaus. 2002. "Museums and Virtuality." *Curator: The Museum Journal* 45 (1): 21–33. https://doi.org/10.1111/j.2151-6952.2002.tb00047.x.

———. 2013. "Museums and Virtuality." In *Museums in a Digital Age*, edited by Ross Parry, 295–305. Abingdon, UK: Routledge.

Parker, Eryn, and Michael Saker. 2020. "Art Museums and the Incorporation of Virtual Reality: Examining the Impact of VR on Spatial and Social Norms." *Convergence* 26 (5–6): 1159–73. https://doi.org/10.1177/1354856519897251.

Petridis, Panagiotis, Martin White, N. Mourkousis, Fotis Liarokapis, Maria Sifiniotis, Anirban Basu, and Christos Gatzidis. 2005. "Exploring and Interacting with Virtual Museums." In *Proceedings of Computer Applications and Quantitative Methods in Archaeology (CAA)*, edited by A. Figueiredo and G. Leite Velho, 73–82. Tomar, Portugal.

Pitzalis, Denis, Franco Niccolucci, Maria Theodoriou, and Martin Doerr. 2010. "Lido and Crm Dig from a 3d Cultural Heritage Documentation Perspective." In *Proceedings of the 11th International Conference on Virtual Reality, Archaeology and Cultural Heritage*, 87–95. Aire-La-Ville, Geneva: Eurographics Association.

Rashid, Hani. 2017. "Learning from the Virtual." E-Flux Architecture. Last Modified January 28, 2020. Accessed July 14, 2014. https://www.e-flux.com/architecture/post-internet-cities/140714/learning-from-the-virtual/.

Relph, Edward C. 1976. *Place and Placelessness*. London: Pion.

Roettgers, Janko. 2019. "Virtual Worlds Startup High Fidelity Lays Off 25% of Staff, Pivots to Enterprise Communication." Variety. Last Modified May 8, 2019. Accessed January 22, 2020. https://variety.com/2019/digital/news/high-fidelity-layoffs-1203208860/.

Santos, Pedro, Sebastian Pena Serna, André Stork, and Dieter Fellner. 2014. "The Potential of 3D Internet in the Cultural Heritage Domain." In *3D Research Challenges in Cultural Heritage: A Roadmap in Digital Heritage Preservation*, edited by Marinos Ioannides and Ewald Quak, 1–17. Berlin: Springer.

Saunders, Carole, Anne F. Rutkowski, M. van Genuchten, D. Vogel, and J. Molina Orrego. 2011. "Virtual Space and Place: Theory and Test." Special issue: New Ventures in Virtual Worlds, *MIS Quarterly* 35 (4): 1079–98. https://doi.org/10.2307/41409974.

Siwek, Stephen, E. 2017. *Video Games in the 21st Century: The 2017 Report.* Washington, DC: Entertainment Software Association. https://www.theesa.com/wp-content/uploads /2019/03/2017-EIR-National-Report.pdf.

Somers, Anna C. 2018. "Top Museum Directors on the Challenges of Climate Change and Mass Tourism." *Art Newspaper.* Last Modified October 30, 2018. Accessed January 30, 2020. https://www.theartnewspaper.com/news/fixes-for-flood-quake-and-sheer -popularity.

Stone, Robert J., and Takeo Ojika. 2000. "Virtual Heritage: What Next?" *IEEE Multimedia* 7 (2): 73–74. http://ieeexplore.ieee.org/document/848434/.

Sylaiou, Stella, Katerina Mania, Ioannis Paliokas, Vassilis Killintzis, Fotis Liarokapis, and Petros Patias. 2013. "Exploring the Effect of Diverse Technologies Incorporated in Virtual Museums on Visitors' Perceived Sense of Presence." Paper presented at the Ninth International Conference on Intelligent Environments (Workshops), Athens, Greece, 16–17 July 2013.

Sylaiou, Styliani, Fotis Liarokapis, Kostas Kotsakis, and Petros Patias. 2009. "Virtual Museums, a Survey and Some Issues for Consideration." *Journal of Cultural Heritage* 10 (4): 520–28.

Ukie. 2021. "Ukie UK Consumer Games Market Valuation." Last Modified April 8, 2021. Accessed April 25, 2021. https://ukiepedia.ukie.org.uk/index.php/Ukie_UK _Consumer_Games_Market_Valuation.

Walsh, Aaron E., and Mikaël Bourges-Sévenier. 2001. *Core Web3D.* Upper Saddle River, NJ: Prentice Hall Professional.

Warman, Peter. 2016. "2016 Global Games Market Report." Newzoo. Last Modified June 2016. Accessed August 3, 2017. https://cdn2.hubspot.net/hubfs/700740/Reports/Newzoo _Free_2016_Global_Games_Market_Report.pdf.

Wazlawick, Raul S., Marta C. Rosatelli, Edla M. F. Ramos, Walter A. Cybis, Bernd H. Storb, Vera R. N. Schuhmacher, Antonio C. Mariani, Tereza Kirner, Claudio Kirner, and Lea C. Fagundes. 2001. "Providing More Interactivity to Virtual Museums: A Proposal for a VR Authoring Tool." *Presence: Teleoperators and Virtual Environments* 10 (6): 647–56.

Wijman, Tom. 2019. "The Global Games Market Will Generate \$152.1 Billion in 2019 as the U.S. Overtakes China as the Biggest Market." Newzoo. Last Modified June 18, 2019. Accessed January 22, 2020. https://newzoo.com/insights/articles/the-global-games -market-will-generate-152-1-billion-in-2019-as-the-u-s-overtakes-china-as-the-biggest -market/.

Williams, Dmitri, Nicolas Ducheneaut, Li Xiong, Yuanyuan Zhang, Nick Yee, and Eric Nickell. 2006. "From Tree House to Barracks: The Social Life of Guilds in World of Warcraft." *Games and Culture* 1 (4): 338–61.

Wired Staff. 2000. "Guggenheim Going Virtual." WIRED. Last Modified June 9, 2000. Accessed January 28, 2020. https://www.wired.com/2000/06/guggenheim-going -virtual/.

chapter three

ARCHITECTURE
Places without People

Introduction

Virtual environments are designed, but are they architect designed? Are they architected, as in, programmed through design as an interface (*English Oxford Living Dictionaries* 2017)?

Designing virtual places would surely be best undertaken by specialists who design real-world places, such as urban designers and architects. Architects are multiskilled and specialize in three-dimensional software. They have great spatial-visualization skills and the honed ability to sketch, render, and automate highly detailed plans and drawings. Schools of architecture typically have very high entrance requirements, and architectural graduates undertake very long degrees in myriad fields.

In this chapter, I question such a simple yet apparently commonsense suggestion: Would architectural training help the understanding of interactive places? If games are virtual places, are they comprehensively understood and handled well by architects? I argue no based on six claims (which the reader is of course free to agree with, modify, or refute): architectural theory is typically essentialist; architectural tools are instrumentalist; architectural media is often people-free; architects are not typically trained in interactive media; architects are not trained in user-experience design and evaluation; and finally, although traditional architectural craft is embodied and sited, takes time, and requires care, these attributes are too often missing in digitally created architecture.

Given these claims, applying theories of architecture, or practices of architectural design, to interactive digital media to create virtual places may well leave some gaps. How do we resolve these in the design of virtual places? Could we modify, twist, and turn thoughts about real-world design? Employ fancy theories and sophisticated-sounding terms like *postmodernism*? No, virtual places are helped more by exploring the concepts of embodiment, multimodality, and role-play (and thematic affordances), allowing user infill and environmental change to affect the design environment and digital personalized patinas: materials that show the effect of time, wear, and care.

Keiichi Matsuda believed that due to mobile computing (phones and tablets), architecture would merge into two streams: a construction-centric one and a user-experience-based one (Hobson 2014). Matsuda predicted a near-future bifurcation of architecture: "I see the architectural profession splitting into two parts," he said. "On the one side, you'll have the people that design the physical support structure of the building. On the other you'll have people who are making the experience of a building—the way that we perceive it in the virtual layer. They'll be much closer to game designers or filmmakers."

Modernity has created experiential cocoons that we should study so we don't repeat them in virtual place design. I hope to show that architecture is more than spaces, shapes, and forms. Architecture also affords experiences, building perceptual relationships between places, paths, and centers. It is not merely the recapture of artifacts or archetypes, for it is our experience of living that is the fundamental relationship, not forms that simply capture these experiences (Savile 1982). Society is shaped by individuals' coming together to share and debate, modeled by places. Culture records, shapes, and responds to these social forces, pulls, and eddies.

Archaeology needs to study changes over time and how space material and form change due to encounters, and architecture helps provide the material framework for these encounters. Architecture has a long tradition of archetypes, which inspire countless digital architectural prototypes and projects. For archetype frameworks, consider Marc-Antoine Laugier's *Primitive Hut* (1977), David Mitchell and Gillian Chaplin's *Elegant Shed* (1984), or Thiis-Evensen's floor-wall-roof conceptual system (Thiis-Evensen, Waaler, and Campbell 1987).

Following such systems, it might seem self-evident and logical to study shapes and grammars based on historical archetypes and generate them via computer algorithms, but the oversight here is people: they don't fit neatly into a shape grammar. Modern architecture is focused on the interrelationship of spaces but underplays the importance of community feedback and social change.

Essentialist Theories That Limit Architecture[1]

My first claim is that architectural theory is typically essentialist and hence has trouble with self-verification and adopting other theories or parameters to improve and be appropriate for different environments and varying conditions. Architectural theory also tends toward the vague (some might say the poetic); it fails to fully describe the experience of place, or it does not directly address the design and understanding of *virtual* places except as direct representations of architecturally designed spaces in the real world. These issues are also apparent in game design. Part of architecture's uncomfortable relationship to interactive media is due to the inflexible yet often vague theories of what architecture should be, particularly in the area of art and aesthetics.

For example, I suggest the following argument: that with one notable exception, major architectural theories are fundamentally representational. These theories can be summarized as theories of semiotics, empathic projection, material symbolism (as the glorification of buildings or territorial protectionism), or reflections of a community (and the related notion of archaeological structuration).

Is Architecture a Language?

Semiotics in architecture is often associated with postmodernism. Semiotics is the study of meaning-making or the interpretation of signs, and architecture is here seen as a self-contained, self-referential, or culturally positioned system of signs—that is, a language. While semiotics has decreased in popularity, it did highlight the concern that there were symbolic elements to architecture; however, it dealt with elements that were symbolic to architects brought up on a classicist vocabulary, not necessarily those elements that were symbolic to the environmental memory of the public. For instance, Martin Donougho (1987) attacked the notion that architecture is a language (as did Nelson Goodman), arguing that architecture-as-language failed to meet the criteria that a language must meet to be considered a language. If Donougho was correct—and even Umberto Eco (1997) found it problematic when discussing architecture—one wonders why the phrase is still popular.

Aesthetic Empathy

The aesthetic experiencing of architecture is sometimes described in terms of empathic projection. According to Nancy Eisenberg and Janet Strayer (1990), empathy is often confused with sentiment and thus not identified with architecture or any other visual art. However, there is a distinction between aesthetic empathy (empathy via association) and sympathy or personal empathy (empathy through feeling). Aesthetic empathy can only be developed by a discriminative ability to "label affective states to others" and "assume the perspective of another person" (or, in this case, ascribe affective states or perspectives to an object, such as attributing personal qualities to columns).

Nineteenth-century aesthetics, according to Morgan (1996, 321), had two further divisions of empathy. The first involved the breaking down of the perceived boundaries between subjective and objective states—that is, one person imaginatively "fuses" their consciousness with that of the object they are perceiving at the time. The second division was the theory of perception, "in which human feeling is projected into forms through the eye's construction acts of visual interpretation."

We could also talk of pantheist and projective theories of empathy. For example, Adolf Hildebrand viewed the appreciation of art as involving projected empathy (Hildebrand, Meyer, and Ogden 1909). Just as watching someone weep induces in us a similar feeling, viewing artwork portraying specific emotions or scenes conjures up within us similar bodily reactions.

Empathic projection, espoused by nineteenth-century German aestheticians, such as Heinrich Wölfflin, was in direct response to the formalist charge that there was no emotional or physiological content to the experiencing of architecture. However, it fell out of favor, for it lacked prescriptive clarity and ignored the distinctive and nonsculptural qualities of architecture, such as the expression of space and the complex interrelationships of facades with external and internal spaces.

Tectonic Representation

Architecture has been described as the glorification or ennobling of building as a craft (Shiner 2007) through ornamentation or the expression of tectonic technology, or it has been described as a celebration of buildings in use (i.e., symbolic demonstration of) with or without an expression of the building as "fighting" the elements and the environment. For example, consider the Colosseum of Rome: the higher the floor, the lighter the half column and order (Tuscan, Ionic, and Corinthian) that was chosen to decorate it (fig. 3.1).

Arthur Schopenhauer's doctrine was that art presents the ideas of nature and that the principal ideas of architectural matter (I would replace *matter* with *form*) are gravity and rigidity; the task of art (and architecture), therefore, is "to present these antithetical ideas." Architecture for Wölfflin is not just a matter of representing load and support; for Wölfflin, the Greek column instead demonstrates "a living, upward striving." Wölfflin believed Schopenhauer neglected to view architecture as representing or embodying the human body's imagined physiological reactions to gravity.

Architecture may also be seen expressing resistance to its place, its *topos*. Those espousing a "tectonic" architecture that fights its surrounds (fig. 3.2) have not sufficiently espoused whether architecture is essentially or contingently tectonically representational and, if it is the former, whether its essence dictates what it "should" be or exactly how architecture must "express" an apparent tectonic essence and "fight" or "resist" its environment (Frampton 2014). And this theory does not appear relevant to urban built environments.

Architecture may also be seen as a vehicle to celebrate craft and traditional detail, although Andrew Ballantyne (2013) suggested that debating whether architecture is art or craft is a distinction only of import to followers of Robin George Collingwood. I would make two points here. First, only in architecture's built form do we see craft *performing*, and for the sake of educating future generations and not losing knowledge of building as craft, this performance needs to be emphasized. To suggest, as Ballantyne does, that craft is the responsibility of the builder and not the architect is not my understanding of current legal responsibility, nor is it advisable that architects design without knowledge of building as craft. This takes on even more import in virtual reality (VR), where construction and the experience of that construction are often lost. Second, the philosophical

Figure 3.1 Colosseum in Rome, Italy, April 2007. Photo by David Iliff. License: CC BY-SA 3.0. The image was converted to grayscale from the original Wikipedia image.

Figure 3.2 Dipoli, Otaniemi, Finland. Erik Champion.

issue of art versus craft is important because the bifurcation is pertinent to both architecture and philosophy: craft as intention or art as creative innovation (Richmond 1995). For example, in *The Question Concerning Technology* essays, Martin Heidegger distinguishes between techne and technology, the boundaries of the creative process, and the care and intentions of the artisan (in this case a silversmith). The creation of art is intrinsically linked with the care and intentions of the maker and the attempt to "bring something into appearance," which Heidegger said is a type of freedom (Heidegger and Lovitt 1977).

Social Space and Community Embodiment

Architecture has been described as "reflections of a community," or archaeological structuration—that is, architecture as an artifact that reflects and modifies the society that builds it. Architecture as "social space" and architecture as an embodiment of a community have also been advanced, yet even if such theories proved one way of appreciating architecture, they have so far not provided a clear prescriptive outline of how architecture is to be critiqued or created.

The Play of Space, Detail, or Material

The previously described theories were representational (does virtual place architecture need to be representational?). The major nonrepresentational view of architecture is formalist: the play of spatial configurations, details, and materials, without reference to historical, environmental, or personal connotations. In this theory, architecture is independent of direct representation of other forms, images, or ideas. Architecture in essence is the play (and interplay) of spaces and/ or of materials, or architecture in essence is the detail: where two or more materials come together.

Adolf Göller (1994) elaborated on the first claim in 1887. He believed that architecture was "pure visible form": It does not trigger associations, for intellectual content is the domain of painting and sculpture. And gravity does not affect its beauty, for it is "an inherently pleasurable, meaningless play of concrete things that we encounter in life" (8). He was not alone. The nineteenth-century Herbartian school and early Greek geometrical studies and ideologies were kindred spirits. Architect and theorist Bruno Zevi (1957, 9) may also be said to be a follower of this school of thought, but with an emphasis on architecture as spatial experience. Scruton (1979, 1983) may be considered a proponent of the second claim.

The philosopher Anthony Savile (1982) claimed modern architecture predominantly (and mistakenly) viewed the aesthetic value of a building as a work of sculpture. Modern architecture is linked by such critics to an overemphasis on formal sculptural elements, a play of combined space, material, and detail independent of a feeling of use. There are, however, strong historical links between architecture and sculpture (Hildebrand, Meyer, and Ogden 1909, 102).

Problems with Essentialism

Deconstructionist architecture was also a conundrum. Is the attempt to show, in architectural form, the questioning of strongly held, fundamental beliefs a type of essentialism? Thomas Leddy (2002) has argued that Jacques Derrida's concepts of *disunity, difference,* and *différance* have no inherent privilege over unity and sameness. Paradoxically, a theory that aims to cut through or destabilize mainstream and institutional thought and practice, and remind us of multivocality, cannot argue it has the mandate to be heard *above* other voices. In practice, deconstruction in architecture quickly led to pastiche and whimsy.

Essentialism may appear in many forms. For example, essentialism may be suggested when writers such as John Haldane (1999) talk of the "enduring" aspect of architecture. So here the essential attribute is the last enduring aspect left in architectural form. A counterclaim that may be raised, appropriate to Kantian aesthetics, is that it suggests we only need to build ruins (Graham 2006).

Alternatively, essentialism may be the view that architecture has to be experienced in a certain way or that it must afford a certain type of experience to be considered architecture. In an extreme sine qua non form, essentialism may be the premise that architecture can *only* exist, or only be thought of, if it contains, affords, or is designed or built with a central essence.

The *evaluative* essentialist view of architecture may be that architecture can only be worthy of being compared to others as architecture, to stand as architecture, or it can only be worthy of criticism if it suggests or can be interpreted in a certain predefined way or, conversely, in some unspecified multitude of ways.

My problem with the aforementioned theories is not that they are wrong; they all have a kernel of truth. However, they have a common and recurring issue, for they seldom explain their parameters—where and when they should *not* be used—or if there is a test to determine their validity. It is highly desirable that we explain border conditions to our theories and determine whether they are falsifiable.

The built environment is complex; therefore, architecture, and our understanding of what is architecture, is complex. If a theory wilfully excludes or attacks criteria or case studies without solid reasoning, such a theory is likely to be guilty of essentialism. And essentialist theories could well lead to impoverished architectural experience for the sake of an argument.

Given these problems, one may ask why some defend essentialism. Perhaps a few architects feel under attack and wish for autonomy, or maybe essentialism has connotations of purity or transcendence. To argue that architecture is building without definite or fixed function may suggest there can be such a thing as a pure form of architecture, which in turn has Platonic, even religious, implications.

On reflection, the concept of architecture as an essence, a pure artwork, is highly debatable. A belief that a building, or a built environment, can only be considered to be a work art if it purifies itself, stripping any affordance of functional use, may not be such a good idea. And constraints often inspire creative people to design unique and engaging responses.

If essentialism is difficult to defend, does that leave nihilism as the only alternative? For example, as far back as 1991, Margaret Sołtan saw that architectural theory had two new aspects: the conflict between the painful realities of getting buildings built versus the increasingly ethereal nature of architectural discourse and its ever-increasing attempt to subvert readings of symbolic values of buildings.

William Hayes (2002) criticized the vagueness of much architectural criticism: terms are not clear, and sometimes deliberately confusing. Sołtan (1991) attacked the language of many architectural theorists, such as Stanley Tigerman's (1992) "inscrutable English." Ironically, even Tigerman vented against the verbiage of the profession.

Verbosity or not, architects do experience architecture directly. Daniel Kaufman (2002) suggested philosophers keep their prescriptions to first-order philosophy (epistemology, metaphysics, ethics, etc.) and leave prescription of second-order philosophy (science, language, arts) to the content experts. His reasons were partially cynical; he asserted philosophers do not highly value philosophy delving into second-order philosophy, and they are likely to be ignored by content experts because they lack firsthand experience in the field.

Kaufman advised they should merely try to describe and clarify theory in such second-order fields as architecture. This may be helpful; however, architects themselves love quoting philosophers, and philosophers can be both astute and concise in diagnosing problems and weaknesses in argument (Fisher 2015).

Mary Carman Rose (1976) defined meta-aesthetics as "philosophical inquiry about aesthetic inquiry." Perhaps philosophers could propose guidelines to architects to enable clearer terms and more reasoned debate on this topic, a type of meta-aesthetics. Can we propose guidelines on what would constitute a sound theory of virtual place based on architectural aesthetics without stipulating what those architectural aesthetics had to dictate and instead indicate only criteria that it must address? Unfortunately, this is unlikely: I agree with Mark W. Rowe (2000) that such a goal, to give principle independently of content, is difficult, if not impossible.

There are, however, smaller steps we can undertake. As critics, we should be wary of using an invalid teleological argument that the future is progress and, therefore, intrinsically good or that what has been dictates what must be. This is persuasive cajolement through a perceived aura of teleological inevitability. Conversely, suggesting VR scenario A is not worthwhile because it does not mirror real-world scenario B may be an empty assertion (Dreyfus 2001; Thompson 2016).

Similarly, using a word like *architecture* without specifying if one means a building, a built environment, a profession, or something else can lead to confusion. And so, too, can assuming the audience is defined and understood by the reader or listener. We should avoid using connotative words to sway people to our way of thinking without explaining to them the pros and cons of the alternatives. *Pure, organic, primeval, primary, fundamental,* and *originary* are all dangerous words, as is the Heideggerian compulsion to believe the ancient Greeks knew the authentic meanings of words and therefore the authentic meaning of life.

These are all simple rules of thumb, but too often do I see reductio ad absurdums (a form of argument that attempts to disprove a statement by showing that its most extreme examples inevitably lead to a ridiculous, absurd, or impractical conclusion), causal fallacies, straw man attacks, and so on. Essentialism seems to invite conflict rather than reasoned debate.

Phenomenological Problems

To be skeptical of essentialism in architecture is not to be skeptical of any attempt to ever find or create meaning and value. To quote Friedrich Nietzsche, "That my life has no aim is evident even from the accidental nature of its origin; that I can posit an aim for myself is another matter" (Kaufmann 1955, 40).

To create an aim for oneself is also a theme in early modernist architecture. My previous research was on Nordic architecture and how architects created details and spatial arrangements in order to pique curiosity during the long Nordic winters. To combat cabin fever, being stuck inside buildings for up to three months a year with very few hours of natural light, they decided to create a "dissolved" architecture. They deliberately aged the appearance of the building so that it would appear older, worn, and more loved.

While architecture is often seen as permanent and material, architects have to account for changes in light, temperature, sound, social groups, lifestyle preferences, and function and have to consider variety to combat potential boredom. Some architects, like the Finn Alvar Aalto and his partners, created rippling walls to reflect light so that phototropia would guide people around large buildings. Stylistically, various materials and forms would appear to roll over each other. Swedish architect Sigurd Lewerentz installed periscopes to insert beautiful indirect light and holes in his ship-hulled ceilings so they looked like abandoned factories with piercings of light through damaged roofs. Brick walls were made of bricks that were never cut to meet in corners.

Erik Gunnar Asplund sawed the exterior of the Woodland Crematorium marble columns in Stockholm to create a beguiling patina of apparent age (fig. 3.3). He also hung lights in his crematorium off apparently bending wires so that they appeared to float. In his Gothenburg Law Courts renovation, he designed the rise of the stairs so panicking defendants could not rush up the stairs and arrive breathless; the height of the rise slowed them down, and they would enter the courtroom calm and relaxed. He also created various stylistic layers of building so that the building appeared to be built on top of previous eras—a "buried typology," if you will.

Others, like Danish architect Arne Jacobsen, designed large areas of fenestration that reached down just past the knee, resulting in a sense of vertigo. These

Figure 3.3 Asplund: Woodland Crematorium, Stockholm. Erik Champion.

architects tried to dissolve the building in terms of light, changes in texture, the roles of spaces (functional versus ceremonial), the ways material met, or even ornamentation—for example, at the Stockholm Public Library, the door handles told the story of Adam and Eve: when you enter the library, Adam is about to bite the apple (of knowledge); when you leave the library, the library's exit door handles show Adam mid-bite.

For these architects, the interactivity of the place arose from the fusion of interstitial space and the body, the passage of time, the history of patina, thematic allegories, and implication of usage and care through wear (real or artificially created). That is not to say that they were postmodernists, for the buildings could be extended and provide transitions between old and new, engagement was not provided by esoteric juxtapositions, and movement was rewarded with the exploration of space.

Real-world places have unavoidable challenges: the necessity of different floor levels, the daylighting constraints of nearby buildings, acoustic and fire separation requirements, the flow of water, varying light and temperature, the movement of soil, the inevitability of time, and not least the need to create thematic experiences as people move between different spaces. Architecture is not frozen music, but it can contain shards of narrative, fragmented stories.

In Hamar Museum, near Oslo, Sverre Fehn executed the opposite: long concrete ramps were built suspended over a medieval farm building, and holes in the fifteenth-century structure were glazed but were otherwise left as is. Sigurd

Lewerentz created churches where not a single brick could be cut (to the chagrin of the workers) and left holes in the roof to let in light and evoke the poked chiaroscuro effect of abandoned warehouses with their ceiling perforated by time and wear. In Finland, Aalto created the untreated Nordic pine look, actually inspired by traditional Japanese architecture. Aalto would also select the old and battered for exterior finishes, such as the hand-beaten bricks on the red exterior wall of the Säynätsalo Town Hall. Jørn Utzon selected timber beams with splits and cracks for his housing project in Fredensborg, Denmark.

This is an organic architecture of expression, form, and function; the aim is not primarily to resemble organic shapes in nature or to use only biodegradable materials. It can be decorative but for psychological reasons. Organic design is particularly useful for tackling the persistent architectural challenge of how to provide for formal and more static spaces and functions as well as changing and dynamic ones. One answer is to provide head and tail spaces: the "head" spaces are formal and typically more regular, dealing with more ceremonial roles, while the "tail" spaces are more irregular, informal, and dynamic, catering for more dynamic, changeable social functions.

The solution may be decorative and thematic, not just structural. The architect may decide that all factors that go into the building process be thematically expressed as interdependent parts of the "character" of the building. If architecture is the thematically imagined relationship of individually perceived space, structure, and symbolism to the overall nature of the building, organic architecture is the process of orchestrating design, construction, and building performance as an interactive and self-referential system of sensory perception.

In the book *Organic Design in Twentieth-Century Nordic Architecture* (Champion 2019), I defined organic architecture as "a method of design whereby every problem attempts to be individually answered by a coherently identifiable design process that in turn must be altered, changed, and extended to address every necessary particular issue without destroying the continuity of the process itself as a self-evident organic entity."

However, these architects not only prematurely aged the appearance of materials but also skewed the buildings' windows and corridors toward the light and symbolically bifurcated the interiors into dynamic, nondecorated paths and peaceful, highly decorated centers. They were encouraged by architect Carl Petersen's theoretical teachings and inspired by John Ruskin's Byzantine dictum: "Wherever you can rest, there decorate: where rest is forbidden, so is beauty."

Many of the architects were inspired by Nietzsche's Apollonian-Dionysian bifurcation of classical architecture and by Heidegger's talk of clearing: to design spaces separated by phenomenological intuitions. For example, Sverre Fehn commented (via P. O. Fjeld), "A boundary is not that at which something stops, but as the Greeks recognized, the boundary is that from which something begins its presencing. That is why the concept is that of horismos, that is, the horizon, the boundary. Space is in essence that for which room has been made, that which is let into bounds. That for which room is made is always granted and hence is joined, that is gathered by virtue of location, that is by such a thing as a bridge. Accordingly, spaces receive their being from locations and not from 'space'" (Fjeld and Fehn 1983, 10).

Can computer-aided design (CAD) provide this phenomenological boundary making? Maybe, but not easily. Why do I mention this theory of architectural design? Unlike the earlier theories mentioned, it is open and adaptable. Computer-simulated spaces may encourage us to design machinelike environments, but the many ongoing failures of modernist architecture indicate that this design aesthetic is increasingly unfulfilling; "star" modernist, high-tech or futurist architecture (designed by celebrity architects, "starchitects") is unlikely to be flexible, incorporate personalization, or respond to the symbolic needs of its users or the aesthetic and associative qualities of the landscape and surrounds. So why must we incorporate the machine-aesthetic or an essentialist architectural theory to the design of virtual places when the real-world examples fail to capture, support, and evoke the richness of place?

Architectural Design Tools: The Limitations of CAD

Architectural tools are instrumentalist; architects typically do not work on or near the site, as they need specialist tools connected to databases, not experiences, to complete their work. Architects have also complained that CAD, which allows them to create three-dimensional models and fly throughs and produce detailed drawings for the builders, are not very helpful as design tools. Although some have argued that verbalization is more important than freehand sketching for design ideation (Jonson 2005), others have disagreed and stated CAD is limited as a creative design tool (Dorta, Perez, and Lesage 2008; Robertson and Radcliffe 2009).

For example, Jean Thilmany (2019), associate editor for the American Society of Mechanical Engineers and its website, noted that mechanical engineers have mixed feelings in regard to CAD. CAD experts she interviewed told her that while CAD improved the overall quality of design, it limited creativity (as designers tended to choose geometry that they knew was easier to model in CAD), was slower than sketching, and did not prevent design ideas that proved impractical when built.

These concerns also affect architecture, but here, a major concern seems to regard the amount of time and software required for full design creativity with CAD tools. In "Design Too Important to Leave to CAD," Tara Roopinder (2016) recounts a talk by an expert at Skidmore Owings Moore (SOM), the eleventh-largest architecture firm in the world; the expert told the architects that CAD tools alone were not enough and that they needed to know many more tools and programming to be fully creative.

In the online article "Digital Design in 2016: An Industry Snapshot of Australia," Ben Coorey (2016) surveyed architects and found that "the single biggest challenge for designers is finding the time to learn new software and keep up to date." Most had to learn about the software themselves, had to educate others on their project teams, and were stronger in two-dimensional documentation, three-dimensional modeling, and building information modeling than more advanced applications like rendering, parametric design, scripting, and animation. Perhaps because of the continual self-training needed, and the time-poor nature of the architectural profession, most respondents were fairly conservative in terms of the software they hoped to use soon.

These concerns in the architectural profession also affect the development of games and virtual environments (and thus, by extension, virtual places) when undertaken by architects. Tools like CAD are genuinely interactive digital tools, but they don't create experientially rich, *thematically immersive*, and *interactive* virtual worlds. Unlike a typical software package, which ideally is designed to be easy to learn and easy to master, a virtual place is elusive in boundary and contrary in nature: humans wish to experience both the periphery and the center, simultaneously.

Interactive Media

Given the time required for developing CAD skills, the specific software experience required for digital games is not yet well taught in many architectural education institutes, but it is not only an issue of specific software skills. Digital games are not only virtual environments; they are challenging but engaging goal-based activities that afford agency and thematic interaction and provide rewards. Unlike typical software, a digital game is often designed to be *challenging*, difficult to learn, and difficult to master but even more difficult to put down (Brown and Bell 2004).

Architects can and do use game engines (Donath and Regenbrecht 1999; Boeykens 2013; Dalton 2016). They offer analyses of architecture and architectural place-making inside games (Ljungström 2005; McGregor 2006) and suggest architecture will move closer to game design (Hobson 2014). Some have also provided expertise to game designers (Van Buren 2015) or have moved into the fields of game design, online world creation, and machinima (Shaw 2015; Fairs 2016), but I argue they are the exception rather than the rule. Hopefully, this will change, and when architects learn more about game design, this knowledge will help them in turn. As architect Deanna van Buren (2015) wrote on the cross-industry collaboration behind the game *The Witness*, "The rules of The Witness with regards to gameplay were rigorous and finite in many ways. As architects, we had to learn about what this meant. It is one of the things architects need to understand when working with developers and an aspect that developers can more rigorously apply to environmental design."

Nor are architects trained in interactive media; their tools (see the earlier paragraphs on CAD) are typically instrumentalist and passive. Unfortunately, designing interactive, real-time, immersive, and imaginative places with new media is far more complicated and tortuous than many new designers anticipate. For virtual places, some academics have also argued that they must have a persistent state, something architectural communication courses typically do not cover.

Take, for instance, Richard Bartle's book *Designing Virtual Worlds*. One section lists the minimum requirements for designing a virtual world (Bartle 2003), and it is quite demanding! Yet even though his book was described (perhaps self-described) as "the most comprehensive treatment of virtual world design to-date from one of the true pioneers and most sought-after design consultants," it defines a virtual world as no more than a space that "continues to exist and develop internally even when no people are interacting with it." Bartle's requirements would need to increase if his definition of virtual worlds were as demanding as that of this book (expanded on in chapter 8).

People

Architectural media seem reluctant to include people even if architectural spaces do not work as places without people (e.g., famous modern architectural "masterpieces" tend to be presented in architectural publications without people). The "peopling" in architectural presentations is not meant to reveal the building in all its architectural glory but to sell the building independently of how it will be used. There is an old architectural joke that new hospital buildings would be perfect if they did not have people using them.

This tendency also seems to be reflected in virtual simulations. Laia Pujol Tost (2007) has warned, "Consequently, VR applications have consisted mainly of reconstructions of monuments where people accomplish a decorative function instead of being shown as agents of change.... CAA07 has definitively established the spreading of VR's more scientific uses. However, all these applications, even the experimental ones, relate to the site and not to the social and natural agents behind the formation of the archaeological record."

Juan Barceló (2012) has argued for the addition of people in computer simulations:

> Computer simulation should allow us to understand archaeological observables in terms of a priori affordances: relationships between observed properties and the inferred properties/abilities of people having generated those properties.... In other words, people having lived in the past do not appear as passive museum objects. Inside the computer simulation, and as well as they did in their real world, they act as influenced by other people having lived at the same time and any other change in the social or physical environment, for instance, climatic change, social transformation, etc. People interact, influence others, reinforce some actions, interfere with others, and even sometimes prevent the action of other people. People consciously and deliberately generate contexts (activities) in part through their own objectives.

French director Antonin Artaud was the first to use the term *virtual reality* (in 1933). Jaron Lanier is, however, famous for coining the term in English, but he has revealed that *virtual reality* was inspired by the philosopher Susanne Langer (Leddy 2018), who was describing the "virtual worlds" of modernist painting. Lanier envisaged VR as "an extended version of virtual worlds" (Evenden 2016), which means it included a sense of embodiment, with an avatar that could interact with virtual objects or with other people in a social environment. The key point here is that the early pioneers envisaged VR as a doorway into social worlds. When we think of virtual places, I suggest we also consider how an experience of place, even virtual place, is either inhabited by people or suggests how it could be inhabited by people. Carole Saunders and colleagues (2011) perhaps said it best: "The starting point should not be what is possible with the current technologies but how to allow people to find a place for themselves in the space that is provided."

Terrain

In 2001, Brian Orland, Kanjanee Budthimedhee, and Jori Uusitalo wrote, "VR deserves far more than the scant attention it has received from geographers." I'd suggest this statement is still valid, but this is not the fault of geographers. While technical developers are moving quickly to integrate natural spaces into their workplaces (Hawken 2017), there are few devices that fully exploit the multisensory variety of the world around us (Eve 2017), and research and consumptive media are focused on the visual. Although audio is highly immersive (Whitelock et al. 2000), I'd contend that it is not greatly explored in immersive virtual environments. Dynamic characteristics of the space, such as changes in the terrain's slope or texture or to the lighting and weather or the realistic movement of wind, sea, planets, and stars, all have computational costs.

To save on these issues, virtual worlds are usually never-ending terrains (suburbs) or discrete units (islands). Our planet, on the other hand, varies according to geophysical isolation, assimilation, and change, with the growth, bridging, and disappearance of land affecting the size, uniqueness, and success of both animal and plant life through evolution, specialization, and migration. These micro and macro changes in soil and stream affect our settlements and therefore our societies.

Phenomenology of Landscape

The architect Frank Lloyd Wright would demand architects sleep on the site they aim to build on, while Christopher Tilley's (1994) *A Phenomenology of Landscape* provides an example of an archaeologist asking researchers investigating traditional societies to inhabit, explore, and test the landscape in situ, with all our senses. Tilley argued these experiences could not be conveyed by two-dimensional media like maps, but I would also extrapolate this warning to virtual environments based purely on sight, for landscapes are not only visual experiences. Even on archaeological sites, archaeologists have told me they want the site to be visualized in VR but that it was imperative to "feel" the soil via a shovel or a trowel.

As Tim Ingold (1993) noted in his abstract, "Landscape and temporality are the major unifying themes of archaeology and social-cultural anthropology"; however, he also declared that "human life is a process that involves the passage of time" and famously defined a *taskscape* as an array of activities analogous to the variety of features of a landscape, but a landscape is also an enduring record of "the lives and works of past generations who have dwelt within it, and in doing so, have left something there of themselves." The landscape is thus a memory, remembered by experiencing it not as an object but as an experience through the dwelling, through journeying. And this raises problems.

For Ingold, the landscape is not land: it is qualitative, not quantitative; heterogeneous, not homogenous. The landscape was created before us, but it affords for us bounded experiences. And our interaction with it leaves traces after we are gone. It is hard to see how these characteristics are also made available in virtual landscapes.

Time

Design takes time, construction takes far more time, and inhabitation takes time and understanding. Digital places are conceived, reconfigured, and deployed in different time scales to real places. In the real world, a sense of placeness is enhanced through apparent signs of embodiment, multimodality, and role-play (and thematic affordances). These dynamic and modifiable features allow inhabitants to add infill, while climate, usage, and age also help create localized and personalized patinas, materials that show the effect of time, wear, and care.

Like place, architecture provides a *betweenness*, not just inside and outside, but also between constancy and change. For just as settlements were traditionally built between at least two different ecosystems (different providers of food in case one ecosystem weakened), so too should architecture, as a cultural activity, be built *across* eras.

Architecture aims for immortality and carries the immortal hopes and values of past generations whether they are engraved via graffiti or plaques, but the roar and pageantry of these painted dreams eventually fade into dust and the gleaming steel and marble crumble into ruin. Yet functional modernist architecture avoided expressing an awareness of its lifespan as either style or built object. As Sverre Fehn (Almaas 2009) drily remarked, "The bird nest is absolute Functionalism, because the bird is not aware of its death."

I would like to thank these architects for reminding me that architecture is not just building places but also building in a place and between places; it is spatial and material, interstitial, and often interplatial, but it is also *across* time. Creating spaces with unique character and thematically linking between them is a demanding challenge, coupled with the need to consider how materials deform and alter over time and with environmental changes.

An architectural theory must, I believe, consider the issue of time and change. To be visualized *virtually*, these breadcrumbs of inhabitation require much more work to express procedural decay and user-based erosion as well as afford richer forms of learning about the built environment than crashing crates or shooting temporary holes into digital walls.

Genius Loci: Care, Time, and Sacrifice

The notion of a virtual environment as a process rather than a presentation seems lost. Traditional architectural craft is embodied, sited, takes time, requires care, and records care (or at least leaves traces, signs of care). This is less and less the case with modern, fast-track construction techniques.

Genius loci is an ancient Roman term meaning a daemon, an interface between mortality and the gods. The siting of ancient Greek temples to seat certain gods in certain types of landscapes (Scully 2013) has been mentioned in architecture. While it may not be a rigorous or accurate interpretation of Heidegger (Auret 2015), Christian Norberg-Schulz's (1980) *Genius Loci: Towards a Phenomenology of Architecture* is probably the most famous publication of this theme, and it has been widely used and cited, from architectural theory (Haddad 2010; Otero-Pailos 2010; Habib, Mohammad, and Sahhaf 2012) to place-based education projects (Schneider and Ark 2016).

There has been some trenchant criticism of this reading of genius loci in architecture, from Richard Coyne (2007, 75–76; Snodgrass and Coyne 2013) to Alberto Pérez-Gómez (2007). My point is that Norberg-Schulz's book is very light on the topic of care. It seems more concerned with the architect's intention. Genius loci as a reference to the (deific) spirit of place, and the sense of a specific spirit that cares for that space's unique character, seems to have been lost in modern architectural theory.

Care is a key aspect of cultural heritage, but it is also, in a sense, important to players sharing virtual worlds. Michael Nitsche (2008, 200) wrote, "A genius loci is often defined by subjective experience of the location. To establish some measure, three indicators for placeness are suggested: identity, self-motivated and self-organized action, and traces of memory." He saw the relevance of earning the *worth of place*, noting, "Placeness is not a quality of a virtual space per se, but one that can be achieved for it through the inhabitants: the game's players. Virtual placeness has to be earned. The indicators presented here showed that virtual places can be traced in the changing character identity, self-motivated goals and actions, and memory recollection of localized game world events" (210).

User-Experience Design and Architecture

Why has modernist architecture suffered so many criticisms over its lack of human scale, functionality, or a satisfactory user experience? My first point is that many exemplars of the modern movement of architecture were pavilions rather than houses, they were temporary and functionally limited showcases. The most famous architectural works by the most famous architects of the twentieth century have arguably been predominantly buildings of spectacle rather than buildings of inhabitation. Pavilions exemplify the so-called twentieth-century masterpieces by the masters, typically including Frank Lloyd Wright, Ludwig Mies van der Rohe, Le Corbusier, Walter Gropius, and possibly also Alvar Aalto (Goldberger 1976; Hoag and Hoag 1977; Peter 1994).

Not many buildings are pavilions (much less in the sense of a secondary building), but those featured in twentieth-century modernist books typically were pavilions or were factory and warehouse inspired (Le Corbusier, Gropius). Jonathan Hill (2006) declared the (capital P) Pavilion to be an architectural icon because it is perceived as an artwork, first serving as an exhibition building between 1929 and 1930 (probably referring to Asplund's Stockholm Exhibition), for the next fifty-six years being known through photographs, and then later being seen as reconstruction, "both exhibit and gallery, the reconstruction reinforces the status of the architect as an artist and implies that contemplation is the experience most appropriate to the building." The form and detailing of the Pavilion is typically symmetrical, smaller, and sleeker and does not carry complex signs of inhabitation; it is easier to model and to render, but computer environments are *typically* not as suitable for contemplation as real-world examples.

Secondly, post-occupancy evaluation (POE) has not always been effectively taught, maintained, or commissioned in the design of real-world places. While it is true that architects and other specialists do this, it is still not that common. Many architecture schools do not have extensive courses and specialists in POE, and (in my opinion) not enough developers pay for it.

The problems are to do with the industry overall rather than the architects. Thankfully the previously mentioned issues are changing, but my conversations with architects as well as academic and industry publications over the last four decades suggest to me these are still problems. Ian Cooper (2001) goes further back, detailing "the stalled development of post-occupancy evaluation (POE) in Britain since the 1960s." Wolfgang Preiser (1995) decried POE as "something that has been neglected for too long." Alex Zimmerman and Mark Martin (2001) criticized its fragmentation and lack of benefits as well as its "exclusion from professional curricula." More recently, in 2010, Mike Riley, Noora Kokkarinen, and Michael Pitt (2010) wrote, "The general uses of POE are discussed alongside the potential benefits that would come from having it as a mainstream process. For this to happen, the barriers against the process need to be overcome. . . . The industry need[s] to make changes to the organizational culture by either delineating what best practice would [be] or [by starting to include] POE as a part of [its] regular services[,] therefore taking away the issue of who conducts it" (Bordass and Leaman 2005).

The lack of POE is a problem. Evaluation is crucial not only for real-world place design but also for the design of *virtual* places.

Summary

Real places evoke memories, they are unique, and they are part of our identity. Simulations can provide space for contemplation and reflection, but real-world places are not simulations of other places, even if they borrow and reorganize elements from other places. You might argue that some places *are* replicated, and while, yes, that is true, this replication can erode the *placeness* of the original.

Many modern Western banks are designed to look like Greek temples. Greek temples were sited according to characteristics of the landscape or the dedicated deity of the city or other buildings and oriented to the sun or heavenly bodies (Boutsikas and Ruggles 2011; Hannah, Magli, and Orlando 2015; Liritzis et al. 2017). But the Greek temple's construction was also designed stylistically as an homage to early wooden temples. The temple was approached from a sacred path of pilgrimage that oriented the walker to views in the landscape. The exterior was not white; polychromatic paint emphasized key parts of the building. Greek temples did not typically have an interior focus as worshippers gathered outside (interiority was a hallmark of Roman architecture). They also represented not just ceremonial sacrifice but also sacrifice in terms of the huge efforts required just to build them (Scully 2013).

Yet later architects copied the classical Greek temple canon slavishly—externally, that is, and only in its formal aspects. The result: cultural dilution. The uniqueness, sense of sacrifice, and aura of venerability were lost. Modern Grecian-style banks have an interior (unlike Greek temples); they aren't sited in a profound way, covered in the polychromic paint commemorating ritual and mythology, or dedicated to a deity (for a Greek temple the characteristics of the house of the revered deity would dictate its scale, order, and proportion). They don't honor the history of their construction and hence the originary intention of creating a permanent landmark to sacred space.

This is not just a blunt criticism of neoclassical and postmodern banks. Apart from the fuzziness created by the cultural appropriations of the stylistically schizophrenic, recent architecture has lost its sense of engagement, intentionality, and care. You can see the hands of a thousand workers in the rippled or textured brickwork of a cathedral; you can marvel at the bravery of the workers at the Duomo of Florence or the Hagia Sophia of Istanbul (possibly an inspiration for European gothic). And you can feel the sense of ceremony and atmosphere of a building by merely examining what has been worn and what has been taken care of. Engagement, care, and the representation of these two factors happen *less often* in virtual environments when we view them as virtual place.

What is required for designing virtual places? An understanding not just of design but also of digital- and internet-based models, formats, and limitations. What does architecture theory leave out? Most of the importance of movement, agency, playful engagement (a lusory attitude), and any resulting interactivity. A refined theory needs to be critical but flexible; it would be informed by affordances of the environment but also by specific challenges of the design medium. It needs to be based on an understanding of games (interactivity, navigation, challenge, imagination, reward, agency), a further understanding of interactive narrative and space (games, films, theme parks), and an understanding of the limited and unlimited embodiment of digital environments and the creative development potential of spaces using the latest interfaces.

Architectural theory is often rigidly essentialist, but I argue it would be better served by being flexible, component-based related to goals, evaluation-friendly, and focused on its audience and setting. For example, Kelly Lynch's theory of how we navigate in the city using our mental maps (collected from our memories of the city's paths, edges, districts, nodes, and landmarks) does not apply equally to everyone and hence how we navigate has been hard to determine using virtual environments.

Hopefully, some guidelines may save us from some endless debates on what is essential, necessary, or sufficient.

1. Acknowledge that comparing virtual to real or past to future is problematic.
2. Parameters to definitions help us concentrate on key arguments behind definitions.
3. Theories should have room for growth and modification, especially in the fast-growing but contestable area of virtual places.
4. Develop, where possible, theories that could be explored, test, and repeated.
5. Where results could be disseminated, disseminate as widely as possible.

Teaching architecture (design, history, theory, construction, user experience, etc.) through simulating traditional forms of "learning by doing" is an incredibly understudied research area and is of vital importance to a richer understanding of place (Roussos et al. 1997). However, the actual spatial implications of siting learning tasks in a virtual environment are still underresearched, as typical evaluation of virtual environments has been relatively context free, designed for user freedom and forward-looking creativity. It is much more difficult to create a virtual place that brings the past and present alive without destroying it.

Rybczynski notes that according to Christopher Alexander, there is a real danger in computer-based architectural design; it distorts our view of the problem so that we tend to think of the solution in terms of what is most convenient to solve computationally (Rybczynski 2013). I see both danger and opportunity. Be they VR systems or game editors, digital media technologies provided to architects can provide virtual places that are evanescent, ephemeral, experientially immersive, and atmospheric. In return, architects could show our digital media colleagues the importance of key architectural concepts of interrelated and interstitial space, inhabitation-derived wear and tear, territoriality, kinesthetically learned narrative, proprioceptive feedback, phototropic signifiers, and head-tail spatial design.

What would this mean for metacriteria and for understanding the architectural design of virtual places? Any theory that cannot take on parts of other theories is likely to be too vague or, conversely, too inflexible to be of much use, for architectural experience is rich, varied, and complex. If it cannot be falsified (if no conditions could prove it wrong), then I wonder how useful it could be.

Inhabitation, world, place, and interaction are all interrelated in the real world; it is up to us as architects and designers to interpret and transfer their power and potential to virtual environments. In doing so, we should be more critical of the superficial application of these key terms, for they are critically important. If architecture cannot help us understand how it helps its inhabitants to *individually and collectively* inhabit space, transform space, and be transformed by it over time, architecture may as well be limited to the description of frozen music. Let us creatively resist: the next phase in virtual world design is before us, and architects can do much more than design pretty polygons.

Note

1. Partially derived from a conference paper: Erik Malcolm Champion, "Essentialist Polemics in Architectural History," paper presented at SAHANZ 2006, Melbourne, AUS, September 29–October 2, 2006.

References

Almaas, Ingerid Helsing, ed. 2009. *Sverre Fehn: Projects and Reflections*. Oslo: Norske arkitekters landsforbund.

Auret, Hendrik Andries. 2015. "Care, Place and Architecture: A Critical Reading of Christian Norberg-Schulz's Architectural Interpretation of Martin Heidegger's Philosophy." PhD thesis, Architecture, University of the Free State. http://scholar.ufs.ac.za:8080/xmlui/handle/11660/2242.

Ballantyne, Andrew. 2013. "Introduction." In *What Is Architecture?*, edited by Andrew Ballantyne, 9. London: Routledge.

Barceló, Juan A. 2012. "Computer Simulation in Archaeology: Art, Science or Nightmare?" *Virtual Archaeology Review* 3 (5): 8–12.

Bartle, Richard A. 2003. *Designing Virtual Worlds*. Indianapolis: New Riders.

Boeykens, Stefan. 2013. *Unity for Architectural Visualization*. Birmingham, UK: Packt.

Bordass, Bill, and Adrian Leaman. 2005. "Making Feedback and Post-Occupancy Evaluation Routine 1: A Portfolio of Feedback Techniques." *Building Research & Information* 33 (4): 347–52.

Boutsikas, Efrosyni, and Clive Ruggles. 2011. "Temples, Stars, and Ritual Landscapes: The Potential for Archaeoastronomy in Ancient Greece." *American Journal of Archaeology* 115 (1): 55–68. https://doi.org/10.3764/aja.115.1.0055.

Brown, Barry, and Mark Bell. 2004. "CSCW at Play: 'There' as a Collaborative Virtual Environment." Paper presented at the ACM Conference on Computer Supported Cooperative Work, November 6–10, 2004, Chicago, IL.

Champion, E. 2019. *Organic Design in Twentieth-Century Nordic Architecture*. New York: Routledge.

Cooper, Ian. 2001. "Post-occupancy Evaluation—Where Are You?" *Building Research & Information* 29 (2): 158–63. https://doi.org/10.1080/09613210010016820.

Coorey, Ben. 2016. "Digital Design in 2016: An Industry Snapshot of Australia." Architecture & Design. Last Modified November 1, 2016. Accessed July 2, 2017. http://www .architectureanddesign.com.au/features/features-articles/most-popular-digital -design-tools-in-australia.

Coyne, Richard 2007. "Thinking through Virtual Reality: Place, Non-Place and Situated Cognition." Special issue, *Techné: Research in Philosophy and Technology* 11 (1). Accessed May 20, 2021. https://scholar.lib.vt.edu/ejournals/SPT/v10n3/coyne.html.

Dalton, Ruth. 2016. "Want to Build Better Computer Games? Call an Architect." The Conversation, May 6, 2016. Last Modified May 27, 2017. Accessed August 3, 2017. https:// theconversation.com/want-to-build-better-computer-games-call-an-architect-58912.

Donath, Dirk, and Holger Regenbrecht. 1999. "Using Immersive Virtual Reality Systems for Spatial Design in Architecture." Paper presented at the AVOCAAD Second International Conference, Brussels, BEL, April 8–10, 1999. Accessed March 20, 2020. http://papers.cumincad.org/cgi-bin/works/paper/fd35.

Donougho, Martin. 1987. "The Language of Architecture." *Journal of Aesthetic Education* 21 (3): 53–67.

Dorta, Tomas, Edgar Perez, and Annemarie Lesage. 2008. "The Ideation Gap: Hybrid Tools, Design Flow and Practice." *Design Studies* 29 (2): 121–41.

Dreyfus, Hubert L. 2001. *On the Internet*. London: Routledge.

Eco, Umberto. 1997. "Function and Sign: The Semiotics of Architecture." In *Rethinking Architecture: A Reader in Cultural Theory*, edited by N. Leach, 173–195. London: Routledge, 1997.

Eisenberg, Nancy, and Janet Strayer. 1990. *Empathy and Its Development*. Cambridge: Cambridge University Press.

English Oxford Living Dictionaries. 2017. "Architect." Accessed July 3, 2017. https://en .oxforddictionaries.com/definition/architect.

Eve, Stuart. 2017. "The Embodied GIS: Using Mixed Reality to Explore Multi-sensory Archaeological Landscapes." *Internet Archaeology* 44. https://doi.org/10.11141/ia.44.3.

Evenden, Ian. 2016. "The History of Virtual Reality: Step Back in Time to See How Art Fused with Cutting-Edge VR Technology to Create Entire Worlds. . . ." *Science Focus: The Online Home of BBC Focus Magazine* (blog), November 6, 2016. Accessed March 20, 2020. https://www.sciencefocus.com/future-technology/the-history-of-virtual-reality/.

Fairs, Marcus. 2016. "Video Games Will Become 'New Tools' to Solve Architecture's Global Challenges." De Zeen Magazine, March 7, 2016. Last Modified May 27, 2017. Accessed August 3, 2017. https://www.dezeen.com/2016/03/07/jose-sanchez-block-hood-video -game-tools-solve-global-challenges-architecture/.

Fisher, Saul. 2015. "Philosophy of Architecture" *Stanford Encyclopedia of Philosophy*. Stanford. Accessed January 30, 2020. https://plato.stanford.edu/archives/win2016/entries /architecture/.

Fjeld, Per Olaf, and Sverre Fehn. 1983. *Sverre Fehn: The Thought of Construction*. New York: Rizzoli International Publications.

Frampton, Kenneth. 2014. "Towards a Critical Regionalism." In *Post Modernism: A Reader*, edited by Thomas Docherty, 268–80. London: Routledge.

Goldberger, Paul. 1976. "Alvar Aalto Is Dead at 78; Master Modern Architect." *New York Times*, May 13, 1976. Last Modified June 29, 2017. Accessed August 3, 2017. http://www.nytimes .com/1976/05/13/archives/alvar-aalto-is-dead-at-78-master-modern-architect.html.

Göller, Adolf. 1994. "What Is the Cause of Perpetual Style Change in Architecture?" In *Empathy, Form, and Space: Problems in German Aesthetics,* edited by H. F. Mallgrave and E. Ikonomou, 1873–93. Chicago: Getty Center for the History of Art and the Humanities.

Graham, Gordon. 2006. "Can There Be Public Architecture?" *Journal of Aaesthetics and Art Criticism* 64 (2): 243–49.

Habib, Farah, Sayyed Mohammad, and Khosro Sahhaf. 2012. "Christian Norberg-Schulz and the Existential Space." *International Journal of Architecture and Urban Development* 1 (3): 45–51.

Haddad, Elie. 2010. "Christian Norberg-Schulz's Phenomenological Project in Architecture." *Architectural Theory Review* 15 (1): 88–101.

Haldane, John. 1999. "Form, Meaning and Value: A History of the Philosophy of Architecture." *Journal of Architecture* 4 (1): 9–20.

Hannah, Robert, Giulio Magli, and Andrea Orlando. 2015. "Understanding the Meaning of Greek Temples's Orientations: Akragas Valley of the Temples as a Case Study." arXiv .org. Last Modified November 2015. Accessed July 27, 2017. http://adsabs.harvard.edu /cgi-bin/bib_query?arXiv:1511.02497.

Hawken, Scott. 2017. "Blurred Lines: Landscapes That Bridge the Physical and Virtual Worlds." *Foreground* (blog), June 23, 2017. Accessed June 12, 2021. https://www .foreground.com.au/public-domain/virtual-real-worlds-youth-future-public-space/.

Hayes, William H. 2002. "Architectural Criticism." *Journal of Aesthetics and Art Criticism* 60 (4): 325–29.

Heidegger, Martin, and William Lovitt. 1977. *The Question Concerning Technology, and Other Essays.* New York: Harper & Row.

Hildebrand, Adolf, Max F. Meyer, and Robert Morris Ogden. 1909. *The Problem of Form in Painting and Sculpture.* New York: G. E. Stechert.

Hill, Jonathan. 2006. *Immaterial Architecture.* New York: Routledge.

Hoag, Edwin, and Joy Hoag. 1977. *Masters of Modern Architecture: Frank Lloyd Wright, Le Corbusier, Mies Van Der Rohe, and Walter Gropius.* Indianapolis: Bobbs-Merrill.

Hobson, Ben. 2014. "Architects Could Become 'Closer to Game Designers or Filmmakers.'" De Zeen Magazine, October 15, 2014. Last Modified May 27, 2017. Accessed August 3, 2017. https://www.dezeen.com/2014/10/15/keiichi-matsuda-architecture-augmented -reality-architects-become-game-designers-filmmakers/.

Ingold, Tim. 1993. "The Temporality of the Landscape." *World Archaeology* 25 (2): 152–74. https://doi.org/10.1080/00438243.1993.9980235.

Jonson, Ben. 2005. "Design Ideation: The Conceptual Sketch in the Digital Age." *Design Studies* 26 (6): 613–24. https://doi.org/http://dx.doi.org/10.1016/j.destud.2005.03.001.

Kaufman, Daniel A. 2002. "Normative Criticism and the Objective Value of Artworks." *Journal of Aesthetics and Art Criticism* 60 (2): 151–66.

Kaufmann, Walter. 1955. *The Portable Nietzsche.* New York: Penguin Books.

Laugier, Marc-Antoine. 1977. *An Essay on Architecture (Essai sur l'architecture).* Translated by W. Herrmann and A. Herrmann. Documents and Sources in Architecture, no. 1. Los Angeles: Hennessey and Ingalls.

Leddy, Thomas. 2002. "Shusterman's Pragmatist Aesthetics." *Journal of Speculative Philosophy* 16 (1): 10–16.

———. 2018. *The Extraordinary in the Ordinary: The Aesthetics of Everyday Life.* Peterborough, CAN: Broadview Press.

Liritzis, Ioannis, Evgenia Bousoulegka, Anne Nyquist, Belen Castro, Fahad Mutlaq Alotaibi, and Androniki Drivaliari. 2017. "New Evidence from Archaeoastronomy on Apollo

Architecture

Oracles and Apollo-Asclepius Related Cult." *Journal of Cultural Heritage* 26:129–43. https://doi.org/10.1016/j.culher.2017.02.011.

Ljungström, Mattias. 2005. "The Use of Architectural Patterns in MMORPGs." Paper presented at the Aesthetics of Play conference, Department of Information Science and Media Studies, University of Bergen, NOR, October 14–15, 2005. Accessed August 3, 2017. http://www.aestheticsofplay.org/ljunstrom.php.

McGregor, Georgia Leigh. 2006. "Architecture, Space and Gameplay in World of Warcraft and Battle for Middle Earth 2." CyberGames '06: Proceedings of the 2006 International Conference on Game Research and Development. Murdoch University, Perth Australia, December 6, 2006.

Mitchell, David, and Gillian Chaplin. 1984. *The Elegant Shed: New Zealand Architecture since 1945.* New York: Oxford University Press.

Morgan, David. 1996. "The Enchantment of Art: Abstraction and Empathy from German Romanticism to Expressionism." *Journal of the History of Ideas* 57 (2): 317–341.

Nitsche, Michael. 2008. *Video Game Spaces: Image, Play, and Structure in 3D Game Worlds.* Cambridge, MA: MIT Press.

Norberg-Schulz, Christian. 1980. *Genius Loci: Towards a Phenomenology of Architecture.* London: Academy Editions.

Orland, Brian, Kanjanee Budthimedhee, and Jori Uusitalo. 2001. "Considering Virtual Worlds as Representations of Landscape Realities and as Tools for Landscape Planning." *Landscape and Urban Planning* 54 (1–4): 139–48.

Otero-Pailos, Jorge. 2010. *Architecture's Historical Turn: Phenomenology and the Rise of the Postmodern.* Minneapolis: University of Minnesota Press.

Pérez-Gómez, Alberto. 2007. "The Place Is Not a Postcard: The Problem of Genius Loci." *Architecture Norway: An Online Review of Architecture,* June 5, 2007. Accessed February 3, 2020. https://architecturenorway.no/questions/cities-sustainability/perez -gomez-genius/.

Peter, John. 1994. *The Oral History of Modern Architecture: Interviews with the Greatest Architects of the Twentieth Century.* Vol. 1. New York: Harry N. Abrams.

Preiser, Wolfgang F. E. 1995. "Post-occupancy Evaluation: How to Make Buildings Work Better." *Facilities* 13 (11): 19–28. https://doi.org/10.1108/02632779510097787.

Richmond, Sheldon. 1995. "Meta-Aesthetics and Meta-Methodology: A Response to Andy Sanders Review Essay." *Tradition and Discovery: The Polanyi Society Periodical* 22 (2): 36–37.

Riley, Mike, Noora Kokkarinen, and Michael Pitt. 2010. "Assessing Post Occupancy Evaluation in Higher Education Facilities." *Journal of Facilities Management* 8 (3): 202–13. https://doi.org/doi:10.1108/14725961011058839.

Robertson, B. F., and D. F. Radcliffe. 2009. "Impact of CAD Tools on Creative Problem Solving in Engineering Design." *Computer-Aided Design* 41 (3): 136–46.

Roopinder, Tara. 2016. "Design Too Important to Leave to CAD." Engineering.com. Last Modified August 15, 2016. Accessed June 12, 2021. http://www.engineering.com/BIM /ArticleID/12893/Is-Design-Too-Important-to-Leave-to-CAD.aspx.

Rose, Mary Carman. 1976. "Nature as Aesthetic Object: An Essay in Meta-Aesthetics." *British Journal of Aesthetics* 16 (1): 3–12.

Roussos, M., A. E. Johnson, J. Leigh, V. A. Vasilakis, C. R. Barnes, and T. G. Moher. 1997. "NICE: Combining Constructionism, Narrative and Collaboration in a Virtual Learning Environment." *SIGGRAPH Computer Graphics* 31 (3): 62–63.

Rowe, Mark W. 2000. "How Do Criticism and Aesthetic Theory Fit Together?" *British Journal of Aesthetics* 40 (1): 115–32.

Rybczynski, Witold. 2013. "Parametric Design: What's Gotten Lost amid the Algorithms." Architect, July 11, 2013. Accessed July 2, 2017. https://www.architectmagazine.com /design/parametric-design-whats-gotten-lost-amid-the-algorithms_o.

Saunders, Carole, Anne F. Rutkowski, M. van Genuchten, D. Vogel, and J. Molina Orrego. 2011. "Virtual Space and Place: Theory and Test." Special issue: New Ventures in Virtual Worlds, *MIS Quarterly* 35 (4): 1079–98. https://doi.org/10.2307/41409974.

Savile, Anthony. 1982. *The Test of Time: An Essay in Philosophical Aesthetics*. London: Clarendon Press.

Schneider, Carri, and Tom Vander Ark. 2016. "Genius Loci: Place-Based Education & Why It Matters." Getting Smart: Place-Based Education. Last Modified July 28, 2016. Accessed January 30, 2020. http://www.gettingsmart.com/2016/07/genius-loci-place-based -education-why-it-matters/.

Scruton, Roger. 1979. *The Aesthetics of Architecture*. Vol. 8. London: Methuen.

———. 1983. *The Aesthetic Understanding: Essays in the Philosophy of Art and Culture*. London: Methuen.

Scully, Vincent. 2013. *The Earth, the Temple, and the Gods: Greek Sacred Architecture*. San Antonio, TX: Trinity University Press.

Shaw, Dougal. 2015. "The Architects Using Animation Skills to Build Film Careers." BBC News, August 6, 2015. Last Modified June 9, 2017. Accessed August 3, 2017. http://www .bbc.com/news/business-33757862.

Shiner, Larry. 2007. "Architecture vs. Art: The Aesthetics of Art Museum Design [1]." *Contemporary Aesthetics* 5 (1): 9.

Snodgrass, Adrian, and Richard Coyne. 2013. *Interpretation in Architecture: Design as Way of Thinking*. Abingdon, UK: Routledge.

Sołtan, Margaret. 1991. "Architecture as a Kind of Writing." *American Literary History* 3 (2): 405–19.

Thiis-Evensen, Thomas, Rooth Waaler, and Scott Campbell. 1987. *Archetypes in Architecture*. Oslo: Norwegian University Press.

Thilmany, Jean. 2019. "Pros and Cons of CAD." Mechanical Engineering. Last Modified March 29, 2019. Accessed June 12, 2021. https://www.asme.org/topics-resources /content/pros-and-cons-of-cad

Thompson, Janna. 2016. "Why Virtual Reality Cannot Match the Real Thing." The Conversation, March 13, 2018. Last Modified March 14, 2018. Accessed March 4, 2019. https://theconversation.com/why-virtual-reality-cannot-match-the-real-thing-92035.

Tigerman, Stanley. 1992. "Has Theory Displaced History as a Generator of Ideas for Use in the Architectural Studio, or (More Importantly), Why Do Studio Critics Continuously Displace Service Course Specialists?" *Journal of Architectural Education (1984-)* 46 (1): 48–50.

Tilley, Christopher Y. 1994. *A Phenomenology of Landscape: Places, Paths, and Monuments*. Vol. 10. Oxford: Berg.

Pujol Tost, Laia. 2007. "Does Virtual Archaeology Exist?" In *35th International Conference on Computer Applications and Quantitative Methods in Archaeology (CAA)*, edited by A. Posluschny, K. Lambers and I. Herzog, 101–107. Berlin: Dr. Rudolf Habelt GmbH.

Van Buren, Deanna 2015. "Architecture in Video Games: Designing for Impact." Gamasutra. Last Modified May 27, 2017. Accessed July 2, 2017. http://www.gamasutra.com/blogs

/DeannaVanBuren/20151012/254238/Architecture_in_Video_Games_Designing_for
_Impact.php.

Whitelock, Denise, Daniela Romano, Anne Jelfs, and Paul Brna. 2000. "Perfect Presence:
What Does This Mean for the Design of Virtual Learning Environments?" *Education
and Information Technologies* 5 (4): 277–89.

Zevi, Bruno. 1957. *Architecture as Space. How to Look at Architecture*. New York: Horizon
Press.

Zimmerman, Alex, and Mark Martin. 2001. "Post-occupancy Evaluation: Benefits and
Barriers." *Building Research and Information* 29 (2): 168–74. https://doi.org/10.1080
/09613210010016857.

chapter four

THEORIES OF PLACE AND CYBERSPACE

Place Theory

This chapter starts with a discussion of the philosophy of place, applied to real places. Place definitions and arguments for how to explain, use, or reject philosophical definitions of place will be proposed from a slightly more philosophical viewpoint. By virtual place, I mean a virtual environment (a digital environment with aspects of three-dimensional space) that has "place" qualities. The overall argument in this book is that aspects of culture are missing from many virtual environments, but there are other related aspects that are also often overlooked.

The Issue of Definitional Clarity

Theorists in architectural and game space have not yet created a convincing overarching theory that both describes and prescribes. For example, in Michael Nitsche's (2008) book on the subject, his overarching diagram describes game space as including rule-based space, mediated space, fictional space (what the player imagines they are seeing), play space (the physical space the player is in), and social space (when other players are physically present). Where is the cognitive space? It is not exactly the fictional space the player imagines, it is more the past experiences and future projections the player is extracting, collating, interpreting, and predicting.

Thinking beyond Space toward Place

Writers in architecture, urban planning, philosophy, and geography have defined place in myriad ways. Edward Casey (1993, 1997, 2002) and Ed Relph (1976) have both written extensively on the definition and characteristics of "place." Casey focused on the experiential sensation of place as an extension of the body. On the other hand, the cultural geographer Ed Relph tended to view "place" as that which surrounds the viewer existentially, in terms of attitude and intention. Relph defined many different types of place and how each offered a mix of experiences.

Yi-Fu Tuan (1979), another cultural geographer, proffered yet another viewpoint: "Place incarcerates the experiences and aspirations of a people." Tuan argued that personal and cultural places may be seen as distortions compared to the more objective geometrical space but that this viewpoint was misleading; geometrical space is a cultural concept, "a sophisticated human construct." He also suggested that culture was a form of escapism (Tuan 1998, 387). Following Tuan, David Seamon and Jacob Sowers (2008) claim that "space and place are dialectically structured in human environmental experience since our understanding of space is related to the places we inhabit, which in turn derive meaning from their spatial context."

While the emphasis is understandable, in practice, just as with the use of the term *presence* (Witmer and Singer 1998; Slater 1999; Schuemie et al. 2001), the use of the term *place* seems to vary, so I am less inclined to view place and space as dialectically structured (if dialectic is meant in terms of Hegelian dialectic). Rather, it seems to me that the word *space* in common linguistic usage means outer space, volumetric capacity, or a particularly "not-yet" place; it is more a universal measurement—the absence of place or the potential to have a place—than a dialectical counterpoint to place. If a place is, broadly speaking, a spectrum of loosely associated meanings, this does make the goal of defining place and placeness more difficult. Perhaps we could talk about aspects of place rather than the essence of place?

For example, when you ask someone how to get to a location—say, a restaurant—they are unlikely to refer to it as a place if they have not taken part in the experience of it (eaten there rather than just walked past). Imagine that you ask them if there is a restaurant they can recommend nearby. They are, I suspect, much more likely to say, "When in town, there is a place I go to eat" than, "When in town, there is a location I go to eat." Most importantly, why don't most people reply with "When in town, there is a restaurant I go to eat"? Would they refer to the restaurant as a place if they had not been there? I doubt it. "Place" is an experiential category; it is experienced space or identifying space (an experience identifying us or others) or inhabitable space. In virtual worlds, in cyberspace, do we have the same level and variety of placeness?

Cyberspace

The term *cyberspace*[1] appears to date back to the nineteenth century (Johnson 2014). Some have traced it back to Stefan Odobleja in 1938 or 1939, others to Norbert Wiener in 1948 (Coe 2015), but historically the concept is millennia-old. Cybernetics appeared in Plato's *The First Alcibiades*, or *Alcibiades I*, to mean "the study of self-governance" (Vocabularist 2016). There were also artificial people in the ancient Greek world: the robot Talos, the artificially created fembot Pandora, and the mechanical servants of the crippled Greek god, Hephaistos, also known as Vulcan (Vulcānus) in Latin (Mayor 2018a, 2018b).

The mythical inventor Daedalus also designed artificial servants. Even in mythical tales, robots are described as possessing impressive, almost godly, skills. Robotic ethicists have since claimed history has blinded us to what robots can do, we load far more responsibility onto their artificial shoulders than they are designed to even be aware of (Mudry, Degallier, and Billard 2008).

The role in virtual reality (VR) of cyberspace came via science fiction in the book *Burning Chrome* (1982) by William Gibson. But it was probably perhaps via Gibson's 1984 book, *Neuromancer* (Kaplan 2016), that "cyber" became "official," appearing in the 1997 Marsh report "Critical Foundations Protecting America's Infrastructures," which warned of cyberterrorism. In the 1990s, the term *cyber* seems to have blossomed into a variety of meanings (Newitz 2013). But *cyber* does not just mean terrorism committed via cables; it can describe the experience of visiting and partaking in a virtual world.

There are many other definitions of cyberspace (Benedikt 1991; Novak 1991; O'Connor 1996; Kitchin 1998; Jiang and Ormeling 2000; Bryant 2001; Strate 2009; Devriendt et al. 2011). For instance, Thomas Folsom (2007) has a particularly rigid view of cyberspace: "an embodied switched network for moving information traffic." Then, of course, there is Margaret Wertheim's *Defining Cyberspace (Finding Real Virtue in the Place of Virtual Reality)* (2000).

In the conference paper "Mapping Cyberspace: Visualizing, Analysing, and Exploring Virtual Worlds," Bin Jian and Ferjan Ormeling (2000) proposed an interesting threefold definition of cyberspace as "physical anchorages," "topological relationships," and "an animated 3D computer-based model." They did not define place or world, but they seemed to think virtual worlds could involve agents and activities and typically represented the real world. However, for them, cyberspace, especially for applications like ActiveWorlds, was distinct from virtual worlds. Although I am not convinced these early online worlds were a marriage of internet and VR technologies, I mention this paper here as it occurs to me that the notion of cyberspace as the navigation and visualization system between virtual worlds (drawing on the origins of *cyber* as the Greek word for "steersman") is an interesting one that has largely disappeared from the academic literature.

In their paper "The Role of Place in Cyberspace," Yehuda Kalay and John Marx (2001) proposed several attributes of places that may be features of place in cyberspace. They proposed that place affects and is affected by both social and cultural behavior. Places cue social interaction and cultural behavior, allowing and affording inhabitation and framing appropriate and inappropriate actions and individual behavior in general.

Barry Wellman coined *cyberplace* at least as far back as 2001, but in the same year, in their paper "The Role of Place in CyberSpace," Kalay and Marx (2001) identified eight features of cyberspaces (as virtual places) by extrapolating from architectural and urban design theory. They declared that places are settings for complex and rich events, require presence (although presence here is not defined), afford relative location (i.e., orientation), are imbued with a sense of authenticity (and authenticity is not defined), are adaptable, afford a variety of experiences, offer much greater richness than physical space because of user choice and control over transitions from place to place, and are "well-designed places [that] are inherently memorable."

In 2006, Kalay and Marx elaborated on this concept of place: "Places, in the physical world, are filled not only with artifacts, tools, and representations of our work, but also with other people and the signs of their activities. The sense of other people's presence and the ongoing awareness of their activity allow us to structure our own activities, and to seamlessly integrate them with those of others. They give *meaning* to our own actions and behaviors."

I gather here that for Kalay and Marx, these are also desirable if not essential characteristics of cyberspaces. Cyberspace allegedly has some "peculiarities" not shared with real-world places, but Kalay and Marx (2006) do not elaborate on these peculiarities. Further, citing Thomas Chastain, they say he "defined [cyberspace] as a territory whose boundaries are defined by a sense of being 'inside' thus supporting the feeling of being somewhere as opposed to just anywhere." Places are not just social: they argued that place use requires the users to "have a shared 'sense of place.' This shared understanding helps them to orient themselves with respect to the space they occupy and with respect to each other, and thereby establish social references that direct their behavior in a way that gives meaning to their activities."[2]

Others defined cyberspace as a virtual place, identifiable in terms of the activities it hosts. For example, in "Place-Making in Online Virtual Environment: The Case of Second Life," Beng-Kiang Tan and Stephen Lim Tsung Yee (2009) wrote, "A place is a space with experiences based on its physical setting and type of activities carried out." I have followed a similar path, but from 2001 onward, I categorized virtual places into three broad categories: visualization based; activity based; and hermeneutic (interpretation rich).

Kalay and Marx (2006) proposed four categories of cyberspace, but their categories apply more to modes of digitally simulated realism than to place activities. Hyper reality attempts to mimic the physical world in every detail (which helps with ease of use, comfort, and familiarity); abstracted reality "obeys enough laws of nature to engender believability, but does not attempt to create a 'perfect' reality," with three-dimensional multi-user domains (MUDs) being the obvious examples; hybrid cyberspace "freely mixes 'real' and 'virtual' experiences"; and "Hyper Virtuality drops all relationship to the physical world and the Laws of Nature." The spectrum of realism is distinguished by how closely it maps to either physical laws, expectations, or genre conventions.

Although all four are categories of cyberspaces, only the first one has much to do with a sense of place, but it misleads, as hyper reality "captures only the *spatial* qualities of Architecture, without its *place* qualities" (emphasis in original). I would advise reading this article several times, as it is hard to grasp their message. Were they aiming to design a full sense of place or find the type of cyberspace that gives designers the most freedom? In their 2006 paper, they proposed the most suitable type of cyberspace to be the imaginative but defamiliarizing hyper virtuality.

Five Aspects of Real-World Places

In 2005, I wrote that the usefulness of "place" can be considered a key feature of virtual communities in at least five major ways, based on real-world places (Champion 2005). A sense of place can be evoked by its apparent uniquenesss, by evocation of memories and associations, by its ability to identify and reflect individual participants, by its ability to induce sheer awe, or by its ability to act as either a stage or framework on which communal and individual activities can "take place."

Uniqueness

Doreen Massey (1994) made the interesting point that a place may be unique not because of individual elements but due to the history, combination, or selection of those elements. These elements may also be associated with other places, but the way they are experienced together can form a new sense of place or afford a distinct sense of placeness. For example, Emperor Hadrian's Villa in Tivoli near Rome (fig. 4.1) is both unique and a showcase of Roman, Egyptian, and Greek architecture (UNESCO World Heritage Organization 2021).

In other words, a place can have nonunique landmarks, standard activities, repetitive layouts, and unremarkable environmental surroundings, but it is the combination of these features and how they relate to each other that provides a specific place with its identity.

Associations and Memories

Place as a field or center of unique associations and memories has been suggested by many writers (Relph 1976; Johnson 1997). Some indicate geography indirectly highlights our schemas of place—be they telluric, projected, or urban landforms (Relph 1976). When triggering mental associations to theses schemas, "place" is evocative of remembered sensations of its previous versions or of related activities or even of similar places (Johnson 1997).

Sublimity and Awe

By linking to "heavenly" architecture in the introduction of his book, Michael Benedikt (1991) may have foreseen cyberspace in the third sense, as an environment that awes and inspires or as a unique artwork (with a sense of the sublime and overpowering and inspiring awe). A place can awe through infinite scale and size or possibility, "unthinkable complexity" (Gibson 2000); through immutability; through the materialization of perfection or demonstration of an unstoppable, vast force (Kant 2007); or through complete indifference to human visitation (an Ozymandian or perhaps monumental sublime?). It may also terrify us or force us

Figure 4.1 Canopo, Villa Adriana, Tivoli, Italy. Wikimedia Commons, License: CC-BY-SA-4.0. The notice from Wikimedia reads, "Author died more than 100 years ago public domain images." https://commons.wikimedia.org/wiki/File:Canopo_-_Villa_Adriana_-_Tivoli,_Italy_-_DSC03650.jpg.

to feel not inside a place but outside it or, conversely, trapped inside a place with no center or no end (a Piranesian or Escherian space). The philosopher and phenomenologist Edward Casey (1993) wrote a that place could be a noninhabitable site, and therefore a nonplace, and he defined *placescapes* as places that surround and dwarf us.

The use of place as an evoker of previous or imagined places is used by many virtual environments including those of computer games. Yet writers who have noted the atmospheric "sense of place" have not yet fully described how it may be created (Neumann and Albrect 1996; Johnson 1997; Kalay and Marx 2001). Other writers have investigated this mysterious "sense of place" but their studies relied on questionable premises (discussion on this topic is covered in chapter 9).

Storehouse and Museum

Cultural geographers, anthropologists, and archaeologists often view place as an artifact that records traces of its owners. For them, place is the slate on which historical interactions are inscribed by intent, by accident, or by ritual and habit. Some writers have described a place as a storehouse of users' meanings and identity rather than the architects' intentions. Places are artifacts and "trace" museums,

Figure 4.2 Xochicalco in Mexico shows the influence of different cultural beliefs, art, and calendars. Erik Champion.

recording imprints of inhabitation (Canter 1974; Rapoport 1982; Beckmann 1998; Crang 1998; Tuan 1998; Schiffer and Miller 1999).

Stage or Social Framework

Place as the stage has been posited by architects such as Richard Coyne (2014) and geographers such as Relph (1976). Coyne suggested deliberately constructing constraints to force people to act in certain ways, a clear change from the suggestion of architect Marcos Novak (1991) that virtual environments be "Liquid Architecture."

Place as a constraint for the body is a common feature of three-dimensional games, yet it also has a central place in theoretical writings. Casey (1997) seems to favor the definition of place as that which provides boundaries, affords rest, is unique, and is related to the human body. Marisa Ponti and Thomas Ryberg (2004) argued a virtual place should act as a playground and space for negotiations for a sense of community to develop.

Place as the stage can be a metaphor for either place recording significant ceremonial actions or choreographing (restricting) ways in which we move while inside it. For the cultural geographer Doreen Massey, a place was not static but a dynamic matrix or series of social interactions. (For example, figure 4.2 shows a temple wall in Mexico that acts as a translator between the calendar systems and art styles of different Mexican cultures.) The place is a process, not a product, and hence can consist of multiple interpretations and conflicts and a unique combination of borrowed histories (Massey 1994).

A Modification to the Five Aspects of Place

Fundamental-level, real-world places identify, gather, or evoke. Real-world places are typically unique or distinctive or may impress themselves on us by their capacity to identify and reflect individual participants. A place may evoke specific memories and associations. A place may also induce extreme and dramatic emotions: a sense of awe, shock, or horror. A place may also develop a special character and identity by its capacity to act as either stage or framework on which communal and individual activity can "take place." It can also act as a storehouse or a repository. Originally from Latin (*repositiō*), *repository* means repositioning: a placing back of artifacts.

The previously outlined fivefold schema could be improved on. I never clearly explained whether all these aspects are essential (they are not), and I did not explain how frequently they appear or which aspects are necessary for an experience of place. I suggest that a place has to have a concept of inner and outer, offer identifiable aspects, have a sense of the persistence of past or current actions, and be in some way modifiable. (If it is not modifiable, then the sense that it is a place will not be as deep and rich as it could be.) Modifiability could, however, pose a problem for virtual place design: How do we simulate it with current digital technology?

Another point I had not mentioned earlier was the relation of place to the community. Communities identify and are identified by not just the clothes they wear, the language they speak, or even the way their members greet each other. Communities are often identified by where their activities take place, how they use spaces to construct meanings, and the traces left by their social interactions. These "trigger" regions are thus not just points in space; they are also landmarks, havens, homes, ruins, or hells. Communities are identified and identify with or against not just space but also place. Places do not just organize space; they orient, identify, and animate the bodies, minds, and feelings of both inhabitants and visitors.

I suggest that a place typically has to be distinctive; it has to evoke specific memories *or* associations, *or* it has to create the sense that after experiencing it, there will be identifying memories or associations. I don't believe it has to evoke specifically dramatic feelings inside of us, but sometimes a place does just that. Only certain types of place act as a stage (a theater auditorium in the literal sense, a piazza in the figurative sense) or as a framework, but all places create a sense of inner and outer.

Not all places act as a storehouse or repository, but some do. Almost all carry evidence of encounters or other forms of human interaction; they are geographical palimpsests (Simm and Marvell 2015; Marvell and Simm 2016). They not only collect and interrelate objects, sometimes from other places, but also act as a meta-artifact of artifacts *and* the patinas of wear and usage of people, their traffic, their encounters, and their creations.

Place and Interpretation

We saw how places are crafted, but places are also open to interpretation. A place is a web of existential alternatives as well as a record of existential choices, chances, triumphs, and tragedies. I have argued that real-world places have up to five major characteristics, but here I will also touch on five major issues concerning virtual places: presence in virtual space; whether hermeneutics offers anything valuable for design or criticism; realism and the relationship between the real and the virtual or whether the virtual is parasitical on the real; the question of authenticity; and the question of whether phenomenology is useful in describing the experience of virtual places.

Presence in Virtual Space

Place itself may refer to many different types of location, the feeling that one is in or surrounded by a type of location, or the intensity of the feeling of being in a particular place. One may well feel spatially surrounded, or be able to say an event happened in a certain position in a virtual environment without feeling that one was experiencing a strong or unique experience of place. Because presence relates to place and presence is typically an evaluation of the success of virtual environments, "place" is of central concern to the design of virtual environments. To understand how and why people can feel a sense of presence, then, we need to have a clear and appropriate sense of place.

If we do not have a strong sense of place, then perhaps we do not have a strong sense of presence. Many writers (frequently from architecture) have made the distinction between place and cyberspace and suggested that virtual environments usually lack the former (e.g., Benedikt 1991; Johnson 1997; Kitchin 1998; Kalay and Marx 2001; Champion and Dave 2002).

Realism

What is the relationship between the real and the virtual? Is the virtual parasitical on the real? In an online article titled "Why Virtual Reality Cannot Match the Real Thing" in The Conversation, Professor of Philosophy Janna Thompson (2016) argued that virtual reality attempts to provide accurate and equivalent *realistic* interactive simulations of the existing real world.

But VR is not only a possible mirror to the current world, as Sir David Attenborough noted about the Natural History Museum's Hold the World VR application (Hamilton 2018). VR supports a richer understanding of the process; people can move and view virtual objects that are otherwise fragile, expensive, or remote. VR applications can also exaggerate actions and behaviors to help rehabilitate people with disabilities or reveal processes behind the visualization of objects and events.

VR can reveal beliefs and interpretations behind and of the real world. Mythology can replace the laws of physics, ghosts can become more or less tangible, religious beliefs can be shown, contrasting views of the world can be chosen or compared, and new interfaces can be developed that appear to mesh with the real world to create an "enabled landscape." VR can allow us to share experiences

Figure 4.3 Two players share one character, controlling different parts of the avatar's body, during a 2018 summer intern project. Agathe Limouzy, Toulouse University, and Erik Champion.

with others in a way impossible to us in the so-called real world. While collaborative learning in the real world can help teams to see the bigger picture, our actions or decisions via virtual reality can be augmented and incorporated into the experience for others.

Figure 4.3 shows one of the possibilities: In 2018, intern student Agathe Limouzy created two different interface devices for the same virtual avatar in a virtual environment. Player 1 watched a large monitor and the player's real-world hands were tracked by a cheap Leap Motion camera strapped to a bandanna around the player's head. Player 1's real hands were matched to an avatar's virtual hands, and thus the player could point and grab. Player 2 was in a head-mounted display and controlled the avatar's legs. The views of the players could be shared or moved independently of each other; control of the limbs could also be distributed between the two players. As the virtual character was controlled by two players who could be looking in different directions, the players had to learn to coordinate and develop an idea of what the other player was experiencing. One could imagine extrapolating this culturally or chronologically, where each player sees a different aspect of the same world and controls different parts of the same virtual avatar.

VR does not only have to copy what is there; it can allow people to reconfigure, view underlying hypotheses and processes, or mix and match contested views or clashing interpretations. VR (and augmented reality [AR]) allows you to examine places before you go there. VR can reveal past events, like the AR app Dilly Bag, which connects the history of Indigenous servicemen by triggering stories via a smartphone (Lodge 2018). VR, mixed reality, and AR can show you, on site or remotely, what you would not have seen, contested, inferred, amalgamated, or extrapolated from a more locally situated or past point of view. Stories can be told from the perspective of flying animals (Gidley 2017). And VR can provide thrills and spills, such as the VR rollercoaster theme park in China (Campbell 2017), which appears far more dangerous, immediate, and visceral than the real thing. Will virtual tourism prove to be only a pale imitation of the real thing? It depends on how imaginative we are.

Authenticity

Authenticity can refer to the authenticity of what is made and how or to the authenticity of an experience or character. These are all fundamentally different. I argue ownership is authentic both of cultural affinity and also in terms of where it is made or how it parallels experience.

Authenticity leads to more questions, but when detected, it can lead to increased engagement: "Visitors who perceived the rabbits as authentic were more likely to ask a question than those who judged them as inauthentic. Perceived authenticity also promoted more why questions" (Bunce 2016).

Some might declare virtual places to be parasitical on real places. Well then, so are literature and art. Real places also cite, allude to, and steal from each other. Authenticity can be related to how an object is made, who owns it, who understands the culture from which an object is made or intangible heritage is performed or shared, or the experience itself. Virtual place designers need new ways to test authenticity, social judgment, and a hierarchy of authenticity. Is this possible? Or do virtual places have an indexical relation to authenticity?

Hermeneutic Aspects: Interpretation and Contestation

According to Ranald Lawrence (2007), Sverre Fehn favored the following story about walking in the Norwegian landscape: "When you go to untouched nature, you always cause some destruction, if only by stepping on grass. The traces of your footsteps lead the next man to follow the same route. The footsteps are a kind of architecture, because they mediate the walker's feeling for the landscape, telling the follower which view pleases him."

In VR, where are the trails, traces, and footprints? Such a level of personalization and inscription is not typically available to us in the design and use of virtual environments: they lack responsive, granular, and agglutinative interaction. Perhaps we have just forgotten key elements of real-world places.

I mentioned that the usefulness of place can be considered a key feature of virtual communities in at least five major ways (Champion 2005). Unfortunately, virtual worlds typically lack a sense of place in any of those ways. For creating a virtual environment with a notion of "place" (a region recognizable to a user as a culturally coded setting), we need to have more than merely identifiable or evocative virtual environments. Where these virtual environments simulate the past, the challenge is to design a place that evokes and identifies cultural indications of inhabitation driven by a different cultural perspective to that of our own.

This virtual place should suggest ideas of thematically related events, evidence of social autonomy, notions of territorial possession and shelter, and focal points of artifactual possession, of "ready-to-hand" objects (Ables 2016). In other words, the virtual environment must provide a perspective of a past culture to a user. Such a perspective is normally only deduced by trained archaeologists and anthropologists from material remains (fossils, pottery shards, ruins, etc.).

Real places can also afford a sense of inhabitation and "home," but this is seldom found in virtual places. This concern led me to the work of Ed Relph (1976), who examined the issue of place and placelessness. He classified these types of places as shown in table 4.1.

Relph wrote that "existential insideness" was one approach to place not fully covered in earlier classifications of cyberspace and virtual environments in general (Kalay and Marx 2001). Instead, I and my coauthor Bharat Dave (2002) extended and applied Relph's classification of urban places to virtual places, dividing virtual environments into the three major types I mentioned earlier: visualization based, activity based, and hermeneutic.[3] One could also label this third category interpretative, an interpretative framework for different cultural beliefs, individual perspectives, and worldviews (table 4.2).

Virtual Heritage Environments (VHEs) as Test Case

If games are the most interactive and successful form of digital environment, it would seem logical to marry game design with the most cultural of virtual environments, VHEs, to encourage engagement *and* meaningful cultural immersion. A critic may respond that virtual heritage has gamified itself (Stone 2005), and as games are cultural artifacts and practices, we could consider virtual heritage to have accepted and embraced its cultural role. But while it is true that certain types of virtual environments such as games are engaging, they are not meaningful cultural experiences.

For example, many fantasy role-playing games portray previous cultures or cultural beliefs, real or imaginary. The games may feature named characters, treasure, three-dimensional objects, goals, and so forth, but they often lack distinctly cultural places, which is perhaps because there are no identifiers as to how to behave in another culture. Culture implies materially embodied beliefs that could identity yet outlive a maker; play, on the other hand, suggests an eternal changing of form without thought as to the consequences. Because of these reasons, I still believe that virtual environments *lack* place.

Phenomenology, Alterity, and Empathy

Evoking cultural significance may be helped by a philosophical consideration of how specific human experiences can be understood and conveyed. The *Dictionary of Philosophy* (Mautner 1996, 464) says *phenomenology* "is the attempt to describe our experience directly," but phenomenology and virtual places, as far as I know, are seldom discussed.

Table 4.1. A Schematic of Relph's Classification of Place

Type of Virtual Environment	Relph's Categories	Features	Personal / Cultural Attachment
Spatial visualization	Existential outsideness (objective)	Locational (links)	Locates setting.
		Navigational (orients)	Locates paths and centers.
Activity based	Vicarious-behavioral-empathetic insideness (activities and events).	Memorable (and unique)	Has uniquely occurring events.
		Territorial (protects)	Locates shelter for repose and protection against a dynamic environment.
		Modifiable (the environment can be modified)	Contains artifacts and surroundings that can be modified.
Hermeneutic (symbolic)	Existential insideness (culturally coded)	Perceived affordances (signifies cultural value and meaning)	Supports an idea of agency-directed symbols; reveals the secrets of the environment.
		Abandoned inhabitation	Evokes an idea of social agency and past inhabitation.
		Lived-in inhabitation	Supports interpersonal social behavior through human and/or computer agents.
		Home	Affords personal shelter, primary orientation, identification, possession, and collection of artifacts.

Given the problems with questionnaires, and the defining of *presence* as being there (a place concept surely?), can phenomenology help? Hermeneutics, the *Dictionary of Philosophy* says, "explores the kind of existence had by beings who are able to understand meanings, and to whom the world is primarily an object of understanding (rather than, say, of sense-perceptions)" (Mautner 1996, 274–75).

Phenomenology appears to have had some form of practical use and success in medical and therapeutic circles and also in performance (Ladly 2007; Renaud et al. 2013), but when it is mentioned in the design and evaluation of virtual environments, it is only in passing and, I suggest, rather superficially. One example of

Table 4.2. Virtual Place Interaction and Place Features

Virtual World	Goals	Interaction (Over Time)	Features
Observational (audiovisual worlds)	Navigate and recognize	Physiologically inactive to reactive	Objects, background, navigation metaphors, time recording (sometimes).
Process driven (activity worlds)	Enact, test skill level, and learn	Physiologically reactive to intentionally proactive	As above, plus artifacts and performance recording.
Hermeneutic (culturally / personally identifiable worlds)	Inhabit, identify otherness (alterity), and communicate	Personally and socially symbolic	As above, plus the perception that one can either personalize artifacts or that artifacts have been personalized by distinct individuals or societies.

a simplification of phenomenology is in Robert Govers and Frank Go's (2009, 43) declaration: "Constructivism . . . is further emphasized by existentialists such as Kierkegaard, Husserl, Brentano and Heidegger, who believe that all that matters is that humans participate in the world: 'being there' [Dasein, in German]."

This is strange to me for two reasons. First, a virtual environment lends itself directly to issues of subjective experience and world construction. Second, phenomenology offers a potentially useful type of evaluation of experience in virtual worlds where other forms of evaluation (such as questionnaires) are not reliable (Slater 2004).

Why is phenomenology of potential import to virtual places? The ethnographic techniques used by researchers may be effective in recording activity, but they do not directly indicate the potential mental transformations of perspective that result from being subjectively immersed in a different culture. Using phenomenology, we may be able to extract different perceived affordances and understandings from visitors and, at those crucial junctures of varying perspectives, change the mechanics that would allow visitors to feel comforted in their worldviews.

If we are simulating past or distant cultural settings, how can users learn via interaction the meanings and values of others? Must we interact as the original inhabitants did? How can we find out how they interacted and, through the limited and constraining nature of current technology, help interaction become more meaningful, educational, and enjoyable?

How do we even know when meaningful learning is reached? Through "interpretative translucency," we can test for "mild" hermeneutic immersion in a virtual world, where a participant begins to use and develop the codes of other cultures and societies to orient and solve tasks and to communicate the value and significance of those tasks and goals to others. However, we may also need refined or newly developed phenomenological methods to ensure participants have grasped an experience of a culture different from their own.

Summary

Philosophical notions of place typically feature the concept of centering; creating an experiential interiorization is the most common aspect. Yet places also evoke, identify, and store. Places are unique and memorable, reflect individuals, gather communities, induce awe, and store artifacts.

I have given some brief forays and scenarios for investigating whether virtual place design can be helped by phenomenological inquiry and hermeneutical affordances. Such an investigation would attempt to understand how individual societies experience the world, how they interpret the world to themselves and to each other, and how their cultural signs are made, modified, and learned. It would also attempt to discover how the horizons of current visitors could be nudged out of balance by being either overwhelmed by encounters with genuine alterity (that is, sense of otherness) or by gradually learning how to be accepted in this vastly different phenomenological world.

A recurring issue in the design of virtual places, and especially in the design of VHEs, is to avoid the "museumization" and "Westernization" of digital simulations as forewarned by Ziauddin Sardar (1996) and others. I suggest, by contrast, that virtual environments do not have to subjugate and conquer and homogenize; the current use of this technology does not define and limit their potential, at least for virtual heritage.

The past might remind us that not only is there our personal concept of home but there are also different concepts of home that are worth trying to express and understand, even if—in fact particularly if—they evade full familiarity compared to our own (the concept of alterity). For place gets some of its power from *not being* other places. Historically, and virtually, the simulation of past places and past cultures is not a "being there" but a "being not quite here but somewhere else"—an idea explored in chapter 8.

Contestation is also missing from many virtual places. Alterity and difference, not just homogeneity, are hallmarks of real-world places; why can they not be of virtual-world places as well? Fundamental aspects of culture and cultural affordances are missing from virtual places. Perhaps mechanics, gamification, or procedural rhetoric can help? The following chapters will examine this question.

Notes

1. In this book, I will use *cyberspace* rather than *Cyberspace*, as the latter implies an authoritative definition has been determined.

2. In their earlier work, *social presence* was enough; later, Yehuda Kalay informed me he could see the reasoning for a distinction between *social presence* and *cultural presence* (discussed in chapter 7).

3. Perhaps "interpretation-affording environments" is a less confusing if still clumsy label.

References

Ables, Brent. 2016. "Myst and the Truth of Objects." Kill Screen. Last Modified May 24, 2016. Accessed July 27, 2017. https://killscreen.com/articles/myst-truth-objects/.

Beckmann, John. 1998. *The Virtual Dimension: Architecture, Representation, and Crash Culture.* New York: Princeton Architectural Press.

Benedikt, Michael. 1991. *Cyberspace: First Steps.* Cambridge, MA: MIT Press.

Bryant, Rebecca. 2001. "What Kind of Space Is Cyberspace?" *Minerva: An Internet Journal of Philosophy* 5. Last Modified June 12, 2017. Accessed July 27, 2017. http://www.minerva .mic.ul.ie//vol5/cyberspace.html.

Bunce, Louise. 2016. "Appreciation of Authenticity Promotes Curiosity: Implications for Object-Based Learning in Museums AU." *Journal of Museum Education* 41 (3): 230–39. https://doi.org/10.1080/10598650.2016.1193312.

Campbell, Joseph. 2017. "Inside China's First Virtual Reality Theme Park." IT News, November 27, 2017. Last Modified October 22, 2017. Accessed January 22, 2020. https:// www.itnews.com.au/news/inside-chinas-first-virtual-reality-theme-park-478484.

Canter, David V. 1974. *Psychology for Architects.* London: Applied Science Publishers.

Casey, Edward S. 1993. *Getting Back into Place: Toward a Renewed Understanding of the Place-World.* Bloomington: Indiana University Press.

———. 1997. *The Fate of Place: A Philosophical History.* Berkeley: University of California Press.

———. 2002. *Representing Place: Landscape Painting and Maps.* Minneapolis: University of Minnesota Press.

Champion, Erik. 2005. "Virtual Places." In *Encyclopedia of Virtual Communities and Technologies,* edited by Subhasish Dasgupta, 556–61. Hershey, PA: Idea Group.

Champion, E., and B. Dave. 2002. "Where Is This Place." In *Proceedings of Acadia 2002: Thresholds between Physical and Virtual,* edited by George Proctor, 87–97. Pomona, CA: ACADIA.

Coe, Taylor. 2015. "Where Does the Word Cyber Come From?" *OUPBlog* (blog). Oxford University Press. Accessed April 26, 2021. https://blog.oup.com/2015/03/cyber-word -origins/.

Coyne, Richard. 2014. "Back of Shop." In *Reflections on Technology, Media & Culture,* edited by Richard Coyne. Accessed April 26, 2021. https://richardcoyne.com/2014/09/27 /back-of-shop/.

Crang, Mike. 1998. *Cultural Geography.* London: Routledge.

Devriendt, Lomme, Andrew Boulton, Stanley Brunn, Ben Derudder, and Frank Witlox. 2011. "Searching for Cyberspace: The Position of Major Cities in the Information Age." *Journal of Urban Technology* 18 (1): 73–92. https://doi.org/10.1080/10630732.2011.578410.

Folsom, Thomas. 2007. "Defining Cyberspace (Finding Real Virtue in the Place of Virtual Reality)." *Tulane Journal of Technology & Intellectual Property* 9: 75. https://ssrn.com /abstract=1350999.

Gibson, William. 2000. *Neuromancer.* London: Voyager.

Gidley, Sophie. 2017. "Virtual Reality: Tourism Firms Use VR to Attract Visitors." BBC. Last Modified October 22, 2017. Accessed January 22, 2020 https://www.bbc.com/news/uk -wales-41635746.

Govers, Robert, and Frank Go. 2009. *Place Branding: Global Virtual and Physical Identities, Constructed Imagined and Experienced.* Basingstoke, UK: Palgrave Macmillan.

Hamilton, Isobel. 2018. "David Attenborough's VR Project 'Hold the World' Is Absolutely Astonishing." Mashable. Last Modified May 24, 2018. Accessed March 21, 2020. https://mashable.com/2018/05/24/david-attenborough-hold-the-world-vr/.

Jiang, Bin, and Ferjan Ormeling. 2000. "Mapping Cyberspace: Visualizing, Analysing and Exploring Virtual Worlds." *Cartographic Journal* 37 (2): 117–22.

Johnson, Christopher. 2014. "'French' Cybernetics." *French Studies* 69 (1): 60–78. https://doi .org/10.1093/fs/knu229.

Johnson, Steven. 1997. *Interface Culture: How New Technology Transforms the Way We Create and Communicate.* San Francisco: HarperEdge.

Kalay, Yehuda, and John Marx. 2001. "The Role of Place in Cyberspace." In *Proceedings Seventh International Conference on Virtual Systems and Multimedia,* edited by Hal Thwaites and Lon Addison, 770–79. Los Alamitos: IEEE Press.

———. 2006. "Architecture and the Internet: Designing Places in Cyberspace." *First Monday.* Accessed July 27, 2017. http://firstmonday.org/ojs/index.php/fm/article/view/1563 /1478.

Kant, Immanuel. 2007. *Critique of Judgement.* Edited by Nicholas Walker and James Creed Meredith. Oxford: Oxford University Press.

Kaplan, Fred. 2016. *Dark Territory: The Secret History of Cyber War.* New York: Simon and Schuster.

Kitchin, Rob. 1998. *Cyberspace: The World in the Wires.* Chichester, UK: Wiley.

Ladly, Martha. 2007. "Being There: Heidegger and Thephenomenon of Presence Intelematic Performance." *International Journal of Performance Arts and Digital Media* 3 (2–3). https://www.academia.edu/229511/Being_there_Heidegger_and_the_phenomenon _of_presence_in_telematic_performance.

Lawrence, Ranald. 2007. "Building on the Horizon: The Architecture of Sverre Fehn." Last Modified May 24, 2016. Accessed July 27, 2017. http://www.presidentsmedals.com /Entry-11320.

Lodge, Jess. 2018. "Anzac Day 2018: Indigenous Diggers' Stories Shared through Augmented Reality App." ABC News. Last Modified April 25, 2018. Accessed January 22, 2021. www.abc.net.au/news/2018-04-25/app-shares-forgotten-stories-indigenous-anzacs /9690766.

Marvell, Alan D., and David Simm. 2016. "Unravelling the Geographical Palimpsest through Fieldwork: Discovering a Sense of Place." *Geography* 101 (3): 125–36.

Massey, Doreen B. 1994. *Space, Place and Gender.* Cambridge: Polity.

Mautner, Thomas. 1996. *The Dictionary of Philosophy.* London: Wiley-Blackwell.

Mayor, Adrienne. 2018a. "An AI Wake-Up Call From Ancient Greece." *Project Syndicate; Prague.* Accessed April 25, 2021. https://www.project-syndicate.org/commentary /artificial-intelligence-pandoras-box-by-adrienne-mayor-2018-10?barrier =accesspaylog.

———. 2018b. *Gods and Robots: Myths, Machines, and Ancient Dreams of Technology.* Princeton, NJ: Princeton University Press.

Mudry, P. A., S. Degallier, and A. Billard. 2008. "On the Influence of Symbols and Myths in the Responsibility Ascription Problem in Roboethics: A Roboticist's Perspective." Paper presented at the the the Seventeenth IEEE International Symposium on Robot and Human Interactive Communication 9 (RO-MAN 2008), Munich, August 1–3, 2008.

Neumann, Dietrich, and Donald Albrect, eds. 1996. *Film Architecture: Set Designs from Metropolis to Blade Runner.* New York: Prestel.

Newitz, Annalee. 2013. "The Bizarre Evolution of the Word 'Cyber.'" Gizmodo, September 16, 2013. Last Modified September 16, 2013. Accessed March 3, 2020. https://io9.gizmodo .com/today-cyber-means-war-but-back-in-the-1990s-it-mean-1325671487?IR=T.

Nitsche, Michael. 2008. *Video Game Spaces: Image, Play, and Structure in 3D Game Worlds.* Cambridge, MA: MIT Press.

Novak, Marcos. 1991. "Liquid Architectures in Cyberspace." In *Cyberspace: First Steps*, edited by M. Benedikt, 225–54. Cambridge, MA: MIT Press.

O'Connor, Diane Vogt. 1996. "Exhibitions in Cyberspace: Museum Exhibition Documentation at the Millenium." *Art Documentation: Journal of the Art Libraries Society of North America* 15 (1): 17–19. https://doi.org/10.1086/adx.15.1.27948813.

Ponti, Marisa, and Thomas Ryberg. 2004. "Rethinking Virtual Space as a Place for Sociability: Theory and Design Implications." Paper presented at the Networked Learning Conference 2004, Göteborg University and Aalborg University. April 5–7, 2004. Lancaster, UK. Accessed June 12, 2021. http://www.networkedlearningconference.org.uk/past/nlc2004/home.htm.

Rapoport, Amos. 1982. *The Meaning of the Built Environment: A Nonverbal Communication Approach*. Tucson: University of Arizona Press.

Relph, Edward C. 1976. *Place and Placelessness*. London: Pion.

Renaud, Patrice, Sylvain Chartier, Joanne-Lucine Rouleau, Jean Proulx, Mathieu Goyette, Dominique Trottier, Paul Fedoroff, John-P. Bradford, Benoît Dassylva, and Stéphane Bouchard. 2013. "Using Immersive Virtual Reality and Ecological Psychology to Probe into Child Molesters' Phenomenology." *Journal of Sexual Aggression* 19 (1): 102–20. https://doi.org/10.1080/13552600.2011.617014.

Sardar, Z. 1996. "alt.civilizations.faq: Cyberspace as the Darker Side of the West." In *Cyberfutures: Culture and Politics on the information superhighway*, edited by Z. Sardar and J. Ravetz, 14–41. London: Pluto Press.

Schiffer, Michael Brian, and Andrea R. Miller. 1999. *The Material Life of Human Beings: Artifacts, Behavior, and Communication*. London: Routledge.

Schuemie, Martijn J., Peter Van der Straaten, Merel Krijn, and Charles A. P. G. Van der Mast. 2001. "Research on Presence in Virtual Reality: A Survey." *CyberPsychology and Behavior* 4 (2): 183–201.

Seamon, David, and Jacob Sowers. 2008. "Place and Placelessness (1976): Edward Relph." In *Key Texts in Human Geography*, edited by Phil Hubbard, Rob Kitchin, and Gill Valentine, 45–52. London: SAGE.

Simm, David, and Alan Marvell. 2015. "Making Sense of Place: Unravelling the Geographical Palimpsest of Barcelona." Paper presented at the Royal Geographical Society, West of England & South Wales Regional Branch Talk Series, University of South Wales, Pontypridd, UK, February 17, 2015. https://www.academia.edu/10893354/Making_sense_of_place_unravelling_the_geographical_palimpsest_of_Barcelona.

Slater, Mel. 1999. "Measuring Presence: A Response to the Witmer and Singer Presence Questionnaire." *Presence: Teleoperators and Virtual Environments* 8 (5): 560–65. Accessed August 3, 2017. https://doi.org/10.1162/105474699566477.

———. 2004. "How Colorful Was Your Day? Why Questionnaires Cannot Assess Presence in Virtual Environments." *Presence-Teleoperators and Virtual Environments* 13 (4): 484–93. https://doi.org/10.1162/1054746041944849.

Stone, Robert J. 2005. "Serious Gaming - Virtual Reality's Saviour?" In *Proceedings of the Eleventh International Conference on Virtual Systems and Multimedia: Virtual Reality at Work in the 21st Century: Impact on Society*, edited by Harold Thwaites, 773–86. Ghent: Ename.

Strate, Lance. 2009. "The Varieties of Cyberspace: Problems in Definition and Delimitation." *Western Journal of Communication* 63 (3): 382–412. https://doi.org/10.1080/10570319909374648.

Tan, Beng-Kiang, and Stephen Lim Tsung Yee. 2009. "Place-Making in Online Virtual Envionment: The Case of Second Life." Paper presented at CAADFUTURES 2009, "Joining Languages, Cultures and Visions," Montreal, June 17–19, 2009.

Thompson, Janna. 2018. "Why Virtual Reality Cannot Match the Real Thing." The Conversation, March 14, 2018.. Accessed March 4, 2019. https://theconversation.com /why-virtual-reality-cannot-match-the-real-thing-92035.

Tuan, Yi-Fu. 1979. "Space and Place: Humanistic Perspective." In *Philosophy in Geography*, edited by Stephen Gale and Gunnar Olsson, 387–427. Dordrecht: Springer.

———. 1998. *Escapism*. Baltimore, MD: Johns Hopkins University Press.

UNESCO World Heritage Organization. 2021. "Villa Adriana (Tivoli)." UNESCO WHO. Accessed April 26, 2021. http://whc.unesco.org/en/list/907.

Vocabularist. 2016. "The Vocabularist: How We Use the Word Cyber." BBC News, March 15, 2016. Accessed March 3, 2019. https://www.bbc.com/news/magazine-35765276.

Wellman, Barry. 2001. "Physical Place and Cyberplace: The Rise of Personalized Networking." *International Journal of Urban and Regional Research* 25 (2): 227–52.

Wertheim, Margaret. 2000. *The Pearly Gates of Cyberspace: A History of Space from Dante to the Internet*. New York: W. W. Norton.

Witmer, Bob G., and Michael J. Singer. 1998. "Measuring Presence in Virtual Environments: A Presence Questionnaire." *Presence: Teleoperators and Virtual Environments* 7 (3): 225–40.

chapter five

RATS AND GOOSEBUMPS
Mind, Body, and Embodiment

Introduction

This chapter surveys literature in psychology, neuroscience, and cognitive science to address new developments in our understanding of how the brain distinguishes between virtual space and real space, and the importance of mind and body in virtual reality (VR). In terms of the physical, how can crude digital interfaces convince us of complex simulated realities? In terms of the mind, how can it be compelled to react to simple affordances and phobic triggers? I also discuss a critique of embodiment (or lack thereof) of internet-based learning and virtual worlds (such as *Second Life*) by the philosopher Hubert Dreyfus (2008).

VR: Illusive Control of the Very Real?

Is VR an illusion? Critics may declare that VR has no mental, physical, or social consequences, but we already have examples of people dying from an excessive length of time in digital games, suicides due to abuse in online societies, and serious accidents from augmented reality (AR) games.

On the other hand, VR can be an excellent therapeutic method, according to various researchers (Granic, Lobel, and Engels 2014; Chen et al. 2016; Powell 2017). VR can and has trained people; it can relieve or reduce pain via distraction or provide some indication as to how or why different people think and act the way they do. While proponents claim that VR is healthy and good for you, there are dissenting voices: Nicola Davis (2016) has reported that the long-term effects of virtual reality are severely underresearched.

There are continuing worries about overengagement in a virtual world (Griffiths 2015) and withdrawal from the real one (Bajarin 2017). Tim Bajarin quoted John Hanke, the CEO of Niantic (the company behind the AR game *Pokémon Go*): "'I'm afraid [VR] can be too good, in the sense of being an experience that people want to spend a huge amount of time in,' said Hanke. . . . 'I mean I already have concerns about my kids playing too much Minecraft, and that's a wonderful game.'"

Apart from legal issues and privacy issues, and the blurring of fantasy and reality (Gent 2016; West 2016), there is also an ethical concern over the risk of *embodiment control* or a designed VR experience verging on mental torture (Oberhaus 2016). These concerns led philosophers Michael Madary and Thomas Metzinger (2016) to propose a detailed (ethical) code of conduct.

Scott Stephan, who designed the VR game *Anamnesis*, warns of a major difference between VR and normal media: the body becomes the interface, and the feeling that the experience is completely voluntary quickly evaporates (Parkin 2016). Designers have had to create sliders so users can control the level of horror, and they create enemies no "bigger than a small dog" as the experience can become personally frightening with any larger size of adversary. Stephan adds, "We haven't yet found an effective way to scare people in V.R. without making it a personal transgression. Long-term, perhaps it's a case of building literacy in players and viewers so they understand when the scares are coming. For now, I think that means taking it slow."

There are also health concerns. There is an increased chance of germs and contagions (Giardina 2016) due to the sharing of equipment so close to the body, and germs from touch have also been an issue with touch-screen displays on smartphones and tablets; however, this has not dented public enthusiasm. And furthermore, there are far greater off-putting issues, such as eyestrain, motion sickness, and vertigo.

In a 2014 *New York Times* article entitled "Virtual Reality Fails Its Way to Success," Virginia Heffernannov recounted how in 2012 a hobbyist VR headset made her (literally) sick, yet just two years later, in 2014, the Oculus Rift proved to be a revelation in user comfort. But in 2017, in a lengthy *ScienceNews* article entitled "Virtual Reality Has a Motion Sickness Problem: People Prone to Nausea May Opt Out of Immersive Experiences," Betsy Mason returned to the topic. In the year 2020, this problem has not disappeared, but in the long term, VR may become a distractive solution to car sickness in self-driving cars.

Consumer-based head-mounted display (HMD) technology is also relatively recent, and there are still concerns about potential long-term damage to human vision, both for adults and for children (Gent 2016). One startling research experiment on rats in VR showed major hippocampus activity changes (Lewis 2016), including neurons shutting down when rats are in VR due to a lack of changing body location data (Boddington 2017). Professor Mayank Mehta, a University of California, Los Angeles, professor of physics, neurology, and neurobiology, has also conducted experiments of rats in a visual-only VR environment, with results published in *Nature Neuroscience* (Aghajan et al. 2015). Mehta and his colleagues found over half of the rats' hippocampi neurons shut down when navigating in the virtual world but not when navigating in the real world (Wolpert 2014). Could the same thing happen to humans?

As VR HMD manufacturers aim to provide more interactive, standing, and even moving environments, these issues become ever more pressing. A second issue is a technological holy grail: HMDs with no wires, such as the Oculus Quest, is currently appearing on the consumer market. Even with wired VR headsets, you will generally find people in demo headsets closely watched, in safe and uncluttered environments. What will happen when people take wireless and portable VR headsets home?

Health and safety issues will be heavily dependent on context. According to Virginia Heffernannov (2014), "But whatever its 'use' might be, V.R. is not fundamentally a pragmatic technology, which is why it begins with gamers. If it works, if it catches on, it must first give pleasure—and be fun." While consumer VR does seem to be currently dominated by gamers (which makes the selling of meditation and therapy-oriented VR games harder to sell), long-term markets suggest VR has great potential for the elderly (Granic, Lobel, and Engels 2014; Simor et al. 2016; Nguyen et al. 2017), those who are bedridden, and those with a disability: "'For some gamers with disabilities, virtual reality might be a godsend,' said Mark Barlet from The AbleGamers Foundation in an interview with ARC at GDC 2016. 'One of the core philosophies of the AbleGamers charity is that games allow disabled people to do things that they wouldn't in real life. And that includes ablebodied people—in virtual reality you can climb Mount Everest, or be an NFL player ... most of us can't do that'" (Langtree 2016).

The Senses

The academic literature around VR has predominantly focused on two senses: sight, and hearing, particularly the former. Does that mean virtual reality is best served by a focus on sight and then hearing? How many senses do we have? This is the title of an interesting online BBC article, which is also an extract of the book *Great Myths of the Brain* by Christian Jarrett (2014): "Simply defining what we mean by a 'sense' leads you down a slippery slope into philosophy.... We can simplify the human senses down to just three—mechanical (which takes in touch, hearing and proprioception); chemical (including taste, smell and internal senses); and light."

Learning through Affordances

In his review of the philosopher Robert Schwartz's selected anthology *Perception*, Bruce Bridgeman (2004, 380) notes the pioneering contribution of J. J. Gibson: "The section begins with Gibson defining perceptual systems as opposed to an anatomical set of modalities. The systems are verbs, varieties of visual attention, five things that people do to collect information: seeing, hearing, tasting, touching, and smelling. It's a revolutionary clarification, distinguishing what a system does from what its anatomical components are."

Bridgeman was a professor of psychology at the University of California, Santa Cruz, and reviewed Schwartz's *Perception* book with some trenchant observations. Criticism is evident in the title of his review: "Philosophy of Mind Fails in Generating Progress toward Understanding the Mind." His major criticism was leveled at philosophers unable to get beyond subjective levels of introspection and undertake the discoveries of experimental scientific research.

> To get back to the issue of sensation, laboratory experiments have found that it doesn't exist in the pure form that philosophers such as Hamlyn assume. A "sensation" is always connected with a place, an object, an event. Gibson points out that human subjects are aware first of objects and surfaces in the environment, not of sensations of redness or hardness, and not of the myriad recordings of sensory information in the afferent sensory systems. This is what he [Gibson] means by "direct perception" not that physiological processing of sensory information does not exist, only that we are not aware of it. (Bridgeman 2004, 380)

This is an articulate description of part of Gibson's theory of visual perception (Gibson 1966, 1974, 1986) that led to his conception of affordances (Gibson 1977, 1986), and the topic of affordances will be returned to in a later chapter. But it is also a warning that when evaluating, we may well be tempted to look at the physical properties and observable actions of the senses, but these are experiences we have (sensory experiences), not the senses themselves.

I am not sure that a linguistic simplification of sensory phenomena (or sensory activities) is responsible for an insufficient number of VR peripherals providing for more than digitally transmitted sight and sound, but it is timely advice to go back to the context and ask what sort of technology could provide an appropriate sensory experience rather than try to create a new experience based on new technology. For instance, haptic technology provides us with nonverbal information via the "sense" of touch. But without industry standards, many projects either failed on launch or left a great deal to be desired. If you reviewed historical failures of unusual peripherals produced by the game industry, it is self-evident that one of the common reasons for their failure was the lack of robust showcases that effectively demonstrated the point. There are of course exceptions, but again these haptic projects tend to stress the technical features of the equipment rather than their phenomenological advantages. Which specific examples would they enrich experientially?

You can now buy a haptic suit, for instance, the TESLASUIT suit (TESLASUIT 2021), "the world's first fully integrated smart clothing apparel with Haptic Feedback, Motion Capture, Climate Control and Biometric Feedback systems." Haptic interaction has been a beguiling but challenging area in VR research, but recent results show promise for addressing these challenges in the near future (Culbertson, Schorr, and Okamura 2018).

Unfortunately, haptic technology can inspire and then falter. "This haptic feedback VR suit could complete your VR look," wrote Ashley Carman (2017) about the Hardlight VR suit. The company claimed there were sixteen upper-body haptic feedback zones ready to be triggered by compatible games' actions. In its marketing, the company guaranteed that "every muscle group above your hips is covered." After running a successful Kickstarter campaign, it ran out of money in 2018 or 2019 but then, fortunately, went open-source, providing a software development kit and related applications via GitHub.

Science and Design

Do philosophical explanations of memory and place (Tavanti and Lind 2001; Ihde 2002) reflect recent discoveries in scientific experiments (Farovik et al. 2015)? Can science help us better design virtual places (Moore 2005; Johnson 2013)? Do they explain how people navigate and orient themselves in virtual places (Zimring and Dalton 2003; Cockburn 2004)?

From the examples mentioned earlier in this chapter, it appears that psychology and cognitive science research greatly inspire education leading directly toward advances in human-computer interaction design, but when the scientific experiments begin to be questioned by future verification tests, changes in the viewpoints of the scientific community do not always quickly transfer to changes in the mindsets of those testing and designing virtual environments.

Cognitive Maps

The increasing doubt of scientists that we create a comprehensive cognitive map and the conflicting research into Lynch's theories of the imageability of the city are but two examples of research that has been slow to reach designers of virtual environments. So, there is a need for virtual environment designers to work more closely with related scientific researchers. However, the cost of equipment (such as fMRI [functional magnetic resonance imaging]), the need for specialist researchers who update themselves constantly with scientific advances and retesting, and the need for carefully controlled trials and rigorous evaluation methods (as seen in neuroscience and cognitive psychology) lead me to question how applicable these findings are in terms of mainstream virtual place development.

Are there differences in our experience and recall of episodic space as a scene (via film and literature) to our completed experience and recall of sequential and interstitial space (as places of action) in three-dimensional games (Wang, Johnson, and Zhang 2001; Jørgensen 2004; Werner and Schindler 2004; Dalton, Hölscher, and Spiers 2015)?

In terms of design implications, are there case studies of virtual places used in these experiments? What devices do they use to help capture brain activity and physiological states? Are there affordances in their experimental designs that can also be employed in the design of virtual places more generally? I have found some studies (Parsons, Gaggioli, and Riva 2017) that explain how VR technology can be used with neuroscience research, but in general, the virtual places themselves are not explained in any detail. Could designers develop virtual places that are more usefully evaluated by computer-human interaction experts?

Perhaps the devices employed in the scientific experiments could lead to peripherals and interfaces that are adopted, refined, and marketed by virtual place-making design software and hardware. How accessible and user-friendly is the potential monitoring technology? Will low-cost scientific experiments still provide useful results? Researchers see many configurational and ethical problems in the use of VR for science (Parsons, Gaggioli, and Riva 2017). There are, however, more fundamental conceptual issues. For example, do we need to be physically present to learn?

Advantages of Internet-Based Travel

Sometimes we wish to understand people who live far away or in distant times, not easily accessible to us, or to lessen the crowds, erosion, and pollution resulting from physical visitation. Heritage monuments are now being overrun; I remember once reading the Lonely Planet guide on South America suggesting tourists *not* visit Machu Picchu. Overtourism is here, an increasing global problem (Goodwin 2017; Bourliataux-Lajoinie, Dosquet, and del Olmo Arriaga 2019; Dodds and Butler 2019). Even if travelers can visit isolated and remote sites, they may be greeted by empty shells of buildings. Many ruins are bereft of their artifacts, which sit forlornly in the museums of past colonial powers. When famous historic cities are so overrun by tourists, the user experience is endangered (Koens, Postma, and Papp 2018).

In that respect, internet media may prove more immersive and educational than actually standing at the site where history once took place (Carter 2019). Further, the internet can specify cultural constraints that mediate and strengthen the travel experience far more effectively than viewing the place through a hotel window or by watching PowerPoint slides in a large classroom.

Figure 5.1 shows one example of three-dimensional media: a Kinect camera tracks the narrator and copies real-world narrator's gestures to an in-world narrator inside a Unity 3D environment (Champion et al. 2016).[1] Everywhere the human narrator points, the avatar points as a mirror-reflection, and where the avatar points on the three-dimensional model will trigger slides, movies, or teleportation through the three-dimensional model. No keyboard, joystick, or mouse is required, and the audience doesn't need to work out where the human narrator is pointing (which is very difficult to do on a curved scene). The narrator can also be green-screened inside the environment; there is a physics engine so objects can change or be replaced on being pointed out. This application could also be used as a form of three-dimensional teleconferencing.

Mind and Navigation and Memory

To solve the problem of designing virtual environments many researchers have turned to the theoretical framework of Kevin Lynch, especially his book *The Image of the City* (1960). Carol Strohecker and Barbara Barros (2000, 2) declared:

> In particular, Lynch studied how people think about the structure of their cities. From verbal and pictorial accounts, he derived five basic elements of the city

Rats and Goosebumps

Figure 5.1 Kinect-Tracked 3D Mirror Interface. Erik Champion.

image: districts, paths, edges, nodes, and landmarks. In *The Image of the City*, Lynch describes how people use these elements to organize a mental image of the places they inhabit:

> In the process of way-finding, the strategic link is the environmental image, the generalized mental picture of the exterior physical world that is held by an individual. This image is the product both of immediate sensation and of the memory of past experience, and it is used to interpret information and to guide action.

There is also the overall concept (and goal) of environmental legibility, which Lynch (1960, 2) defined as "the ease with which its parts can be recognized and can be organized into a coherent pattern." Itzhak Omer and Ran Goldblatt (2007) summarize other important concepts: "Spatial knowledge acquisition is often described as comprising three developmental stages . . . or complementary types of knowledge . . . : identification of landmarks, procedural route knowledge formed when traveling between landmarks, and configurational or survey knowledge."

However, different people seem to use different methods when navigating real-world environments and virtual ones. The experimental designs of Florian Röser, Kai Hamburger, and Markus Knauff (2011) suggested that it is difficult to ascertain what ideal landmarks are and that landmarks can interfere with recall of survey knowledge: "Thus, we may assume that humans encode landmarks in multiple ways so that they do not just rely on single characteristics (visual, semantic, or structural)."

Landmarks are considered to have visual *salience*, and the way they are experienced as a sequence aids recognition and memorization (Lynch 1960, 83).

Semantic salience refers to all knowledge-related features, such as the fame of a building (e.g., the Statue of Liberty) or its function (e.g., city halls or churches). Semantic salience is often related to how well a building can be named (language and knowledge components). Structural salience refers to features that are primarily (directly) related to navigation. For example, the number of intersections that need to be passed (surrounding context) and the exact location of a landmark along a route (close to it: local; farther away: global; decision point vs. non–decision point). Röser and colleagues (2012, 3) noted, "Such features are of great importance if there is no possibility to revert to any visual or semantic features for successful wayfinding."

Kai Hamburger and Markus Knauff's (2011) research findings on salience and studying landmarks in spatial cognition appear to have been supported by others, such as David Caduff and Sabine Timpf (2008, 253), who proposed a factor to measure salience of landmarks, the saliency vector. This factor, according to them (Caduff and Timpf 2008, 253), "accounts for the trilateral relationship between observer, observed object, and environment in terms of Perceptual, Cognitive, and Contextual Salience." Unfortunately, overall research experiments have not been conclusive in providing evidence that Kevin Lynch's theory works.

Kellogg Booth and colleagues (2000) agree that the influence of Lynch's theories on real-world city design has not been consistently and regularly corroborated. They noted that "virtual environments are typically sparse, and the relative shortage of local landmarks (such as buildings and signposts) and more global visual contexts (such as a backdrop of mountains) may impede learning" (2–3). They quoted the example of Micronesian oceangoing navigation made famous in the book *Cognition in the Wild*, by Ed Hutchins (1995). Hutchins argued that the early oceangoers used techniques not directly related to the actual physical environment to help them navigate space (the Pacific Ocean). Booth and colleagues summarized, "Given the lack of environmental cues and navigation tools, these models have proven superior to a more realistic mental map of the space in the most direct way possible—by the success of these ocean voyages and the survival of the voyagers. By analogy, it is possible that the most effective methods of wayfinding in sparse virtual environments will prove to be methods that are not extensions of our ways of navigating the physical world, but rather are specific to these unfamiliar spaces."

What can we gather from such "cognition in the wild" studies? First, experienced navigators may use deliberately inaccurate or unrealistic metaphors not easily simplified onto a mental map. Second, research supporting the long-held belief that we create and recall fully formed cognitive maps has been questioned by more recent research. Third, with the development of surround-screen displays, AR devices, and HMDs, navigation issues of virtual environments may well become even more challenging. This has already been raised by game designers and critics (Robertson 2016, 2017).

HMDs

Despite decades of research on navigation in VR and the recent emergence of consumer-level headsets, most research on virtual environments (especially virtual learning environments) has been desktop-based. We still encounter gaps in academic literature comparing new HMDs and AR displays to traditional desktop environments (Sousa Santos et al. 2009). Even though a few researchers have compared different display spaces, these displays have not been tested against a variety of simulated content and varying goals with different audiences. According to Daniel Montello and Corinna Sas (2006), "there is surprisingly little on the human factors of wayfinding for those with visual impairments, despite the powerful social, economic, and emotional importance of independent travel." In "Wayfinding in a Virtual Environment," Booth and colleagues (2000) wrote, "It is clear that the task of learning one's way around a particular environment is qualitatively different from learning a fact (semantic memory) or remembering an event in the past (episodic memory). The key difference relates to the way that memories are formed over time and are mediated by action."

According to Xiaolong Zhang (2008), geographers and cognitive psychologists have stated research into human navigation behavior needs to discover and apply new directions in theoretical models for virtual environments. However, real-world navigation systems do not scale easily to virtual environments, and there have been various proposed solutions, such as creating visible rather than passive landmarks (Pierce and Pausch 2004). Zhang (2008) has tested multiscalar experimental conditions, where maps could be scaled up or down (zoomed) to see different types of information directly relevant to the direction and appropriate to the skill level of people navigating space with specific tasks in mind. Multiscaling is not the same as changing the level of details at different scales; objects can be replaced with text information, and the level of detail of an object is not the only feature that can dynamically change. Zhang called such a virtual environment (or, in his words, a "3D world") using multiscale technology an mVE.

Chao Li (2006) noted the lack of consistent results in many navigation-based research studies in virtual environments. Li reminded us that much of the research has typically not considered the variety of tasks users may wish to follow (rather than those designed for the experiment) and other potentially distracting or confounding features, such as the external environment, the reliability of the technology they use, or, of course, other people. This would be of even more importance for location-based systems with portable technologies. This led Li to suggest we require more "multimodal information" and a wider range of optional user-led strategies.

Further, there appear to be differences, both slight and major, in navigation preferences between individuals and between genders. Judith Gluck and Sylvia Fitting (2003) provided some evidence through tests across three different domains of spatial cognition: mental rotation, testing spatial ability, and environmental navigation and orientation.

There are also other considerations necessary for people who do not use specific senses for navigation. For blind people, navigation is even more important. Orly Lahav and David Mioduser (2004) also noted that helpful navigation cues for blind people included being able to walk the perimeter first or moving from object to object and using echoes to facilitate their navigation. And W. H. Jacobson (1993), too, described the indoor environment familiarization process of people who are visually impaired, similarly noting they commence navigation with the use of a perimeter-recognition tactic: walking along the room's walls and exploring objects attached to the walls, followed by a grid-scanning tactic, aiming to explore the room's interior.

Even here in the real world, researchers like Jianhong Xia, Colin Arrowsmith, Mervyn Jackson, and William Cartwright (2008) remind us of individual preferences in wayfinding and note that "[tourism] management should provide complimentary materials to assist in wayfinding." That also applies to various kinds of shoppers ("adventure shoppers, social shoppers, idea shoppers") in a real-world shopping mall (Chebat, Gélinas-Chebat, and Therrien 2005).

Navigation, Imageability, Cognitive Maps, and Mental Maps

Research into navigation, orientation, and wayfinding has been ongoing for over two decades and has typically included the notion of cognitive maps. Researchers in this area include Ruth Alison Conroy (2001), Makio Ishihara, Saki Higuchi, and Yukio Ishihara (2016), Philip Jeffrey and Gloria Mark (1998), Joshua Julian and colleagues (2016), and Norman Vinson (1999) as well as Rudolph Darken and John Sibert (1993, 1996a, 1996b) and Chen and Stanney (1999).

The theory of cognitive maps goes back more than half a century (Tolman 1948), but more recent research has failed to fully verify its existence. It may be an unproven theory, and some have argued that despite its intuitive charm, it should be modified or even deleted from psychology textbooks (Jensen 2006). Rather than create complete overviews in a map-like form, our minds may instead (according to Jason Goldman [2011]) take photo-like snapshots, "the critical difference is that our *internal* representations of the environment are not map-like." According to Goldman, there is increasing doubt about the actual existence of cognitive mapping in the field of psychology, but unfortunately, this wariness has not reached many academics in digital environments.

As evidence of his skepticism for the existence of cognitive mapping, Goldman cited a study using fMRI that tracked people being shown pictures of scenes, objects, and human faces. fMRI indicated a particular part of the hippocampus, the parahippocampal place area (PPA), is triggered by images of "scenes, very weakly in response to objects, and not at all to faces."

Summary

The start of this chapter briefly outlined issues and challenges in how virtual environments require, enhance, or stymie healthy minds and bodies. Apart from the issues of posture, sedentary activity, and hygiene (Lutz et al. 2017), there is increasing concern over the addictive potential of digital entertainment and social alienation. There is also concern over what HMDs may do to the eyes or what happens to the brain's neurons, which are accustomed to movement, when a realistic stereoscopic visual field moves but the body does not.

Embodiment is an important aspect of experiencing the world, and philosopher Hubert Dreyfus was right to question the richness of interaction offered by online virtual worlds like *Second Life*. His notion of intercorporeality, borrowed from Maurice Merleau-Ponty (Kreisler 2005; Dreyfus 2008), may also be useful in helping improve the sense of embodiment, although I'd like to see separate terms: one for sensing others' bodily presences and the effect of one's own presence on others, and another for a sense of the physical boundaries of an overall group. Internet technology and, by extension, virtual environments do struggle to evoke a sense of intercorporeality. However, I don't believe Dreyfus was aware of recent developments in gestures, facial expressions, physiological trackers, and biofeedback or exertion interfaces, which may help engender not just improved fitness but also more sociability (Mast and de Vries 2017; Mueller and Young 2017).

One issue where our real-world sense of embodiment will be severely tested is in the navigation, orientation, and wayfinding of HMDs in 360-degree environments. Navigation is an essential but often overlooked aspect of useful and engaging *flat-screen* virtual environments. The way we orient, wayfind, and move in the real world differs markedly among people and depending on the context, and while previously virtual worlds were seen to be similar to real-world environments so that theories could be applied across both, this is looking increasingly inaccurate. Context is important here; the cultural background of the participants and the cultural milieu simulated along with thematic goals likely to be appropriate to the setting has typically been underexamined in these virtual environments.

How will new devices and interfaces affect how we experience and otherwise learn about place? More research is required in the emerging and exploding world of AR and HMDs. While being able to spin around and walk through virtual environments poses serious logistic problems in many living rooms, a new range of design methods will be required to stop a repeat of the original Nintendo Wii remote controller debacle, when untethered remotes flew through television screens and windows and hit unsuspecting pets and bystanders (Milawe 2012).

Apart from these accidental displays of embodied consequences, virtual places don't typically have powerful examples of solidity, materiality, and embodiment. Real-world architectural experiences and design techniques might not easily translate to virtual realms. How will these differences affect interaction in VR environments, games, and other types of cyberspace?

Note

1. This summer intern student project was developed thanks to a Pawsey summer intern grant.

References

Aghajan, Zahra M., Lavanya Acharya, Jason J. Moore, Jesse D. Cushman, Cliff Vuong, and Mayank R. Mehta. 2015. "Impaired Spatial Selectivity and Intact Phase Precession in Two-Dimensional Virtual Reality." *Nat Neurosci* 18 (1): 121–28. https://doi.org/10.1038/nn.3884.

Bajarin, Tim. 2017. "I Love Virtual Reality, but I'm Also Afraid of It." *Time*, May 16, 2017. Last Modified July 22, 2017. Accessed May 3, 2021. http://time.com/4780507/virtual-reality-vr-problems/.

Boddington, David. 2017. "Virtual Reality: Recognising the Risks." Science Focus. Last Modified January 23, 2017. Accessed July 22, 2017. http://www.sciencefocus.com/article/future/virtual-reality-recognising-risks.

Booth, Kellogg, Brian Fisher, Steven Page, C. Ware, and S. Widen. 2000. "Wayfinding in a Virtual Environment." Paper presented at Graphics Interface, Montréal, May 15–17, 2000.

Bourliataux-Lajoinie, Stéphane, Frederic Dosquet, and Josep Lluís del Olmo Arriaga. 2019. "The Dark Side of Digital Technology to Overtourism: The Case of Barcelona." *Worldwide Hospitality and Tourism Themes* 11 (5): 582–93. https://doi.org/10.1108/WHATT-06-2019-0041.

Bridgeman, Bruce. 2004. "Review: Philosophy of Mind Fails in Generating Progress toward Understanding the Mind, Perception." *Perception* 33: 379–81. https://doi.org/10.1068/p3303rvw.

Caduff, David, and Sabine Timpf. 2008. "On the Assessment of Landmark Salience for Human Navigation." *Cognitive Processing* 9 (4): 249–67. http://dx.doi.org/10.1007/s10339-007-0199-2.

Carman, Ashley. 2017. "This Haptic Feedback VR Suit Could Complete Your VR Look." The Verge. Last Modified February 24, 2017. Accessed May 3, 2021. https://www.theverge.com/circuitbreaker/2017/2/24/14717776/hardlight-haptic-feedback-vr-suit.

Carter, Jeremy Story. 2019. "The 'Paradigm Shift' of Virtual Reality Tourism." *Blueprint for Living*, April 11, 2016. Last Modified April 12, 2016. Accessed January 22, 2020. https://www.abc.net.au/radionational/programs/blueprintforliving/virtual-reality-technologies-and-tourism/7312152.

Champion, Erik Malcolm, Li Qiang, Demetrius Lacet, and Andrew Dekker. 2016. "3D In-World Telepresence with Camera-Tracked Gestural Interaction." Paper presented at the Eurographics Workshop on Graphics and Cultural Heritage, Genoa, October 5–7, 2016. http://dx.doi.org/10.2312/gch.20161394.

Chebat, Jean-Charles, Claire Gélinas-Chebat, and Karina Therrien. 2005. "Lost in a Mall, the Effects of Gender, Familiarity with the Shopping Mall and the Shopping Values on Shoppers' Wayfinding Processes." *Journal of Business Research* 58 (11): 1590–98. https://doi.org/http://dx.doi.org/10.1016/j.jbusres.2004.02.006.Chen, Jui Lin, and Kay M. Stanney. 1999. "A Theoretical Model of Wayfinding in Virtual Environments: Proposed Strategies for Navigational Aiding." *Presence: Teleoperators and Virtual Environments* 8 (6): 671–685.

Chen, Ling, Wai Leung Ambrose Lo, Yu Rong Mao, Ming Hui Ding, Qiang Lin, Hai Li, Jiang Li Zhao, Zhi Qin Xu, Rui Hao Bian, and Dong Feng Huang. 2016. "Effect of Virtual Reality on Postural and Balance Control in Patients with Stroke: A Systematic Literature Review." *BioMed Research International* 2016: 8. https://doi.org/10.1155/2016/7309272.

Cockburn, Andy. 2004. "Revisiting 2D vs 3D Implications on Spatial Memory." Proceedings of the Fifth Australasian User Interface Conference (CRPIT '04), Dunedin, January 18–22, 2004.

Conroy, Ruth Alison. 2001. "Spatial Navigation in Immersive Virtual Environments." PhD diss., Faculty of the Built Environment, University of London. http://discovery.ucl.ac.uk/1111/.

Culbertson, Heather, Samuel B. Schorr, and Allison M. Okamura. 2018. "Haptics: The Present and Future of Artificial Touch Sensation." *Annual Review of Control, Robotics, and Autonomous Systems* 1 (1): 385–409. https://doi.org/10.1146/annurev-control-060117-105043.

Dalton, Ruth Conroy, Christoph Hölscher, and H. J. Spiers. 2015. "Navigating Complex Buildings: Cognition, Neuroscience and Architectural Design." In *Studying Visual and Spatial Reasoning for Design Creativity*, edited by John Gero, 3–22. Dordrecht: Springer.

Darken, Rudy P., and John L. Sibert. 1993. "A Toolset for Navigation in Virtual Environments." In *Proceedings of the 6th Annual ACM Symposium on User Interface Software and Technology (UIST)*, edited by Scott Hudson, Randy Pausch, Brad Vander Zanden, and James Foley, 157–65. Atlanta, GA: ACM.

———. 1996a. "Navigating Large Virtual Spaces." *International Journal of Human-Computer Interaction* 8 (1): 49–71.

———. 1996b. "Wayfinding Strategies and Behaviors in Large Virtual Worlds." In *Proceedings of the SIGCHI Conference on Human Factors in Computing Systems: Common Ground*, 142–49. Vancouver: ACM.

Davis, Nicola. 2016. "Long-Term Effects of Virtual Reality Use Need More Research, Say Scientists." *The Guardian*, March 19, 2016. Last Modified July 22, 2017. Accessed July 22, 2017. https://www.theguardian.com/technology/2016/mar/19/long-term-effects-of-virtual-reality-use-need-more-research-say-scientists.

Dodds, Rachel, and Richard Butler, ed. 2019. *Overtourism: Issues, Realities and Solutions.* Vol. 1. Berlin: De Gruyter.

Dreyfus, Hubert L. 2008. *On the Internet.* 2nd ed. London: Routledge.

Farovik, Anja, Ryan J. Place, Sam McKenzie, Blake Porter, Catherine E. Munro, and Howard Eichenbaum. 2015. "Orbitofrontal Cortex Encodes Memories within Value-Based Schemas and Represents Contexts That Guide Memory Retrieval." *Journal of Neuroscience* 35 (21): 8333–44.

Gent, Ed. 2016. "A Lack of Data and Guidelines Is Leaving Consumers in the Dark about Virtual Reality's Potential Negative Side Effects for Kids." *Scientific American.* Accessed October 4, 2016. https://www.scientificamerican.com/article/are-virtual-reality-headsets-safe-for-children/.

Giardina, Carolyn. 2016. "The Next Germ Nightmare: Movie VR Headsets." Hollywood Reporter. Last Modified June 16, 2016. Accessed July 22, 2017. http://www.hollywoodreporter.com/behind-screen/next-germ-nightmare-movie-vr-902887.

Gibson, James J. 1966. *The Senses Considered as Perceptual Systems.* London: Allen & Unwin.

———. 1974. *The Perception of the Visual World.* Westport, CT: Greenwood.

———. 1977. "The Theory of Affordances." In *Perceiving, Acting and Knowing: Toward an Ecological Psychology*, edited by Robert Shaw and John Bransford, 67–82. New York: Lawrence Erlbaum Associates.

———. 1986. *The Ecological Approach to Visual Perception.* Hillsdale, New Jersey, USA: Lawrence Erlbaum Associates.

Gluck, Judith, and Sylvia Fitting. 2003. "Spatial Strategy Selection: Interesting Incremental Information." *International Journal of Testing* 3 (3): 293–308. https://doi.org/10.1207 /S15327574IJT0303_7.

Goldman, Jason G. 2011. "Rats, Bees, and Brains: The Death of the 'Cognitive Map.'" *Scientific American.* Last Modified July 12, 2011. Accessed May 3, 2021. https://blogs. scientificamerican.com/thoughtful-animal/httpblogsscientificamericancomthoughtful-animal20110712rats-bees-and-brains-the-death-of-the-cognitive-map/.

Goodwin, Harold. 2017. "The Challenge of Overtourism." Responsible Tourism Partnership. Responsible Tourism Partnership Working Paper. Last Modified October 2017. Accessed April 26, 2021. https://haroldgoodwin.info/wp-content/uploads/2020/08 /rtpwp4overtourism012017.pdf.

Granic, Isabela, Adam Lobel, and Rutger C. M. E. Engels. 2014. "The Benefits of Playing Video Games." *American Psychologist* 69 (1): 66–78. https://www.apa.org/pubs /journals/releases/amp-a0034857.pdf.

Griffiths, Mark. 2015. "Gaming to Death: What Turns a Hobby into a Health hHazard?" CNN, January 21, 2015. Accessed May 3, 2021. http://edition.cnn.com/2015/01/21 /opinion/gaming-addiction-risks/.

Hamburger, Kai, and Markus Knauff. 2011. "SQUARELAND: A Virtual Environment for Investigating Cognitive Processes in Human Wayfinding." *PsychNology Journal* 9 (2): 137–63.

Heffernannov, Virginia. 2014. "Virtual Reality Fails Its Way to Success." *New York Times Magazine*, November 14, 2014. Last Modified July 10, 2017. Accessed May 3, 2021. https://www.nytimes.com/2014/11/16/magazine/virtual-reality-fails-its-way-to -success.html.

Hutchins, Edwin. 1995. *Cognition in the Wild.* Cambridge, MA: MIT Press.

Ihde, Don. 2002. *Bodies in Technology.* Minneapolis: University of Minnesota Press.

Ishihara, Makio, Saki Higuchi, and Yukio Ishihara. 2016. "Effect of Navigation Methods on Spatial Awareness in Virtual Worlds." Paper presented at the International Conference on Human-Computer Interaction (HCI 2016), Toronto, July 17–22, 2016.

Jacobson, W. H. 1993. *The Art and Science of Teaching Orientation and Mobility to Persons with Visual Impairments.* New York: USA American Foundation for the Blind.

Jarrett, Christian. 2014. "Psychology: How Many Senses Do We Have?" BBC Future, November 19, 2014. Last Modified July 10, 2017. Accessed July 27, 2017. http://www.bbc .com/future/story/20141118-how-many-senses-do-you-have.

Jeffrey, Phillip, and Gloria Mark. 1998. "Constructing Social Spaces in Virtual Environments: A Study of Navigation and Interaction." Workshop on personalized and social navigation in information space, Stockholm, March 16–17, 1998.

Jensen, Robert. 2006. "Behaviorism, Latent Learning, and Cognitive Maps: Needed Revisions in Introductory Psychology Textbooks." *Behavior Analyst* 29 (2): 187–209. http://www.ncbi.nlm.nih.gov/pmc/articles/PMC2223150/.

Johnson, Mark. 2013. *The Body in the Mind: The Bodily Basis of Meaning, Imagination, and Reason.* Chicago: University of Chicago Press.

Jørgensen, Anker. 2004. "Marrying HCI/Usability and Computer Games: A Preliminary Look." In *NordiCHI '04: Proceedings of the Third Nordic Conference on Human-Computer Interaction*, edited by Aulikki Hyrskykari, 393–96. Tampere, FIN: ACM.

Julian, Joshua B., Jack Ryan, Roy H. Hamilton, and Russell A. Epstein. 2016. "The Occipital Place Area Is Causally Involved in Representing Environmental Boundaries during Navigation." *Current Biology* 26 (8): 1104–1109.

Koens, Ko, Albert Postma, and Bernadett Papp. 2018. "Is Overtourism Overused? Understanding the Impact of Tourism in a City Context." *Sustainability* 10 (12): 4384.

Kreisler, Harry. 2005. "Hubert L. Dreyfus Interview: Conversations with History; The Disembodied Internet." Institute of International Studies, University of California, Berkeley. Last Modified November 2, 2005. Accessed July 7, 2017. http://globetrotter .berkeley.edu/people5/Dreyfus/dreyfus-con7.html.

Lahav, Orly, and David Mioduser. 2004. "Exploration of Unknown Spaces by People Who Are Blind Using a Multi-Sensory Virtual Environment." *Journal of Special Education Technology* 19 (3): 15–23. https://doi.org/doi:10.1177/016264340401900302.

Langtree, Ian. 2016. "Disability and Virtual Reality Technology." Disabled World, July 20, 2016. Last Modified November 12, 2016. Accessed May 3, 2021. https://www.disabled -world.com/assistivedevices/computer/vr-tech.php.

Lewis, Tanya. 2016. "Samsung Gear VR: Virtual Reality Tech May Have Nasty Side Effects." Livescience. Last Modified February 3, 2015. Accessed July 22, 2017. https://www .livescience.com/49669-virtual-reality-health-effects.html.

Li, Chao. 2006. "User Preferences, Information Transactions and Location-Based Services: A Study of Urban Pedestrian Wayfinding." *Computers, Environment and Urban Systems* 30 (6): 726–40. https://doi.org/http://dx.doi.org/10.1016/j.compenvurbsys.2006.02.008.

Lutz, Otto Hans-Martin, Charlotte Burmeister, Luara Ferreira dos Santos, Nadine Morkisch, Christian Dohle, and Jörg Krüger. 2017. "Application of Head-Mounted Devices with Eye-Tracking in Virtual Reality Therapy." *Current Directions in Biomedical Engineering* 3 (1): 53–56. https://www.degruyter.com/view/j/cdbme.2017.3.issue-1/cdbme-2017-0012 /cdbme-2017-0012.xml.

Lynch, Kevin. 1960. *The Image of the City*. Vol. 11. Cambridge, MA: MIT Press.

Madary, Michael, and Thomas K. Metzinger. 2016. "Real Virtuality: A Code of Ethical Conduct; Recommendations for Good Scientific Practice and the Consumers of VR-Technology." *Frontiers in Robotics and AI* 3 (3). https://doi.org/10.3389/frobt.2016.00003.

Mason, Betsy. 2017. "Virtual Reality Has a Motion Sickness Problem: People Prone to Nausea May Opt Out of Immersive Experiences." *ScienceNews* 191 (5): 24.

Mast, Danića, and Sanne de Vries. 2017. "Cooperative Tetris: The Influence of Social Exertion Gaming on Game Experience and Social Presence." Paper presented at the Eighth International Conference on Intelligent Technologies for Interactive Entertainment (INTETAIN 2016), Utrecht, June 28–30, 2016.

Milawe. 2012. "Wii Remote Accidents: The Dangers of Console Gaming." *Altered Gamer* (blog), July 26, 2017. Accessed May 3, 2021. http://www.alteredgamer.com/wii-gear /42586-wii-remote-accidents-the-dangers-of-console-gaming/.

Montello, Daniel R., and Corina Sas. 2006. "Human Factors of Wayfinding in Navigation." Accessed May 3, 2021. https://eprints.lancs.ac.uk/id/eprint/42335/1/MontelloSas.pdf.

Moore, Keith Diaz. 2005. "Using Place Rules and Affect to Understand Environmental Fit: A Theoretical Exploration." *Environment and Behavior* 37 (3): 330–63. http://eab.sagepub .com/cgi/content/abstract/37/3/330.

Mueller, Florian 'Floyd', and Damon Young. 2017. "Five Lenses for Designing Exertion Experiences." In *Proceedings of the 2017 CHI Conference on Human Factors in Computing Systems*, edited by Gloria Mark and Susan Fussell, 2473–87. Denver, CO: ACM.

Nguyen, Thi Thanh Hai, Diana Ishmatova, Tommi Tapanainen, Tapani N. Liukkonen, Niina Katajapuu, Tuomas Makila, and Mika Luimula. 2017. "Impact of Serious Games on Health and Well-being of Elderly: A Systematic Review." Proceedings of the 50th Hawaii International Conference on System Sciences, 1–10, Waikoloa, Hawaii.

Oberhaus, Daniel. 2016. "We're Already Violating Virtual Reality's First Code of Ethics." Motherboard: Tech by Vice, March 6, 2016. Last Modified May 7, 2016. Accessed July 22, 2017. https://motherboard.vice.com/en_us/article/yp3va5/vr-code-of-ethics.

Omer, Itzhak, and Ran Goldblatt. 2007. "The Implications of Inter-visibility between Landmarks on Wayfinding Performance: An Investigation Using a Virtual Urban Environment." *Computers, Environment and Urban Systems* 31 (5): 520–34. https://doi.org/http://dx.doi.org/10.1016/j.compenvurbsys.2007.08.004.

Parkin, Simon. 2016. "The Coming Horror of Virtual Reality." *The New Yorker*. Last Modified May 15, 2016. Accessed July 27, 2017. http://www.newyorker.com/tech/elements/the-coming-horror-of-virtual-reality.

Parsons, Thomas D., Andrea Gaggioli, and Giuseppe Riva. 2017. "Virtual Reality for Research in Social Neuroscience." *Brain Sciences* 7 (4): 42. https://doi.org/10.3390/brainsci7040042.

Pierce, J. S., and R. Pausch. 2004. "Navigation with Place Representations and Visible Landmarks." Paper presented at IEEE Virtual Reality 2004, Chicago, IL, March 27–31, 2004.

Powell, Wendy. 2017. "Five Ways Virtual Reality Is Improving Healthcare." The Conversation. Last Modified June 20, 2017. Accessed July 14, 2017. https://theconversation.com/five-ways-virtual-reality-is-improving-healthcare-79523.

Robertson, Adi. 2016. "Obduction Is a Beautiful Virtual World That Shows the Limits of VR." The Verge. Last Modified September 10, 2016. Accessed July 13, 2017. https://www.theverge.com/2016/9/10/12864598/obduction-myst-cyan-worlds-virtual-reality.

———. 2017. "Playing Fallout 4 and Skyrim in VR Is Probably a Bad Idea: A Good VR Open World Won't Look Like Anything Out There Today." The Verge. Last Modified June 16, 2017. Accessed July 13, 2017. https://www.theverge.com/2017/6/16/15814724/fallout-4-skyrim-vr-bethesda-hands-on-e3-2017.

Röser, Florian, Kai Hamburger, Antje Krumnack, and Markus Knauff. 2012. "The Structural Salience of Landmarks: Results from an On-line Study and a Virtual Environment Experiment." *Journal of Spatial Science* 57 (1): 37–50. https://doi.org/10.1080/14498596.2012.686362.

Simor, Fernando Winckler, Manoela Rogofski Brum, Jaison Dairon Ebertz Schmidt, Rafael Rieder, and Ana Carolina Bertoletti De Marchi. 2016. "Usability Evaluation Methods for Gesture-Based Games: A Systematic Review." *JMIR Serious Games* 4 (2): e17. https://doi.org/10.2196/games.5860.

Sousa Santos, Beatriz, Paulo Dias, Angela Pimentel, Jan-Willem Baggerman, Carlos Ferreira, Samuel Silva, and Joaquim Madeira. 2009. "Head-Mounted Display versus Desktop for 3D Navigation in Virtual Reality: A User Study." *Multimedia Tools and Applications* 41 (1): 161–81. https://link.springer.com/article/10.1007/s11042-008-0223-2.

Strohecker, Carol, and Barbara Barros. 2000. "Make Way for WayMaker." *Presence: Teleoperators and Virtual Environments* 9 (1): 97–107. http://dl.acm.org/citation.cfm?id=1246868.

Tavanti, Monica, and Mats Lind. 2001. "2D vs 3D, Implications on Spatial Memory." In *INFOVIS 2001: Proceedings of the IEEE Symposium on Information Visualization 2001*, edited by Keith Andrews, Steven F. Roth, and Pak Chung Wong, 139–45. San Diego, CA: IEEE Computer Society.

TESLASUIT. 2021. "TESLASUIT." Accessed May 3, 2021. https://teslasuit.io.

Tolman, Edward C. 1948. "Cognitive Maps in Rats and Men." *Psychological Review* 55 (4): 189–208.

Vinson, Norman G. 1999. "Design Guidelines for Landmarks to Support Navigation in Virtual Environments." Proceedings of the SIGCHI conference on Human factors in computing systems: the CHI is the limit, 278–85, Pittsburgh, PA, May 15–20, 1999.

Wang, H., T. R. Johnson, and J. Zhang. 2001. "The Mind's Views of Space." Paper presented at the Third International Conference of Cognitive Science, Beijing, August 27–31, 2001.

Werner, Steffen, and Laura E. Schindler. 2004. "The Role of Spatial Reference Frames in Architecture: Misalignment Impairs Way-Finding Performance." *Environment and Behavior* 36 (4): 461–82. http://eab.sagepub.com/cgi/content/abstract/36/4/461.

West, Darrell M. 2016. "The Ethical Dilemmas of Virtual Reality." Techtank, April 18, 2016. The Brookings Institution. Last Modified April 18, 2016. Accessed July 22, 2017. https://www.brookings.edu/blog/techtank/2016/04/18/the-ethical-dilemmas-of-virtual-reality/.

Wolpert, Stuart. 2014. "Brain's Reaction to Virtual Reality Should Prompt Further Study, Suggests New Research by UCLA Neuroscientists." UCLA Newsroom. Last Modified November 24, 2014. Accessed Janaury 30, 2020. http://newsroom.ucla.edu/releases/brains-reaction-to-virtual-reality-should-prompt-further-study-suggests-new-research-by-ucla-neuroscientists.

Xia, Jianhong, Colin Arrowsmith, Mervyn Jackson, and William Cartwright. 2008. "The Wayfinding Process Relationships between Decision-Making and Landmark Utility." *Tourism Management* 29 (3): 445–57. https://doi.org/http://dx.doi.org/10.1016/j.tourman.2007.05.010.

Zhang, Xiaolong. 2008. "A Multiscale Progressive Model on Virtual Navigation." *International Journal of Human-Computer Studies* 66 (4): 243–56. https://doi.org/http://dx.doi.org/10.1016/j.ijhcs.2007.09.004.

Zimring, Craig, and Ruth Conroy Dalton. 2003. "Linking Objective Measures of Space to Cognition and Action." *Environment and Behavior* 35 (1): 3–16. http://eab.sagepub.com/cgi/content/abstract/35/1/3.

chapter six

GAMES ARE NOT
INTERACTIVE PLACES

Introduction

This chapter argues that interactivity has significant implications for virtual worlds, virtual places, and serious games, centering on key concepts such as the promise of control, the varied definitions of game mechanics, and the dangerous promise of gamification. Interaction can provide for different types of learning preferences while drawing in the younger (and older) generations. Interaction can also show different aspects of place and the care required to evoke and maintain a sense of place.

As mechanics are a key part of the continually engaging nature of computer games, I suggest that virtual places would be far more effective if designers reexamined and contextually applied game mechanics, but not as they are typically used in games. Related to game mechanics is the relatively recently proposed concept of gamification. However, I will caution against the use of *gamification* and suggest instead *playerfication* as well as provide a workflow guiding the design of interactive environments, including for culturally significant places.

Virtual Reality, Interaction, and Control

Interaction is a major reason why entertainment computing has been so engaging and popular. Virtual environments, by contrast, have focused on pixels and speed rather than on interaction and agency. *Virtual reality* (VR) appears to be a loosely applied term that covers a range of vastly different content and technologies. Proponents and consumers regularly conflate terms such as *virtual* with *digital* or confuse virtual presence with photorealistic ocularcentrism and interaction with control over the simulated environment.

For example, in Philip K. Dick's 1964 science fiction classic, *The Three Stigmata of Palmer Eldritch*, virtuality is a drugged escape route from mortality and existence on the terra-formed but banal planet of Mars. But a long-lost space pioneer (who could be an alien or android in disguise) returns offering more realistic VR and immortality for the physical husk left behind, but only if the colonists accept him as their God inside VR. A detective antihero is sent to chase the strange alien/person in the VR, but there is a twist. The detective is never sure, on leaving the VR, whether he did return to reality or is still trapped inside, convinced that he is free.

The Three Stigmata of Palmer Eldritch is analogous to a Turing test: VR succeeds when you are never sure if you have escaped from it. And this story is an early example of VR as control. This control can be over others (things, forces, and people) or over the self (the body, the mind, relationships between self and the simulated environment or between self, simulation, and others), but it tends to be the former.

The philosopher Martin Heidegger appears to have foreseen this issue of technology as control. Mark Vernon (2009) wrote of Heidegger: "The difficulty with technology, he said, is not that it enhances our lives. It does. Rather, it's that it radically prescribes the life it enhances in the process."

I criticized the focus on control in VRs, but I'd like to clarify here that I criticize the emphasis on the essence of VR as being the control of others. In my area of research, virtual heritage, this issue is of particular relevance, but it is, I think, of interest to virtual environment designers and critics in general. A VR participant does not need to develop mastery over others. There are, for example, serious games that exert, reverse, or "show" control over the player (Palazzi, Roccetti, and Marfia 2010). VR can also help people better understand processes at different scales.

In understanding processes, VR can also help us understand our behavior and the consequences of our behavior. In "Can Virtual Reality Emerge as a Tool for Conservation?," Heather Millar (2016) raises the issue of education and conservation via VR. She proffered the example of Google Expeditions: "Meanwhile, the ocean VR experiences produced by VHIL [Virtual Human Interaction Lab] are building on a decade of social science research that shows people who have a VR experience are more likely to change behavior in ways that benefit the planet."

Games and Interaction

Game Definitions and Classifications, Genres, and Ontologies

How do we see possibilities? Depending on how we define them, games can help. Despite the many definitions of games, computer games are considered by many writers to be rules-based systems. Jesper Juul (2003) wrote that a computer game is "a rule-based formal system with a variable and quantifiable outcome, where different outcomes are assigned different values, the player exerts effort to influence the outcome, the player feels attached to the outcome, and the consequences of the activity are optional and negotiable." In a similar vein, Katie Salen and Eric Zimmerman (2003) defined a computer game as "a system in which players engage in an artificial conflict, defined by rules, that results in a quantifiable outcome."

Table 6.1. Games, Virtual Environments, and Virtual Learning Environments

Factors	Games	Virtual Environments	Virtual Learning Environments
Engagement	Essential	Not necessary	Not that common or consistently found and difficult to sustain when evident
Challenge	Essential	Not necessary	Ideally but not always and seldom scales to the expertise of the player
Failure	Essential and typical learning experience	Not necessary	Usually, not always a learning experience
Risks and rewards	No	Not necessary	Usually rewards, sometimes risks, not often imaginatively themed
Strategy	Yes, ideally more than one strategy, combined creatively	Not necessary	Not common
Telescoping (coordinating the in-game workload of tasks) to reach goals	Yes	No	Seldom
Interaction imaginatively themed	Yes	Not necessary	Ideally, but not always

Considering games as *essentially* rules-based systems is not particularly revealing because many digital applications, such as virtual environments, are also rules-based systems. Interestingly, many computer game definitions don't mention challenge or engagement (fun), which separates games from other computer "rules-based systems," even though challenge is an essential component of why we find games so engaging (table 6.1).

Unlike in much edutainment, in games, players often learn by failure as well as by success, and games reward expertise; more complex games even promote and reward a diversity of strategy. Games involve simulated risks and rewards and the selection of different strategies to solve immediate and long-term goals imaginatively framed within a setting that evokes rather than defines the imagination, and the longer games do so in such a way that engagement and challenge are constantly balanced against the performance of the player. However, games are not typical software applications. Games are easy to learn and difficult to master, while software (and virtual environments) are typically easy to learn and easy to master.

We could rephrase the earlier definition: a game is "an engaging challenge that offers up the possibility of temporary or permanent tactical resolution without harmful outcomes to the real-world situation of the participant." Why is this alternative definition of interest here? It reminds us of the intersubjective nature of game play. A game is not merely a system or a collection of rules and equipment; it is a challenging (but not frustrating) task, offers a range of strategies without permanent penalty, and is a thematically designed experience that encourages the imagination (to find and test out these alternative strategies).

Due to their open-ended nature, game prototypes can provide a great deal of information about game play. In figure 6.1, researchers at the University of Central Florida present a board game prototype on South American family relationships (in a game prototyping workshop at the 2017 Computer Applications and Quantitative Methods in Archaeology [CAA] International Conference, Atlanta, Georgia). Physical multiplayer board games are highly engaging, not just because of the rules and mechanics, but also because of the human-to-human negotiations and character revelations that take place.

However, direct and extensive expertise with different types of games does not necessarily mean one can better analyze or create new types of games. Jose Zagal and Amy Bruckman noted of their students (2008), "In many ways, being expert videogame players interferes with their abilities to step back from their role as 'gamers' or 'fans' and reason critically and analytically about the games they are studying or designing. As Diane describes, 'it's hard for them to break out of being a fan. It's even that much harder to take an objective step back, because they just have so much fun playing games.'"

Another reason to be wary of defining games as essentially rules-based systems is because gamers don't participate in the game as a system of rules but as an experience or series of experiences. A great deal of energy and skill is required to design a complicit, imaginatively themed experiential world that encourages play and elegantly hides any programming or shortcuts that prevents the tantalization of the imagination. It can be very difficult for experienced gamers to forego that enchantment and attempt to dispassionately study the game as a systematic combination of design, psychology, and programming.

Game Classification and Typology

There is no necessary single-origin or shared technology for games. Games offer a range of options and strategies and build their imaginative universes independently of any requirement for discipline-oriented or scholastic "purity" so game ontologies do not have to be clear and distinct. These ontologies pose their own problems; either they continually change their definitions and classification systems to fit as many examples as possible, or they try to cram wildly different types of games into a rigid classification system (Dahlskog, Kamstrup, and Aarseth 2009). Few ontologies cater particularly to serious games (Susi, Johannesson, and Backlund 2007; Marsh 2011), and they certainly don't focus on virtual places.

Figure 6.1 CAA 2017 games prototyping workshop, Atlanta. Erik Champion.

That said, for a relatively new upstart field like game studies, classification systems are alluring but the allure is dangerous. We could classify the potential and the impact of video games in myriad ways: for example, via their subject matter, platforms, genres, learning outcomes, or interaction methods. Or we could simply separate game genres in terms of whether they involve the participant being socially embedded or physically embodied.

We could also classify games in terms of their design elements or components, but they don't always smoothly relate to the desired player experience or the optimal form of interactive game play. Nor do their features necessarily distinguish them. There are so many genres, parodies, and games that blend different genres and game elements that classification by genre becomes a lesson in taxonomic masochism.

Characteristics Common to Games but Not to Places

One characteristic common to all game genres, real or computer-based, is that they are challenging. Many computer games feature increasing complexity: a range of puzzles or situations to overcome (Malone 1980/1990). They have tasks, affordances, and constraints. The mixture of affordances, constraints, and different levels are designed to be challenging in the sense of "hard fun": easy to play, difficult to master. They have to be difficult enough to be intriguing, but not so difficult as to make the user give up in frustration; preferably, they can be solved by different strategies, so players are not bored when replaying the game.

Sometimes winning, lucky guesses, random events, or appropriate strategy selections increase equipment or status, and sometimes more of the environment is uncovered. As an easy way of increasing the sense of challenge, games are also often time based. As challenges, games can develop pattern matching and puzzle-solving skills, predictive thinking, and bluffing.

Rewards are also a universal feature of games, be they internal (game feedback), or external (awards and status conferred by other members of the gaming community). As one progresses, the variety and value of rewards increase, with more sophisticated tools, clothes, or weapons; increasingly difficult levels; and new secrets. In many games, knowledge is unfolded over time and in relation to game play, directly related to the increasing success of the player. Increasing the level of difficulty and matching it to the increasing skill, confidence, and knowledge of different players with different learning preferences is not a trivial design task.

Fantasy is often used to give people an idea of what could or should be expected and to give them the feeling of a specific type of freedom, of agency. Thomas Malone (1980/1990) declared fantasy is a common feature of games. Fantasy indicates what is to be expected in the game, the type of character, and their motivations and goals. Characters' aptitudes for specific skills and behaviors can be expressed to give people an idea of what could or should be expected and to provide them the feeling of inhabiting a specific type of freedom, of agency. Fantasy encourages motivation and imagination; and provides an allegorical overview without restricting the player to specific details.

Malone's concept of fantasy was closer to general imagination than to the popular cultural notion of swords and sorcery, but the latter is popular in games because it offers explicit but schematic examples of what the player might be expected to do as a situated character in a game world with minimal backstory. To borrow the clichéd fantasy of Tolkien-inspired games, when provided with vague details of even mythological creatures, we immediately have some idea of their physical characteristics, location, motivation, interests, and capabilities, but explicit details are dependent on the player's actions.

Place theory seldom clarifies different types of place features and different types of place genres—for example, fantasy places. Some places are considered imaginative places because they don't clearly and explicitly relate to current place objects or interactive place relations, while others are considered imaginative because they don't follow commonsense, lived experience, or known physics. I don't, however, know of a classification that would be suitable to the design of virtual worlds. Indeed, writers have complained about the lack of literature on fantasy genres (Mendlesohn 2008), so it may be a wider issue of a topic that is not taken seriously by many academic authors, even if the field produces highly lucrative returns and frenzied discussion and engagement by its fans.

My issue with computer games is that game play is seldom hermeneutic *inside the game itself*. Games, typically, do not offer a world of interpretative possibilities or the ability to customize the world with the player's intentions and identity. The person-to-person feedback of games in the real world is typically faked. Instructions are delivered via a narrator or book during the introduction, and they cannot be added to, layered, or otherwise modified. Social interactions seldom directly influence or are incorporated into the game design of computer games in the same way that real-world audiences and artists affect and influence each other.

I suspect that a lack of hermeneutical layering (levels of interpretative detail and structure) is not an issue for action-based games, but it does raise potential limitations if we are trying to convey historically layered and contested interpretation rather than action-related instruction. Important places typically have a history of encounters, usage, memorable events, interpretable layers, or a contested past (fig. 6.2). How could we layer interpretations without restricting agency, curtailing engagement, or restricting potential narratives? Perhaps we could treat them as games, as platial possibility spaces?

Games Offer the Promise of Control

Possibility spaces have to allow for failure. In previous publications, I have praised games for embracing failure as a way to learn (Champion 2011). But they also promise control over the game environment to people who pay attention and continually work at improving their performance. With the promise of increasing control, players are compelled to improve their skills, memory, awareness, or knowledge. The promise of control over the environment leads to increased control by the player over themselves.

A lack of personal challenge is unlikely to lead to a rewarding and durably enjoyable game. Games can offer control over others but this is usually balanced

Figure 6.2 Multimedia simulation of Palestine, Dr. Rusaila Bazlamit, Curtin University. Erik Champion.

by a cost. Although there may also be collaborative games that can only be completed by cooperating parties, they appear far less frequently and don't seem to be easy to design.

Games have succeeded where VR has failed because games offer increased control and engaging goals, but neither VR nor games are necessarily interactive *places*. Games are explicitly goal directed, while VR environments encourage spectacle rather than inhabitation.

Are Games Virtual Places?

Even if games are simulations (with something added), they are still not necessarily virtual place simulations. Controversially, perhaps, I suggest that they have features and requirements not relevant to or even at cross purposes with place-making features and components. Games differ from simulations and place simulations in that they have outcomes that the player works toward and dedicates time and effort toward *independent of place*. Players invest and therefore become engaged and attached to the potential rewards, not to inhabitation or ownership of place.

While we may talk to other players about our interpretations of what happens inside these games, this dialogue is seldom possible inside the game itself, nor does the social interactions between players immediately and permanently affect the rules and overall system of the game. The digital simulation of a place is a particularly interesting concept, but the setting of the game is typically more a prop or a stage than a place of cultural significance.

I suggest places are semipermanent (and slowly fading) because the dedication and energy we bring to immortalize records, events, and achievements are partially driven precisely because of the inevitable slide toward oblivion: these cultural markers fade over time. How we attempt to preserve events and experiences of value is also cultural. The slow loss of culture in the real world would have no parallel in a virtual world designed to be a world of persistent data (a typical criterion in definitions of virtual worlds). While our culture in this physical world may outlive us as individuals, culture does not outlive time and is only perfectly preserved in unreal worlds. Persistence in virtual worlds should be reconsidered if genuine culture is to be a component. Culture is passed on, but in doing so it changes, and the original meaning is eventually lost, even if cultural traditions typically (and ironically) try to hold on to the original meaning. This irony is not lost on me, but this bitter-sweet conundrum does not exist in virtual worlds, because they are designed to be persistent.

While virtual worlds are often distinguished from games, games do have interesting and useful features. They have challenging tasks (goals), social embeddedness, and focus; they often leverage physical embodiment; they are metaphorically unified; and they have thematic rewards and direct (and usually explicit) player feedback. Some games have time and space for reflection, but generally, they are designed to distract the mind and engage it in an all-consuming activity.

The relationship between place and game is not always an obvious one. We often take places for granted, but they are not as fixed and consistent as one might think; they are interactive as well. They owe at least part of their identity to their relationship to other places: they typically gain their distinctiveness from how they are used and inhabited. They are like games in that they have constraints and affordances, but they also have feedback. Feedback is written back into the place through interaction.

Games, Virtual Environments, and Virtual Learning Environments

Earlier, I outlined how architecture does not prepare one for game design. Computer games are virtual environments, but nongame virtual environments tend to have other priorities. Games dare you to find out more, while virtual environments prefer to explain everything. Game designers know that many of us are drawn to competition, challenge, and fantasy, but these components are often missing from nongame types of virtual environments. Games also offer procedural knowledge learning rather than the descriptive knowledge (sometimes perhaps prescriptive) proffered in typical virtual environments; this distinction raises problems for educators who wish to leverage games with traditional education content.

One could make the argument that computer games are virtual learning environments (VLEs), but computer games typically don't mind creating objects that have no direct factual relationship to similar objects in the real world. Many computer games allow players to learn through failure, or to learn from play (as experimentation). Computer game rewards compel the player to value the games as intrinsically valuable, but this is not such an important objective in most virtual environments.

Then there is the issue of the player and the player's history. Michela Mortara and colleagues (2014) have noted that few serious games track the progress of the player; they recommend "an appealing and meaningful environment and a suited and intuitive interaction paradigm" (322–23). I have only one question here: What do any of these words mean in this context?

Moving Past Destructive Interaction Scenarios

To bring life back to virtual places for the enjoyment of the spectator, we require more understanding of communication design, specifically, interaction design. This requires meaningful participation for visitors to truly engage with the experience, not the superficial personalization or widespread destruction of commercial game worlds or using games that are reflection friendly and not just trigger-happy. Do they always transfer meaningful knowledge and skills to the real world?

Professor Susan Greenfield (2014) argued that the immediacy and short-term excitement of screen interactions are stripping away our ability to follow narratives and understand the context as well as our ability to interpret facial expressions. Yet this is not a new phenomenon. Vaughan Bell (2008; Jarrett 2008) uncovered an article about the nineteenth-century neurologists George Beard and Silas Weir Mitchell, who were worried about the pace of life and the harmful effect new technologies were having on the brains of American citizens.

Despite misgivings over entertainment media used for educational purposes, we can see various opportunities in which games and virtual environments can be used to augment place-based learning. Participants can learn via resource management style–games, or online worlds can teach them constrained social behavior. Travelers and tourists learn about places by going there, observing events, and being instructed by signs, guides, and printed material. Their objective is to learn about culture through interaction (otherwise they could read a book), and hence a virtual tourist or traveler would be aided by devices that augment their learning experience via interaction.

What can one do? What can one learn? How does one separate the significant from the accidental and the authentic from the spurious? To extrapolate from the book *Where the Action Is* by Paul Dourish (2004), in this situation we must grapple with issues of interaction rather than issues of representation. Dourish goes further, asking why we have reified the computer, and it is a valid question. Highly interactive computer games do not necessarily need the latest and most powerful devices.

Mechanics

Mechanics are central to the interactivity of games. There are many differing, even conflicting definitions of game mechanics (Lundgren and Bjork 2003; Pulsipher 2014), but one I suggest that is fairly well known and not highly controversial is Miguel Sicart's (2008): "A game mechanic, then, is the action invoked by an agent to interact with the game world, as constrained by the game rules." What is missing here is a clear explanation as to who identifies the game mechanics: the player or the designer? Game rules as designed are not necessarily the same as the user's understanding of their actions!

An interesting direction for designers, following Thomas Malone and Mark Lepper (1987) are four individual motivating factors: challenge, curiosity, control, and fantasy. These can be considered motivators for mechanics—that is, the motivators that mechanics try to leverage or the reasons people are stimulated to play games—and are similar to the description of computer game features described by Malone (1980/1990).

Mechanics can be viewed in two ways: the underlying system-based mechanics that change states in the game logic, or mechanics that describe the player's experience from the player's point of view. Another way of looking at how *mechanics* is used as a term is to see how it is understood by fans. On forums, "mechanics" are viewed as tools, techniques, or widgets, akin to "constructs of rules" or as fixed rules that players "are required to possess." Game designers can view them as rules, but they may also view them as "a major chunk of game play" (Stout 2010). Yet another definition says mechanics are the "methods by which the game moves forward, and these methods are the mechanics of the game" (Pulsipher 2014). A variant of this concept is to view mechanics as those decisions that help the player "level up" (Allen 2014).

Given these many differing interpretations, can we define the *game mechanic*? We can, of course, but not in a way that incorporates most definitions and understandings. Lewis Pulsipher (2014) wrote, "In other words it is not clear what a mechanic is and what [it] isn't. This is compounded by the tendency to use categories instead of specifics when discussing a mechanic."

Not only does *mechanics* have different meanings to different people, but there also appear to be unclear divisions within the term itself, such as between mechanics and core mechanics (Paras and Bizzocchi, 2005). And there are gaps or even rifts between the definitions used by game designers and those understood by gamers. Even if we could share an agreed-on definition of mechanics, could we delineate easy-to-translate mechanics for methods, experiments, and investigations that could transform into game mechanics to engage and educate the public?

Extrinsic game play separates game play and content, meaning the structure and genre of the game is more important and the content can change. Intrinsic game play integrates the attributes of the objects with the game play. This is typically much more difficult to implement in games for serious learning purposes than if they chose extrinsic game play. In his paper "Game Mechanics and the Museum: Designing Simple Gameplay around Complex Content," David Schaller (2014) noted that "intrinsic gameplay introduces two major design challenges":

> Step 1: Designing a system of game rules that represents the content with accuracy and integrity. This system might be based on one in the real world or contrived for the purposes of the game, or something in between.
> Step 2: Selecting objects that represent the content, then quantifying and simplifying the functional attributes of those objects to fit into the game rules.

In particular, Schaller gave examples of mechanics for serious games, particularly for museum collections:

> Extrinsic gameplay separates gameplay and content. Essentially, it side-steps the problem by establishing game rules that operate on a different plane than the content. The game is populated with museum content and collections according to general attributes, and the player never delves deep into the details.
> Intrinsic gameplay marries gameplay and content. Inherent attributes of the game objects (e.g. the content) are integrated into the gameplay, requiring the player to pay attention to those attributes to make thoughtful choices throughout the game.

In Schaller's area of business (education, museums, and cultural institutions), identifying and relating cultural values and knowledge of objects and settings to a rules-based system of equipment or tools with attributes is challenging. Another problem is raised here: what are the game-based actions, goals, and mechanics that could elegantly and powerfully equate cultural artifacts as game objects with ludic attributes *and* learning objectives?

In determining what we mean by mechanics, it occurred to me that here again there is a problem of language, for game mechanics can be system related or psychology related. Are we challenged more by creating a system of game states and wondering how the player changes these game states? Or is the design challenge more psychological, changing the behavior and perspective of the player?

Instead of psychology, we might more modestly talk of experience changes caused by mechanics. I distinguish here between system mechanics and experiential mechanics (psychological seems to indicate a higher and more cerebral level of mechanics than may be easily addressed by many games). System mechanics advance game states, while experiential mechanics aim to orchestrate the player's experiences.

Forms of Play, Modes of Play

We may also gain some useful insight from examining games in terms of *experience*. And here I am thinking particularly of Roger Caillois's *Man, Play, and Games* (1961).

Table 6.2. An Extrapolation of Caillois's Forms of Play

Forms	Challenges	Rewards	Imaginative Theme	Experience
Agon (competition)	Humiliation, feeling of inferiority	Feeling of superiority	Gladiator arenas, race car tracks, battlegrounds	Adversity
Alea (chance)	Bad luck	Mastery over chance, acceptance of fate	Casino rooms, boards, and tables	Gambling, risk-taking
Ilinx (vertigo)	Feeling of helplessness, confusion, fear	Control over mental and physical reactions	Towers and skyscrapers, outer space, dystopic cities	Movement
Mimicry (mimesis)	Humiliation	Observation and improvisation skills, social perceptiveness	Parties, interrogation, bribing scenes, impersonation situations	Empathy, social responsiveness

The forms of play are agon (competition and strategy, motivating through competition against people and strategy against risk and chance); alea (chance, the opportunity for handling unpredictability and encountering humor); ilinx (a sense of vertigo, challenging us in commitment, focus, and multitasking); and mimicry (mimesis, relying on observation, control, and role-playing).

These forms give us an idea of what makes these games both challenging (inviting but difficult) and engaging from the player's point of view. They describe the general core experience, but they do not narrowly restrict an understanding of what these games must be in terms of genre or construction.

The forms of play are arguably more useful for seeing what is underrepresented in computer games than as a basis for classification. For example, even though a great deal of cultural learning in the real world is done via mimicry, this is not commonly available in digital games, as we lack the rich and nuanced social feedback of other players through a digital interface and abstraction.

With the aforementioned four forms—or, as I would prefer to describe them, experiential modes of game play—I would extend ilinx to include control over one's mind and body (the players' mastery over themselves as an embodied objects). This also brings Caillois's framework (see table 6.2) closer to the motivators that Malone and Lepper (1987) suggested: challenge, curiosity, control, and fantasy.

Caillois's forms of play do, indeed, seem to feature in most, if not all, nondigital games, and they give an idea of the general challenge and motivation (and perhaps even experience) of that form of play. Just as the forms have a dual nature—they evoke an idea of both the motivating and game-hindering elements (the reward and the risk)—game mechanics are also often used in two major ways: they can be seen as levers to move along game states (mechanics to direct the game system) or they advance the experiential progression of the game from the player's point of view.

Here is another way of viewing interpretations of the term *mechanics*:

1. Game progression mechanics: to progress the player through the game (for the designer or the player)
2. Performance mechanics or rewards and skills mastery mechanics: to encourage the player to improve and extend their range of skills and judgment
3. Narrative mechanics: tools to progress and unfold or bring together one or more apparent story threads as they relate to the game play
4. Behavioral mechanics and role assimilation mechanics: repeated actions that become habits through repeated game play and accustom players to seeing things in certain ways
5. Insight and reversal mechanics: mechanics that disrupt the in-game or real-world expectations and presumptions of the player acquired previously or during the game to reveal to them a viewpoint they may take for granted or to supplant the view created by game play but that the designer wants them to suddenly be alienated from

For example, mechanics that persuade people to reflect on and reconsider ingrained habits could induce them to change their perception and awareness of place. A good example of reflective mechanics appears in an essay on how games portray slavery via mechanics. In "How Historical Games Integrate or Ignore Slavery: And How They Can Do It Better," Amanda Kerri (2017) described how even games that attempt to portray the hidden issues of slavery in games are often undone by their inner mechanics and suggested, "One solution, as in Brenda Romero's physical games Train and The New World, is to make the ethical element a subversion and extension of the intrinsic goals. As soon as the setting is made explicit, to win the game by its own rules is a failure."

The last type of game mechanics is most interesting to me. Chris Baker (2012) wrote, "Will Wright calls possibility space: the scope of actions or reactions a player can undertake. . . . In Wright's best work, players have so much leeway to determine their own objectives that the distinction between game player and game designer blurs." If games are possibility spaces, virtual places are possibility spaces as well. Through the interactive richness of possibility space and adroit use of game mechanics—rather than relying solely on a high-tech ability to reproduce elements of the real world—players as designers can both learn and enjoy the different experiences that different understandings and uses of place afford us. That

Table 6.3. Dimensions of Virtual Place

Old Category	New Category	One Can . . .	Place Feature	Examples
Visualization based	Visualization Cyber	View Navigate	Identifiable Locative	360VR Walking sims
Activity based	Ergodic	Play	Affords exploration	Flight simulators, online spatial games, desktop virtual environments
Collaboration based	Shareable worlds	Coplay	Shareable components	Social worlds, collaborative VR, games inhabited by NPCs
Hermeneutic	Etic	Interpret others	Others can be understood via traces of inhabitation	A few games (*Myst*, nearly *SpyParty*)
	Emic	Interpret self	Self-identity develops through dwelling, creating	A few games (*Myst*, *SpyParty* has some elements)

said, the feedback and reward system of a virtual place is more chaotic, sophisticated, and indirect.

Virtual Environments and Virtual Worlds

This issue brings me back to the issue of classification. To get around the issue that typologies for virtual worlds can be inflexible (Champion and Dave 2002; Champion 2011), in previous writings I suggested that virtual environments could be usefully classified in terms of their purpose: visualization, activity based (such as games), or hermeneutic. I'd like to amend this simple classification. Initially, I thought there were two subcategories of hermeneutic virtual environments: those that reveal things about ourselves to ourselves and those that reveal the intentions and beliefs of others (past or present) to us. For archaeological and heritage purposes, I think we need a further subcategory. There are activity-based virtual environments (computer games) that attempt to reveal the culturally specific ways in which people created, modified, and experienced past environments (table 6.3). Game typologies often forget or place in the background the creative input, influence, and importance of the player.

Despite its philosophical overtones, the concept of a hermeneutic or interpretation-affording virtual world does not appear very often in academic literature. In their online paper "A Typology of Virtual Worlds: Historical Overview and Future Directions," Paul R. Messinger, Eleni Stroulia, and Kelly Lyons (2008) suggested virtual worlds could be classified in terms of "(1) purpose (content of interaction), (2) place (location of interaction), (3) platform (design of interaction), (4) population (participants in the interaction), and (5) profit model (return on interaction). . . . Porter has argued that the five elements of this typology (purpose, place, platform, population, and profit model) meet five criteria for a good typology, established by Hunt (1991)."

This may well be a suitable typology of virtual worlds for e-commerce, but the purpose of the virtual world *for the audience* (apart from profit) and the typical experiences expected are not mentioned in this typology. What most concerns me here, though, is item 2, which they go on to explore: "Place (Location of Interaction): Porter focuses on whether the notion of place is completely, or only partially virtual. We also consider whether players are collocated or geographically dispersed."

Is place merely the collocation or geographical summation of players? This typology may be useful for explaining in terms of the historical development of virtual worlds or for predicting future trends (the aims of the paper), but an understanding *of* virtual worlds and their potential important experiential qualities are not being examined.

SimCity, *The Sims*, and *SPORE* game designer Will Wright suggested that games are a form of possibility space, in contrast to strict essentialist definitions for what games are and what they can do. What sort of mechanics are required for possibility space? I'd suggest flexible, open-ended yet powerful player-directed ones; however, design freedom and player freedom does not necessarily create a great game.

Gamification and Gamifying Place

I have previously defined gamification as either the addition of quantifiable actions to websites and learning environments that can be ranked and processed (with ability to store information), with immediate and vastly exaggerated feedback graphically designed in the idiom of well-known computer game genres, or the use of game-based rule structures and interfaces by corporations "to manage and control brand-communities and to create value" (Champion 2015). The latter definition reveals both the attraction of gamification to business and the derision it has received (Fuchs 2013).

Task performance can be graphically rewarded and socially shared, and key points of interest can be emphasized, leading proponents to argue that gamification can provide deeper, richer and more engaging learning (Betts, Bal, and Betts 2013; Schoech et al. 2013; Hamari, Koivisto, and Sarsa 2014). However, many are opposed to it (Bogost 2011; Deterding et al. 2011; Fuchs 2014).

In regard to these "gamified" projects, I typically do not see the process or understand how the results relate to my input, and I do not recognize the value of my agency as a player in the final outcome. When you compare "gamifications" to

Table 6.4. Gamifications, Games, and Virtual Places

Gamification	Games	Virtual Places, Virtual Worlds
WHY? Goal (badges)	Goal and rewards, imagination	Goals, rewards, imagination, opportunities
WHAT? Actions	Actions and strategies	Actions, strategies, accidents
WHO (for)? Players	Players (varying levels of skills and interests)	Player agency (varying levels of skills), place agency
HOW? System	System and spontaneous emergent behavior	System and spontaneous emergent behavior, persistence, changes in the system

games or to virtual places/virtual worlds, games are far more inviting, challenging, and rewarding (in terms of creative, emergent, and spontaneous "happy accidents"). Virtual places and virtual worlds also differ from computer games in what they promise if not always deliver: the added charms of additional opportunities, strategies, a receptive audience, and a legacy (recorded, engraved, or otherwise immortalized) (table 6.4).

According to V. Manrique (2013), games have spaces, actions, movements, and verbs. For gamification, actions are tasks, duties, or work, so we cannot directly apply game mechanics to gamification. Manrique proposes an enthusiastic if simplified four-point case for gamification. His simple table asks *why* you as the designer need to apply gamification, *what* you as a designer would want the audience to do, *whom* your audience represent (the players you are designing for), and *how* you can design gamification. He stressed the importance of players having fun as an experience, but in my opinion, many gamified projects take boring, monotonous tasks and apply simple tasks and rewards to them. Fun is inherent in games, but gamification makes (or tries to make) things fun.

Gamified projects usually don't have thematic prizes that reward imagination and add to the challenge of the game play; they don't offer a multitude of possible strategies catering to the stage and preferences of players' learning or the ability to support emergent, unexpected, spontaneous play. And there is another important distinction: games are inherently enjoyable and can *afford* to frustrate the player, while gamification applications and websites usually don't have this luxury. They have a primary purpose (improved task performance, engagement, "going viral") that they want their audience to complete.

Where virtual places (and virtual worlds) differ in regards to gamification is that they offer spontaneous uncalculated opportunities, marginal practices, accidental happenings, and serendipitous events; the place may have agency (controls, ameliorates, or interferes with the player's agency), and changes to the system created by opportunities devised or exploited by the player can permanently affect the place. While in games, player actions are generally kept separate from the game world apart from directly game play–related details (bullet marks appear,

Table 6.5. Virtual Place Prototyping Workflow

Steps	Design Questions
Define the goal	What is the goal? Why try to achieve it?
Create a challenge	Why is it an engaging challenge? Does it involve competition/mastery, chance, imitation, controlling vertigo/rush of movement/flight?
Develop an immediate feedback/ reward system	What is the feedback system—the affordances and constraints, rewards and punishments?
Relate feedback to goals	Does it level up/use mechanics to advance?
Provide alternative strategies and options to explore	How does it offer different strategies and options?
Consider how learning can loop back into goals and feedback	What is learned during or after the experience?

enemies stay dead, boxes opened with treasures taken remain open but empty), in richly interactive virtual places, actions and their consequences *semipermanently* affect the world. While games record, they do not commemorate. And digitally simulated rituals, if they exist in a computer game, are presented in a vacuum that makes no demand on the commitment or interest of the player and that makes no judgment of them.

Questions for Prototyping a Game

If I was to attempt a gamification breakdown of how to level up a virtual environment to turn it into a game, especially one with a cultural focus, I would suggest considering the information in table 6.5.

I have run game prototyping panels and workshops with archaeologists, historians, and architects at the CAA2017 conference in Atlanta, Georgia; at two digital summer schools in Turin; and also in Newcastle, Australia. The questions at these workshops were simpler:

- What should be experienced and interacted with, specifically?
- Why are we creating a specific experience in a game? (What are our objectives?)
- Where will the game be played? What is the background environment and the imaginative setting?
- How do we design prototypes to convey the experience of the site, artifact, or model?
- How can the game prototypes be better designed as systems, methods, or findings that interact to produce engaging learning experiences?
- Can the game prototypes reveal what is unknown or debated? (How is knowledge established or contested?)

- Can games be used as interpretative systems or be staged by the player to test or demonstrate the clash of interpretations or to pose or test a scholarly argument?
- When will the player receive suitable feedback?

I contend that virtual environments that are only games do not fully create a rich, rounded sense of place: as games are engaging challenges and addiction machines, one is either in a reflective place or in a game's dynamic magic circle. Places relate to other places and allow one to place oneself toward movement or rest in contrast to games' constant agitation and cajoling of the player to always engage, focus, move, or scheme. To gamify place is to systematize its chaotic, spontaneous, and highly localized and personal interactions.

Priorities for Game Prototyping

We could design a game prototype for archaeology, history, or heritage (fig. 6.3), starting with a game-like formula. The steps to doing so are as follows:

1. Focus on the key cultural, historical, or archaeological facts and interpretations of the site or model that are significant, hidden, or otherwise appropriate, engaging, or transformative to explore.
2. Consider the environment the game will be played in, not just the type of audience, but the audience members' surroundings when they play the game—together, alone, on a bus, in a lecture theater, at a museum?
3. Ensure you are designing a game rather than a virtual environment. We need to find a challenge (it could be based on Caillois's forms of play or some other theory) and how the core game play affects and is affected by the modality of experience. Steps 2 and 3 also give us an idea of a setting and theme.
4. Define the core game play: What does the player typically do? Does the game scale or change the degree of effectiveness and complexity over time? Increasing complexity will help keep the game interesting.
5. Develop a reward and punishment system: How do the rewards and punishments interact with the core game play and move the game along (i.e., trigger its mechanics)?
6. Determine the end state (conclusion of the game): How will the game mechanics help us get there? Does reaching the end state create an intentional specific reflection, knowledge development, interpretation, experience, or other feeling in the player?

But there needs to be another step to ensure there is some sense of place:

7. Where on this game's journey can one rest, regather, reflect, and plan? How do these "clearings" relate to the movement, action, and reward of the game? Do these more reflective places allow the gamer/player to

Figure 6.3 Two participants at the Turin Digital Humanities Summer School's Learning by Game Creation Workshop, 2019. Eric Champion. The URL for the summer school is http://digitalhumanitiesforculturalheritage.polito.it/. The school's official title is International Summer School "Learning by Game Creation: Cultural Heritage, Cities and Digital Humanities" (https://eadh.org/news/2019/06/26/cfp-2019-international-summer-school-learning-game-creation-cultural-heritage-cities).

Figure 6.4 Physical, real-world game playing is far more negotiable, fluid, and creative than most digital game playing. DH Downunder Game Development Workshop 2019, Newcastle, Australia. Erik Champion.

reflect on their achievements or leave behind some semipersistent mark or status regarding their progress, experience, or observations gathered through game play?

Summary

Significant differences exist between interaction, play, and control in the related yet distinctive media of digital games, virtual environments, and virtual places. Virtual environments do not have to subjugate, conquer, and homogenize. Virtual places do not have to apply gamification directly, because gamification tends to focus more on the rules and rewards of the system than on the exploration, creativity, and imagination of the player. But virtual places are created as much, if not more, by collaborating individuals and communities as by a solitary designer. Playerfication, affording more creative interaction to the player, is worth considering as an alternative to gamification when designing virtual places (fig. 6.4).

I like to call this concept playerfication because I intend to focus on more of the interactive features of a place that can be refined via prototypes. I believe conceptual definitions of games can be broken down to help us visualize how place and platial artifacts can be deployed more effectively in the visualization of the past. A workflow of how I have taught game design at the previously mentioned workshops is provided in figure 6.5.

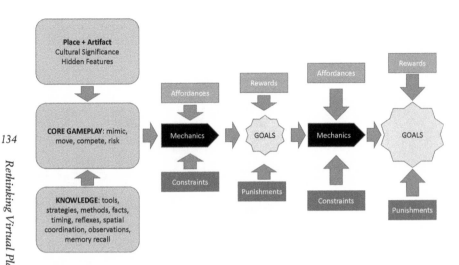

Figure 6.5 Game prototyping schema for games featuring historic places. Erik Champion.

Gamification is still a popular buzzword, and I have probably not convinced many to replace it. Chapter 8 addresses the implication of gamified virtual cultural places; there I argue that gamification threatens to destroy the complicit and messily creative nature of place. Here I have only enough space and time to point out key differences between digital games and virtual places.

The next question is how to leverage the advantages of games for virtual place design, given digital games are often closed systems of rules. Real-world games are more than systems; they are imaginative frames of references that challenge, hinder, create risks, and provide rewards and goal-based activities, and their laws (not set rules) are negotiated in real time and re-created by imagination and groups of people, competitively and collaboratively.

Although Caillois's forms of play are not so popular now in computer game studies, I propose that as modes of experience (and with some tweaking), they provide the reader with a sense of the specific motivators—the challenges, risks, and rewards—from the perspective of the player, not the game-as-system (gamification). Forms of play (or modalities of play) relate to game mechanics, a core part of games as games because richer and more impactful games use game mechanics not only to advance the game as a system but also to advance the game as an experience. We could and should clarify the definition and role of mechanics so we can better understand and implement interaction as a framework of design patterns and build more richly interactive virtual places *thematically* and *psychologically*.

That is not a directive to incorporate gamification in virtual place design. Researchers have already applied principles of gamification to education (Nah et al. 2013): "Gamification is the process of game-thinking and game mechanics to engage users and solve problems." A problem with this approach is that it only explains what games already do: they engage users to solve problems and achieve goals. Gamification also suggests a ready-made formula of heuristics and add-ons, but these don't necessarily augment the experience of the place. Attempting to shoehorn unwieldy educational content into disparate game mechanics for VLEs won't increase player control; it risks destroying the enjoyment of players for both the game experience and the learning experience. According to Ellen Ullman, "We build our computer (systems) the way we build our cities: over time, without a plan, on top of ruins" (Clements 2013). Games, on the other hand, are typically restricted and focused; spontaneity and happenstance are harder to cater to in game design because of their very nature as system-based engaging challenges. Games are not place heavy or world flexible, but aspects of games offer hope to enliven virtual places.

There are mechanics to places, but they are not as structured and teleological as game places (if there are such things as game places), and gamification of place does not easily lead to reflective places where one *dwells*. Games are based on action, while worlds are action and reflection; worlds are collections of places, nonplaces, and semiplaces that link to and from more richly defined or experienced places. A place encountered for the first time provides frustrating challenges; when revisited, even if enemies and treasures are randomly respawned, the game place loses some of its character and interest.

We can separate many places in games as move/attack, rest/defend, but the concept of place is not clear, distinct, or binary. Experiencing a place involves taking a position in a fight, between nature and artifice, between capture and freedom, between immortalization and fading away. They are interactive to some extent, one has to travel to and from them, and consciously experience them (even at risk to one's own comfort).

Experiencing a place evokes a sense of identity, uniqueness, memory, and significance worthy of preserving even though they are mortal and sometimes ephemeral. Virtual worlds, even persistent ones, seldom capture this dynamic and tension. But in games (with some exceptions), the sense of place is even more muted because the challenge is to complete, finish, evade, or overpower as quickly as possible, not to care for, observe, reflect, or blend in with. Games played *as* games don't frequently afford moments of contemplation and reflection or memorialization and commemoration, but when they do, the computer game takes on more of the features of a virtual place.

References

Allen, R. 2014. "Forum Reply To: What Is the Difference between Game Mechanics and Game Dynamics?" Quora. Last Modified January 7, 2014. Accessed July 26, 2017. https://www.quora.com/What-is-the-difference-between-game-mechanics-and-game -dynamics

Baker, Chris. 2012. "Will Wright Wants to Make a Game Out of Life Itself." *Wired Magazine* (online edition). Accessed May 4, 2021. https://www.wired.com/category/gamelife/?p =48115.

Bell, Vaughan. 2008. "Is the Cinematograph Making Us Stupid?" Mind Hacks. Last Modified July 29, 2008. Accessed June 14, 2017. https://mindhacks.com/2008/07/29/is-the -cinematograph-making-us-stupid/.

Betts, Ben W., Jay Bal, and Alan W. Betts. 2013. "Gamification as a Tool for Increasing the Depth of Student Understanding Using a Collaborative e-Learning Environment." *International Journal of Continuing Engineering Education and Life Long Learning* 23 (3): 213–28.

Bogost, Ian. 2011. "Gamification Is Bullshit." *Ian Bogost* (blog), August 8, 2011. http://bogost .com/writing/blog/gamification_is_bullshit/.

Caillois, Roger. 1961. *Man, Play, and Games.* Translated by Meyer Barash. Urbana: University of Illinois Press.

Champion, Erik. 2011. *Playing with the Past.* London: Springer.

———. 2015. *Critical Gaming: Interactive History and Virtual Heritage.* Edited by Marilyn Deegan, Lorna Hughes, Andrew Prescott, and Harold Short. Digital Research in the Arts and Humanities, edited by Dymphna Evans. UK: Ashgate Publishing.

Champion, E., and B. Dave. 2002. "Where Is This Place." In *Proceedings of ACADIA 2002: Thresholds Between Physical and Virtual,* edited by George Proctor, 87–97. Pomona, CA: ACADIA.

Clements, Alan. 2013. *Computer Organization & Architecture: Themes and Variations.* Technology & Engineering. Stamford, CT: Cengage Learning.

Dahlskog, Steve, Andreas Kamstrup, and Espen Aarseth. 2009. "Mapping the Game Landscape: Locating Genres Using Functional Classification." Paper presented at the 2009 DiGRA International Conference, "Breaking New Ground: Innovation in Games, Play, Practice and Theory," September 1–4, 2009, London.

Deterding, Sebastian, Dan Dixon, Rilla Khaled, and Lennart Nacke. 2011. "From Game Design Elements to Gamefulness: Defining Gamification." In *Proceedings of the 15th International Academic MindTrek Conference: Envisioning Future Media Environments,* 9–15. Tampere, FIN: ACM.

Dick, Philip K. 1964. *The Three Stigmata of Palmer Eldritch.* 2007th ed. Kent: Orion Publishing Group.

Dourish, Paul. 2004. *Where the Action Is: The Foundations of Embodied Interaction.* Cambridge, MA: MIT Press.

Fuchs, Mathias. 2013. "CFP: Rethinking Gamification Workshop." Art and Civic Media Lab at the Centre for Digital Cultures. Leuphana University, DEU. Last Modified February 18, 2013. Accessed May 4, 2021. http://www.digra.org/cfp-workshop-rethinking -gamification-leuphana-university-la%C2%BCneburg-15-17-may/.

———. 2014. "Gamification as Twenty-First-Century Ideology." *Journal of Gaming and Virtual Worlds* 6 (2): 143–57.

Greenfield, Susan. 2014. "Neuroscientist Susan Greenfield Warns Young Brains Being Re-wired by Digital Technology." ABC Radio, November 19, 2014. Last Modified November 20, 2014. Accessed January 30, 2020. https://www.abc.net.au/news/2014-11 -20/neuroscientist-warns-young-brains-being-reshaped-by-technology/5906140.

Hamari, Juho, Jonna Koivisto, and Harri Sarsa. 2014. "Does Gamification Work? A Literature Review of Empirical Studies on Gamification." Paper presented at the Forty-Seventh Hawaii International Conference on System Sciences (HICSS), Honolulu, Hawaii, January 6–9, 2014.

Hunt, Shelby D. 1991. *Modern Marketing Theory: Critical Issues in the Philosophy of Marketing Science.* Cincinnati, OH: South-Western Publishing Company.

Jarrett, Christian. 2008. "Is the Internet Changing Our Brains?" *BPS Research Digest* (blog), August 12, 2008. British Psychological Society. Last Modified August 12, 2008. Accessed August 12, 2008. http://bps-research-digest.blogspot.com.au/2008/08/is -internet-changing-our-brains.html.

Juul, Jesper. 2003. "The Game, the Player, the World: Looking for a Heart of Gameness." Paper presented at the 2003 DiGRA International Conference, "Level Up," Utercht, November 4–6, 2003.

Kerri, Amanda. 2017. "How Historical Games Integrate or Ignore Slavery: And How They Can Do It Better." *Rock Paper Shotgun* (blog), January 17, 2017.

Lundgren, Sus, and Staffan Bjork. 2003. "Game Mechanics: Describing Computer-Augmented Games in Terms of Interaction." In *Proceedings TIDSE 03*, edited by S. Göbel, N. Braun, U. Spierling, J. Dechau, and H. Diener, 45–57. Darmstadt: Fraunhofer IRB Verlag.

Malone, Thomas W. August. 1990 (1980). *What Makes Things Fun to Learn? A Study of Intrinsically Motivating Computer Games.* Cognitive and Instructional Sciences. Palo Alto, CA: Palo Alto Research Center. https://www.hcs64.com/files/tm%20study %20144.pdf.

Malone, Thomas W., and Mark R. Lepper. 1987. "Making Learning Fun: A Taxonomy of Intrinsic Motivations for Learning." *Aptitude, Learning, and Instruction* 3 (1987): 223–53.

Manrique, V. 2013. "Gamification Design Framework: The SMA Model." Gamsutra, July 25, 2017. Accessed May 4, 2021. http://www.gamasutra.com/blogs/VictorManrique /20130618/194563/Gamification_Design_Framework_The_SMA_Model.php.

Marsh, Tim. 2011. "Serious Games Continuum: Between Games for Purpose and Experiential Environments for Purpose." *Entertainment Computing* 2 (2): 61–68.

Mendlesohn, Farah. 2008. *Rhetorics of Fantasy.* Middletown, CT: Wesleyan University Press.

Messinger, Paul R., Eleni Stroulia, and Kelly Lyons. 2008. "A Typology of Virtual Worlds: Historical Overview and Future Directions." *Journal for Virtual Worlds Research* 1 (1).

Millar, Heather. 2016. "Can Virtual Reality Emerge as a Tool for Conservation?" *Yale Environment 360.* Accessed May 4, 2021. https://e360.yale.edu/features/can_virtual _reality_emerge_as_a_tool_for_conservation.

Mortara, Michela, Chiara Eva Catalano, Francesco Bellotti, Giusy Fiucci, Minica Houry-Panchetti, and Panagiotis Petridis. 2014. "Learning Cultural Heritage by Serious Games." *Journal of Cultural Heritage* 15 (3): 318–25. Accessed May 4, 2021. https://doi .org/10.1016/j.culher.2013.04.004.

Nah, Fiona Fui-Hoon, Venkata Rajasekhar Telaprolu, Shashank Rallapalli, and Pavani Rallapalli Venkata. 2013. "Gamification of Education Using Computer Games." In *Human Interface and the Management of Information: Information and Interaction for Learning, Culture, Collaboration and Business; 15th International Conference, HCI International 2013, Las Vegas, NV, USA, July 21–26, 2013, Proceedings, Part III*, edited by Sakae Yamamoto, 99–107. Berlin: Springer.

Palazzi, Claudio E, Marco Roccetti, and Gustavo Marfia. 2010. "Realizing the Unexploited Potential of Games on Serious Challenges." *Computers in Entertainment (CIE)* 8 (4): 23.

Paras, Brad, and Jim Bizzocchi. 2005. "Game, Motivation, and Effective Learning: An Integrated Model for Educational Game Design." In *DiGRA '05—Proceedings of the 2005 DiGRA International Conference: Changing Views: Worlds in Play*, edited by Suzanne de Castell and Jennifer Jenson, 1–7. Vancouver: DiGRA.

Pulsipher, Lewis. 2014. "Can We Define 'Game Mechanic?' Not Really." *Board Game Designers Forum* (blog), June 6, 2014. Accessed May 4, 2021. http://www.bgdf.com /node/14642.

Salen, Katie, and Eric Zimmerman. 2003. *Rules of Play: Game Design Fundamentals.[11]*
Crawford, C. *The Art of Computer Game Design, 1982.* Cambridge, MA: MIT Press.
Schaller, David 2014. "Game Mechanics and the Museum: Designing Simple Gameplay around Complex Content." Paper presented at the 2014 annual conference of Museums and the Web (MW2014), Baltimore, MD, April 2–5, 2014. Accessed May 4, 2021. http://mw2014.museumsandtheweb.com/paper/game-mechanics-and-the-museum -designing-simple-gameplay-around-complex-content/.
Schoech, Dick, Javier F. Boyas, Beverly M. Black, and Nada Elias-Lambert. 2013. "Gamification for Behavior Change: Lessons from Developing a Social, Multiuser, Web-Tablet Based Prevention Game for Youths." *Journal of Technology in Human Services* 31 (3): 197–217. https://doi.org/10.1080/15228835.2013.812512.
Sicart, Miguel. 2008. "Defining Game Mechanics." *Game Studies the International Journal of Computer Game Research* 8 (2). Accessed May 4, 2021. http://gamestudies.org/0802 /articles/sicart.
Stout, M. 2010. "Evaluating Game Mechanics for Depth." Gamasutra, July 10, 2010. Last Modified September 15, 2016. Accessed May 4, 2021. http://www.gamasutra.com/view /feature/134273/evaluating_game_mechanics_for_depth.php.
Susi, Tarja, Mikael Johannesson, and Per Backlund. 2007. *Serious Games: An Overview.* School of Humanities and Informatics, University of Skövde (School of Humanities and Informatics, University of Skövde), February 5, 2007. Accessed May 4, 2021. https://www.diva-portal.org/smash/get/diva2:2416/FULLTEXT01.pdf.
Vernon, Mark. 2016. "What's to Fear from Virtual Reality?" *Mark Vernon Philosophy and Life Blog* (blog). Accessed May 4, 2021. https://www.markvernon.com/whats-to-fear-from -virtual-reality.
Zagal, Jose P., and Amy Bruckman. 2008. "Novices, Gamers, and Scholars: Exploring the Challenges of Teaching about Games." *Game Studies* 8 (2). Accessed May 3, 2021. http://gamestudies.org/0802/articles/zagal_bruckman.

chapter seven

DO SERIOUS GAMERS LEARN FROM PLACE?

Introduction

In this chapter, I review the basic terms of serious games, especially in terms of placeness. I cover issues of multimodality, serious games, procedural learning and procedural rhetoric, and various types of learning (through observation, inhabitation, embodiment, and observing and communicating with other people).

There are important issues in pedagogical research that we still do not have answers to, but I won't have time or space to answer here. For example, is the digital interface affecting our notion of identity and our ideas as to what it means to be human? Can we gain a meaningful and worthwhile idea of the social presence of others through the internet? Can we bridge the gap through augmentation or multimodal sensory interface devices or related physical activity? To what extent and for how long is it safe and advisable to allow people to be immersed in these other worlds?

How Do We Learn about a Place?

How do we learn about a place and help place design incorporate and afford learnable experiences? Places include spaces to learn and show that learning takes place. Simulating aspects of past cultures and distant places and determining relationships between those places is surely one area the internet and virtual places can be of use.

I had to tackle this issue about fifteen years ago (Champion 2006) when I needed to design virtual environments to evaluate cultural learning in an online digital environment that simulated a Mayan archaeological site in Palenque, Mexico. To compare different forms of cultural learning, I decided that learning about a specific culture could be broken down into roughly four components: learning through observation, learning through inhabitation, embodiment and physical activity, and learning through taught by others (platial roles and rituals). While this may summarize, very roughly, the types of interaction we use to learn about culture, that does not mean they can be easily evaluated separately to each other, as I once tried to do (Champion, Bishop, and Dave 2012).

Designing a Place

While studying individual places may offer some clues, another approach is to study elements of place as they relate to other places, for worlds are made up of not only collections of places but also the connections between those places, created by people's experiences. And while the start of this book discussed the influence of science fiction settings and no doubt architectural spaces can be studied individually and separately, how places are threaded with paths and references to other places and how they are designed to integrate with or separate themselves from other places is also of use to virtual place design. It is almost too easy to create boundaries in virtual environments, in the real world boundary-making is often complex and richly layered. Real-world places are parasitical, derivative, contested, and fragile.

Some of the answers can be found in relatively small places, such as gardens. Gardens are both spatial and psychological. For example, Dr. Mitsuru "Man" Senda, a practicing architect in Japan, stressed the necessary territorial or thematic "spatial" nature of organic architecture in his doctoral thesis on essential factors for physiologically and psychologically stimulating playgrounds (Senda 1992). But it is not until we also include the organization of spatial relationships in terms of the module, cluster, or hierarchical network—and how they relate to each other and the user-defined environment—that we approach a useful definition of "organic" architecture and understand how the organic relationships of landscapes and gardens are analogous to the social relationships and structuring of human inhabitation, forms shaped by propinquity to and importance of physical functions and features.

I have earlier defined organic architecture as a method of design focusing on accommodating both identity and variety, but it is also concerned with leading people through a building or built landscape; it leverages people's curiosity to explore and solve. The place itself is a complicit puzzle, an unfurling of a self-evident organic entity. Methods for designing this type of architecture could include creating a thematically focused setting, interweaving stylistic fragments or visual clues, implying past visitations and inhabitations (by humans or other creatures), or demonstrating how people can, have, or could inhabit a space and how that place reacts to events or changing environmental conditions or is reshaped over time.

What Characteristics of Place Help Us Learn?

Another approach might be to try to break down the different features of real-world places and how they help us learn about culture:

- Multimodality (and here we can distinguish between how something is learned, not what the learning content is made of)
- Sociability: visitation, uniqueness, enculturation and acculturation, inhabitation, creativity, memetic output (how words, images, gestures, and concepts are spread, contaminate discourse and behavior, and are diffused and integrated into a social activity and cultures), and alterity (encountering others with differing forms of behaviors desires and intentions)
- Encultured physicality: spatial demarcations of roles, statuses, and rituals; laws of physics; constraints of climate and geography; and so on

Multimodality

Roxana Moreno and Richard Mayer (2007) have defined multimodality for instructional design purposes, as

> learning environments that use two different modes to represent the content knowledge: verbal and non-verbal. . . . In multimodal learning environments, students are presented with a verbal representation of the content and a corresponding visual representation of the content. . . . Student understanding can be enhanced by the addition of non-verbal knowledge representations to verbal explanations. . . . The presentation of verbal and non-verbal materials in the visual modality alone is more likely to overload students' cognitive capacity during learning as compared to the presentation of verbal materials in the auditory modality and non-verbal materials in the visual. . . . An interactive multimodal learning environment is one in which what happens depends on the actions of the learner. In short, the defining feature of interactivity is responsiveness to the learner's action during learning.

Kay O'Halloran and her collaborators defined multimodality as "multiple means of making meaning" (Jewitt, Bezemer, and O'Halloran 2016, 2), but they appear to consider mode and modality as congruent, which differs from the terms as used by Moreno and Mayer (2007). In serious games and online worlds the concept of multimodality has been employed (Liarokapis et al. 2017), but it has not yet, as far as I know, been used in the design and critique of virtual places.

Sociability and the Knowledgeable Other

Lev Vygotsky talked about the knowledgeable other, for indeed we learn from each other. In the real world, there is no strict hierarchy of knowledge; even adults can learn from young children. In virtual places, how can this contextual and asymmetrically acquired knowledge be provided? How would we, for example, know that others have read, or traveled to, or learned from books, places, and people that we have not?

There have been various papers and projects conducted on the sociability of virtual worlds (Ducheneaut et al. 2006; Williams et al. 2006; Ducheneaut, Moore, and Nickell 2007). Much of the writing has centered on the idea of virtual worlds as third places (Moore, Hankinson Gathman, and Ducheneaut 2009). There is also emerging work being done on sociability issues with head-mounted displays, wearable computing (Gelsomini et al. 2017), and augmented reality (Cunha et al. 2016).

I mention in chapter 9 that Raph Koster (n.d.) declared that a strict definition of virtual worlds requires a spatial representation, an avatar, and a sandbox (with data persistence). However, spatial representation does not appear to be based on place; Koster (2010) claimed, "Placeness is a feature, not the point." Koster's declaration was based on the failure of his not-really-three-dimensional virtual worlds program and criticism of the value of earlier versions of *Second Life*, which is hardly a comprehensive study. And virtual worlds have not *yet* fully exploited the advantages of virtual places.

It is fair enough for a commercial game designer to see high-hanging fruit and warn others off: "Placeness is a value-add to something else—a game, a community, etc. And adoption is driven by something else, not by the placeness" (Koster 2010). But I question his exploration of "placeness." I did not observe evidence of placeness in the examples he mentioned, and I do not see the concept explored in most of the educational papers on virtual worlds, which tend to explore how people interact through avatars rather than through place.

Some of the limitations of placeness were indicated by a paper on the massively multiplayer online role-playing game *Star Wars Galaxies*. Nicolas Ducheneaut, Robert J. Moore, and Eric Nickell (2007) observed that the cantina in *Star Wars Galaxies* was an identifiable social space, but there was little reason for players to inhabit it as a place, even though or perhaps because the game tried to compel them to regularly spend time there.

Encultured Physicality

In their paper "The Role of Place in Cyberspace," Yehuda Kalay and John Marx (2001) argued that places require:

- Functional appropriateness (a measure of the fit between the activities and the objects or spaces that support it).
- Conceptual appropriateness (a measure of the fit between the form or the environment and the expectations or spaces that support it).

According to their explanation, acculturation includes social conventions, cultural norms, education, and ethnicities. It is not clear to me whether they also view acculturation as an essential quality or feature of places or whether virtual places in particular need to have more emphasis on their spatial qualities. Perhaps the blame lies more with the design of "cyberspace." Kalay and Marx wrote that designers have regarded "cyberspace as a communication medium, rather than as a space." Although they earlier said cyberspace had some unique "peculiarities," they argued that the principles on which the design of real-world places is based can be transferred successfully to the design of virtual places (cyberspaces) as well.

In my reading of Martin Heidegger, enculturated physicality is the third part of his book *Building, Dwelling, and Thinking*, but it specifically refers to the reciprocal nature of place and dwelling (Balstrup 2013). Enculturation is not just socialization (Backhaus and Murungi 2003). The place changes us as we change the place. How cultures are spread over space and how enculturated people make sense of space are interdependent. A visitor perceives space as place, place "perpetuates culture" (frames it, embeds it, erodes it), and thus influences the visitor, coercing them *over time* into becoming an inhabitant. This is more obvious in the real world, where the bounded corporeality, directionality, and needs of our physical bodies are in themselves a sort of place fragment.

How does this relate to the process of enculturation? Where we encounter highly cultural places (places dedicated to cultural beliefs and values), socially understood and valued representations of our body are abstracted, idealized, and demarcated in a way that relates to how we view ourselves and others as essences. Egyptian architecture, Roman architecture, Greek architecture, and even the traditional Maori architecture of New Zealand represent an idealized, abstracted body in terms of proportion, spacing, siting, or metaphorical features.

We also learn about a place from sharing with others, collaborating, annotating and filtering, shortcutting (journeys), or formalizing and safeguarding specific spaces. And we learn about a place from how its values, significance, and features are recorded, transmitted via media and commemorated in practice, in instruction, and via conversation with others. We learn about place spatially, socially, and culturally. Given we proceed through place spatially and architecturally, could place learning be transmitted via the procedures of digital games?

Procedural Rhetoric and Virtual Places

Procedural rhetoric is a relatively well-known expression in game studies yet also an arguably confusing and seldom explored and applied topic. In *Critical Gaming: Interactive History and Virtual Heritage* (Champion 2016), I argued that it is an interesting way of looking at games and significant in particular for the design and evaluation of serious games, but it also has some major challenges.

In this book, I will briefly review my understanding of procedural rhetoric and my major concern that it requires more definitional clarity and exemplars before it can be usefully and applied to not just game theory but also game design. I now think these five major issues need to be: issues of uniqueness and essence, intentionality, transparency, persuasiveness, and externality.

The main question of this section is to explore whether the theory is useful for design critique of serious games and, if so, which issues need to be explored further. Perhaps the theory of procedural rhetoric would even be better employed as a recalibrated meta-epistemic theory of serious games.

Rhetoric involves the art of persuading, not necessarily the art of opening up games as vehicles of critical discourse. Since the time of the ancient Greek philosophers (Rapp 2010), there have been divergent views of rhetoric, such as Aristotle's (dialectical reasoning, universal truths, and then rhetoric) versus his teacher Plato's (rhetoric is dangerous, sophists employ empty rhetoric). The five canons of classic rhetoric (Henrik 2005) were invention (discovery of arguments), disposition (organization and arrangement), expression (mastery of style), memory (ability to recall the argument and its components), and delivery (the ability to develop convincing and compelling arguments). Given that the ancient Greeks acted as their own lawyers, there was a practical need for persuasion, but a conceptual leap is required to follow how rhetoric is understood today.

In the age of the digital computer and the mid-early dawn of game studies, Mike Treanor and Michael Mateas (2009) promoted procedural literacy, and so, too, did Ian Bogost's Georgia Tech colleague, Janet Murray (2001). Murray noted that digital games are procedural, but Bogost extended the claim toward a theory. For Bogost (2007) procedural rhetoric is defined as "a practice of using processes persuasively." However, in his *Persuasive Games* book, Bogost appears to be talking about computer games more generally than serious games in particular.

Uniqueness and Essence

Leaving aside the contemporary recent connotation of rhetoric, if procedural rhetoric ("a practice of using processes persuasively") is an essential and defining component of games, as explained by Ian Bogost (2007, 3), is there a relationship between mechanics and procedural rhetoric that can help the revealing of place? Is procedural rhetoric an essential and defining component of games? Quite simply, no, unless you have a very broad yet selective definition of games. Is tic-tac-toe procedural rhetoric? Not all games have levels; not all games progress the player or attempt to impose a values system on them. I suspect procedural rhetoric is used as both a descriptive (this is what it is) and prescriptive definition (this is what it must be). The more *procedural rhetoric* it has, the more powerfully or clearly or distinctly it is a computer game.

I noted previously that Ian Bogost (2007) defined procedural rhetoric as "a practice of using processes persuasively." But, are computer games unique? (Bogost seems to say no in later writings, at least not in terms of procedural rhetoric.) But it is still useful to ask how the theory of procedural rhetoric distinguishes computer games from other procedurally based mediums and designed experiences. Procedural rhetoric is also in other media and art. In classical Latin, the origin of "procedure" meant to go forward. Architecture can also be processional: examples include classical architectural sites like the Temple of Karnak at Luxor and the Acropolis in Athens. Neoclassicist architectural theorists have written about the importance of path and center and other related allegorical narratives for many decades (Paavilainen 1982).

Purported uniqueness is a generic issue, not only relevant to serious games. And it leads to a further related or even dependent subissue: Does the quantity, intricacy, richness, or singular uniqueness of procedural rhetoric in the particular game form directly determine the uniqueness and artistic or design quality of the games? Is this theory of procedural rhetoric an essentialist theory? Is the procedural rhetoric inherent and essential to computer games per se?

Intentionality

Does the player need to understand and correctly follow the procedural rhetoric? What happens when the player does not follow the intended rules or even transgresses them? Thinking further ahead, can we adjust the mechanics of virtual places with procedural rhetoric to move forward not just the game or narrative but also the understanding of the player and their experience of place?

Mary Flanagan (2013) declared critical gameplay to be the willful subversion of the rules and cited avant-garde art as exemplary precedents. And Ragnhild Tronstad's (2010) review of Flanagan's *Critical Play* said it was the "means to create or occupy play environments and activities that represent one or more questions about aspects of human life . . . characterized by a careful examination of social, cultural, political, or even personal themes that function as alternates to popular play spaces." Given this, an essentialist or formalist view of games appears to be too restrictive and limiting.

The rules or intentions that a player perceives may not be what the designer intended or could be what the rules suggest by accident, by coincidence, or by default independently of the designer's intentions. Even if not rhetorical in the classical art of rhetoric, rhetorical questions arguably contain an implied answer in the question, and rhetorical devices arguably move the player toward a perceivable truth claim, emotional response, or value. Must the player understand the rhetorical intentions in a certain way? Are there death of the author–related philosophical questions? How does procedural rhetoric work with agency?

The emphasis on the designer's viewpoint is questionable. To quote Andrew Robinson's (2011) rephrasing of the theorist Mikhail Bakhtin, "Human consciousness is not a unified entity, but rather, is always conflict-ridden between different consciousnesses. Indeed, a single consciousness separate from interaction with other consciousnesses is impossible." In other words, the conception of procedural rhetoric as discussed in this book appears to be monologic and lacking in polyphony.

The issue is also related to the player. Individual differences and preferences in memory and learning style are crucial problems. What is the role of memory and explicit understanding in gameplay? Do different types of players necessitate different forms of rhetoric, and is this incorporated into procedural rhetoric theory/design?

I mentioned in *Critical Gaming* that I am not convinced that the rules of the game are the rules of the designer or even the rules of the player. The negotiation, changes, and misunderstandings, by the player, about what the rules are exactly

Rethinking Virtual Places

Figure 7.1 *Bust A Cup*, created by Associate Professor Brian Schrank and Briam Gabor Jr. Website: https://shakethatbutton.com/bust-a-cup. Photo permission, Associate Professor Brian Schrank.

are, in my opinion, an important and creative part of games and, by extension, computer games. While it might be reasonable to think that the essence of the game is that it is a rules-based system, it is another thing entirely to not even contemplate the possibility that a rule-based system could be random, changing, or open to change by the player. For example, *Bust A Cup* (Shrank and Gabor n.d.) is a street game with a simple rule: swing your hammer/chain tool to bust the cup on the other player's hammer/chain too; however, how the players negotiate physical proximity and social manners is just as, if not more, entertaining than the stated goal (fig. 7.1).

For games are not just systems; players project themselves into games. They role-play and invest some of their personal goals and vulnerabilities into the game as played. Physical games are renegotiable excitement machines. The way the player creates the boundaries and features of their imagined game space is not explicitly defined in the more famous definitions of games, but that does not mean this process is not important. And while virtual environments have constraints and affordances, digital games have risks and rewards.

Transparency

To be persuasive does not necessitate that the player understands how one is persuaded, but in serious games designed to evoke critical reflection, surely this is of interest. Imagine an advertising game, such as the *McDonald's Videogame satire*, a fast-food video game that is clearly not by the McDonald's company (Molleindustria 2019), exposing the tricks and techniques of corporate capitalist culture or our own cognitive biases. Here procedural rhetoric would surely be more effective if the player begins to realize that they are manipulated and how they are manipulated. Indeed, Bogost's own game company, newsgaming, created a simulation to reveal our unmediated responses, in the game (or simulation), *September 12* (Newsgaming and Gonzalo Frasca 2021). Is procedural rhetoric more successful if people can dissect and deconstruct procedural rhetoric? How transparent should the principles and strategies of procedural rhetoric be to the player?

Persuasiveness

To what extent should a player be persuaded to believe in the value or agree with the belief of something? Could they not be just following instructions or what they perceive to be rules, without consciously or subconsciously believing in these rules or procedures or the reasons for them? Procedural rhetoric does not need to persuade the player, perhaps, but if it is to be used effectively in serious games, then surely persuasion is important. The procedural rhetoric theory does not seem to have much to say about persuasiveness as a required or optional feature or quality or capability, yet the notion of persuasive game design is surely predicated on this.

Externality

Following on from the last issue, to what extent should procedural rhetoric aim to persuade a player inside and/or outside the magic circle? While game designers may not need to persuade the player of something outside the magic circle, serious game designers may well desire to persuade the player once they have left the game. Leaving aside for the moment whether this would break or bend the idea of a magic circle, and whether the term "externality" is suitable (and this is debatable but other more game-specific terms may be confusing), it does seem to me that the term as it stands is unclear on this matter. Does procedural rhetoric refer to the processes that persuade only when the player is in the magic circle (as algorithms seem to be a cornerstone of this theory, and Bogost argued that computer games are specifically unique because of their procedural programmed nature)? However, for serious games, one assumes the designer typically aims for extrinsic value and attention to context or retention of skills or knowledge after the game and game experience, not just during the game experience.

As I wrote in *Critical Gaming: Interactive History and Virtual Heritage* (Champion 2016), Bogost referenced the book *Guns, Germs, and Steel* to declare "Such an approach to history goes far beyond the relation between contemporaneous events, asking us to consider the systems that produce those events." Should the player be led to "consider the system that produce those events" as well? Must the theory force the player to consider the overall system, or is this statement dangerously close to the coercion-by-play approach of gamification, a phenomenon that Bogost (2011) has excoriated? Is procedural rhetoric also running the risk of creating what Bogost has termed "exploitationware"?

The Design Potential of Procedural Rhetoric

Is the aim of procedural rhetoric to design or understand the design of procedural rhetoric in computer games? Bogost's book *Persuasive Games* seems to me to be about the latter, a theory of how to read the games, not how to design them. Despite these concerns, a review of procedural rhetoric as sequential and ordered patterns of affordances, and in terms of how rhetorical devices act concerning specific genres, may uncover useful ways to design serious games as persuasive games or, conversely, as serious games that show us how easily we are led by designers, conventions, or our own cognitive biases and prejudices.

In terms of agency (or confused agency), is it possible for agents to drive procedural rhetoric? Can there be a polyphony of competing procedural rhetoric, such as historians or archaeologist agents all competing to persuade the player with their conflicting theories or opinions? A more focused theory of procedural rhetoric could drive the design of historically contested places and environments and simulations of historical interpretations, but the theory needs more work.

Is Procedural Rhetoric the Key to Virtual Learning Environments?

Is procedural rhetoric essential to the design and evaluation of games and therefore to interactive places? I argue that it is not because procedural rhetoric clashes with the explorative promise of games, and with the agency inherent in place. If a place was to lead you from a scripted event and staged scene to a scripted event and staged scene, the feeling of place will be severely curtailed. According to my earlier criterion for a place, it affords the imagined but framed possibility of past, present, or future experiencing. A canned locative narrative would destroy this sense of place. While procedural rhetoric could hide this sense of staged direction, it is not true of mechanics; for mechanics allows the player to progress (from the designer or the player's point of view).

Serious Games

We call serious games by many labels: (digital) game-based learning (Pivec, Dziabenko, and Schinnerl 2003); learning by stealth (Shute and Ventura 2013); edutainment (Lepouras and Vassilakis 2004); eduventures (Wechselberger 2009); and, of course, serious games (Liarokapis et al. 2017). It does not matter too much what this area is called. Arguably, *serious games* can lay claim to being the most widely used and understood term, but the term does not clearly say where the seriousness resides: in the design of the game, in the experience of the gameplay, or through the postgame reflections. The term *serious games* suggests to me that serious game designers risk undervaluing the educational potential and emotional range of entertainment.

Serious games are often assumed to be *serious* games: people only learn from serious situations, yet entertainment has to be light, happy, and educationally impoverished. Entertainment is much richer and nuanced. Consider humor: a joke is often funny precisely because it is logical, but it is a logic we did not expect until the punchline. Humor can reveal differing, even clashing perspectives, especially perspectives that are unaware they are out of kilter with other perspectives.

Some academics and designers (Van Eck 2006; Charsky 2010; Egenfeldt-Nielsen 2011) attempt to distinguish between serious games and edutainment because the former is good but difficult and the latter is easier but undesirable. For example, Simon Egenfeldt-Nielsen (2011, 18, 62) observed that edutainment titles are usually based on conventional learning theory and simple gameplay and adhere strictly to a curriculum, and later he wrote they tend to have a reward structure (or system) quite separate from the gameplay. I would add that serious games are so focused on explicit end design goals they risk constraining imagination and creativity, the need to set the scene, or compel the player to imagine, explore, and to express.

Don Charsky (2010, 180) went further but in a different direction, declaring that edutainment doesn't teach us much beyond the following: Teaching lower order thinking skills, facts, concepts, and procedures are essential to fields of study, but typically that is all edutainment attempts to teach. Edutainment typically makes little or no attempt at trying to teach gamers how to apply their knowledge, analyze their understanding, synthesize their perceptions, or evaluate their learning; hence, Seymour Papert refers to educational games as "Shavian reversals."

There may well be a simple reason why virtual learning environments (VLEs) in particular have seldom proven to succeed as enjoyable learning environments let alone as digital games or virtual worlds. They are simply not enjoyable enough for the participants. That is why I entitled this chapter "Do Serious Gamers Learn from Place"; the message is not only that place is seldom involved in serious game evaluation (or design) but also that the personal experiences of the participants are not important (who talks about or describes themselves as serious gamers?).

Serious games typically do not focus on the core game play; their mechanics are not intrinsically interesting, they force (rather than compel) participants to learn about objects and events or develop skills that don't directly pertain to either their own interests or to their idea of an interesting game, and their reward systems can seem overly contrived. This is a danger of gamification, trying to force hard-to-play-with content into interaction patterns that don't suit the content. A strictly followed evaluation may also prevent lessons learned by the evaluator from helping the players (as that can confuse evaluation results), but so much of our learning is from collaborating, sharing, or judging and debating the actions and beliefs of others that this constraint seems to be a real drawback.

In the previous chapter, I focused on game mechanics and how they are used to challenge and engage participants. However, the substantive question for educators is less about the mechanics and more about the pedagogy. We could summarize this concern in the following three questions: Do we know if learning has taken place? If it has taken place, has it done so effectively? And if it has taken place, is the knowledge that resulted from this learning is transferrable? In contrast to James Gee (2003), I do not believe that all games are good games and that all games are therefore good learning environments, but I will outline various ways in which games can help people engage with pedagogical objectives of humanities subjects.

Nor am I convinced that the learning potential of two-dimensional games would automatically be enhanced in three-dimensional environments, as many educational games appear to be directly transferred from traditional humanities subjects (Shaffer 2006). I am, however, interested in which pedagogical theories and studies have examined the role and importance of place in virtual learning environments. How can three dimensional–ness help learning acquisition? Is there a relationship between culture, place, and learning? Can gamification of three-dimensional environments dramatically improve the learning experience, and how widely can it be applied? How do we learn about a place, and how do we make place design a learnable experience?

Games motivate, but can a game maximize learning? I have already suggested that learning via gamification is usually best avoided, and it is preferable to embed learning into enjoyable mechanics and useful rewards. Unless the simulation is an accurate and useful reflection of a real-world situation, the challenge is ensuring that what is learned inside the game or virtual place is transferrable. For instance, knowledge of how to identify and use a weapon in a game is knowledge inside the game, but it is not knowledge that is as useful as smelting knowledge is, or that of being able to recognize badly made or environmentally destructive weapons, or that of complex interrelationships of capital, production, wages, and living standards. The game *Heaven's Vault*, for instance, requires the player guess a counterfactual language from glyphic clues (fig. 7.2).

Shoehorning Content into Procedural Learning Environments

Traditional learning environments, especially in the humanities, have focused on prescriptive learning. In contrast, the hugely successful market of computer games (and training simulations) has shown us that unlike traditional media, interactive virtual environments can be highly useful for procedural learning. Traditionally, we learn about history, events, facts, and other cultural perspectives through prescriptive learning. However, procedural learning is arguably more in tune with the recreation of current generations, allowing them to learn by trial and error, with different learning strategies and preferences.

To bring life back to virtual worlds for the enjoyment of the spectator, we require a more nuanced interaction design. This requires meaningful participation for players to truly engage with the experience, not with the superficial personalization or widespread destruction of commercial game worlds or engaging only with games that are reflection friendly rather than trigger-happy. If players can be enticed to stay in the virtual place long enough, procedural learning may help them over time become more aware of (and thus more empathic toward) other peoples from other societies and the ways they lived in different places.

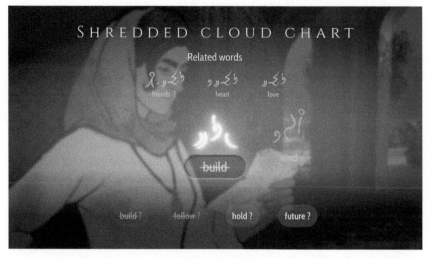

Figure 7.2 Heaven's Vault, 2019. Two-dimensional character, three-dimensional environment narrative game. Copyright Inkle Studios, 2019.

For we also learn spatially. Research into the spatial concepts of Korean and English-language students suggests that children do not have a universal or unique spatial language but begin to reconcile their spatial actions with the space-specific connotations of culture-specific prepositions and actions (Choi et al. 1999; Bowerman and Choi 2003). This seems to be corroborated by later research (Shusterman and Li 2016, 116): "Early philosophers (Kant 1768) and developmental researchers . . . argued that children's spatial representations are primarily egocentric. In contrast to this position, the reports of cross-linguistic variation in spatial language, especially the evidence that some cultures prefer geocentric FoR [frame of reference], raises skepticism about the claim that children's initial FoRs are predominantly egocentric rather than geocentric."

Anna Shusterman and Peggy Li's (2016) paper is a very interesting one. Although it is focused on how four-year-old English-speaking children learn to distinguish left from right, it has some very interesting observations. It suggests that learning about the left-right axes of other people takes far more time but is learned from being able to extrapolate from the directionality of our bodies (Shusterman and Li 2016, 156): "We focused on children's acquisition of two contrasting types of reference systems—an environment-based ('geocentric') coordinate system and a body-based ('egocentric') coordinate system. Our findings generally support Haun et al.'s . . . hypothesis that geocentric representations of space are readily available, and provide the first direct evidence that children's language acquisition draws upon these precursors. The story turns out to be more nuanced: children can represent egocentric left-right, egocentric front-back, and non-egocentric front-back relations quite easily."

Children's' spatial language showed strong developmental improvement from three to five years (Hund et al. 2017), and while it appears that children develop the ability to refer to multiple landmarks when navigating, this is difficult for animals (Ankowski et al. 2012, 2). Language is intimately tied to spatial understanding: "By eighteen months old, children identify language-specific spatial relationships, suggesting that spatial language input helps to construct and order children's view of space from very early in development."

How does this relate to the design of virtual places? I am often asked why a language classroom should use three-dimensional virtual worlds: the aforementioned research papers seem to indicate that culturally specific language in the real world seems to have a direct relation to spatial surrounds. Also, geographically and contextually nuanced virtual places may be required to help either provide cultural specificity and uniqueness of place or develop foreign language learning. Designing specific and characteristic geography and providing social mechanisms to support specific words and phrases to describe them and to communicate how to navigate and wayfind through and around them may be required.

Learning with VR Does Not Have to Focus on Technology

Ryan Morrison (2017) believes that VR does not have to be defined in terms of technical devices. Morrison instead defined virtual worlds as "visual environments that 'have been developed further from three-dimensional (3-D) web-based technologies to form multi-user virtual environments (MUVEs) such as Second Life.'"

Although in the next chapter I will define virtual worlds differently (and specifically note that I don't think they have to be visual), I am mostly in agreement with Morrison on virtual environments, usually known as such even if they are desktop based and don't use VR equipment, and others agree (Wann and Mon-Williams 1996, 833) that "a Virtual Environment (VE) is a representation that 'capitalizes upon natural aspects of human perception by extending visual information in three spatial dimensions.'"

How can we learn in these virtual environments? Morrison quoted Ishbel Duncan, Alan Miller, and Shangyi Jiang (2012, 953), who summarized virtual world learning activities as problem-based learning; inquiry-based learning; game-based learning; role-playing; departing on virtual quests; joining in collaborative simulations (learning by simulation); working on collaborative construction (building activities); designing courses (game, fashion, architectural); teaching and learning language; researching in virtual laboratories; partaking in virtual fieldworks; and attending lectures or classes.

Duncan, Miller, and Jiang distinguished single-user virtual worlds from MUVEs, which is a little unusual but understandable. They employed a virtual world educational usage taxonomy to classify virtual worlds: who the users are (population); what activities they are doing (educational activity); why they are doing them (learning theory); where they are working (learning environment);

and how the system supports the users (supporting technologies). They also surveyed other research areas. Again, although these educational surveys and reports tend to view virtual worlds as mere stages in which genuine learning takes place, other people control digital bodies (avatars), typing to talk to other people represented by virtual bodies (avatars). Their learning is not in-world.

Learning and Features of Games and Game Genres

Game-like environments are seldom taken seriously; students and users can be stuck in "game mode," and engagement can be addictive. There is the issue of authenticity versus interaction: the more interactive the environment, the more likely it could be changed in a way not commensurate with historical evidence or scientific knowledge. From a technological point of view, games can be hijacked, frequently contain serious bugs, and offer only simplistic interaction. Their hardware or software can also disappear or fail to run, and content can be difficult to port to other, better solutions. Meaningfully transferable knowledge and skills are not always obvious.

On the other hand, game genres can give players a fuzzy type of narrative and gameplay affordance: players have some idea of what to expect if they know the particular game genre. A. Frazer, D. Argles, and G. Wills (2008) studied a selection of games from several genres (first-person shooter, role-playing/adventure, puzzle, and strategy). They surveyed whether the games could support the following: conversation, new knowledge, world creation, world exploration, useful feedback, balance difficulty, clear goals, contextualization, curiosity provocation, immersion, reward offerings, united resources, and so on.

They concluded that first-person shooters (FPSs) are generally too fast moving for knowledge acquisition even though they are immersive, encourage exploration, and provide clear rewards. Interestingly (and puzzlingly), the authors believe FPSs offer more conversation than role-playing games (RPGs) but evoke less curiosity and unite fewer resources than RPGs. RPGs "may be better suited to a multimedia-heavy learning area, where learners need to explore a range of different learning resources in a self-motivated manner." Puzzles may be suitable for single concepts and strategy games for "providing new knowledge, uniting different resources, and expressing information extremely clearly."

Frazer, Argles, and Wills claimed, "The FPS genre may be better at providing a setting where the environment itself is the learning resource to explore, with its opportunities for conversation allowing multiple users to be present in it at once." The authors selected three games for each of their four genres, but I could not find a mention of the games in the paper. Although their selection methods are unclear, their approach is interesting.

The Digital Natives Are Restless, and Not That Native

Aren't students of today considered to be "digital natives"? In terms of virtual places and virtual worlds, are we designing and teaching adequately for digital natives? In the 2011 UK report *The Net Generation and Digital Natives*, Chris Jones and Binhui Shao declared there is no clear generational divide, information and communications technology (ICT) skills vary widely, and "students do not naturally make extensive use of many of the most discussed new technologies such as Blogs, Wikis and 3D Virtual Worlds." In fact, they say, "the use of 3D Virtual Worlds is notably low amongst students."

Despite the promise of technology, some radical innovations may lack a clear purpose or a supportive community and will fade away (Scoble 2014). Even though we design for an audience, the media audience is undoubtedly a changing phenomenon. Are recent generations so technologically advanced that education has to be completely rewritten to accommodate them? Do we have to design games or adopt gamification everywhere to connect with the new generation's digital native minds?

According to recent research, it appears that designing games (and specifically virtual environments) for digital natives is not always necessary, and according to Sue Bennett, Karl Maton, and Lisa Kervin (2008), there is little evidence to believe that "these young people [having been] immersed in technology all their lives [has imbued] them with sophisticated technical skills and learning preferences for which traditional education is unprepared."

I earlier noted that Jones and Shao (2011) claimed there was no such clear generational divide, but they also commented that ICT skills vary widely, and students are not automatically experts or even frequent users of "Blogs, Wikis and 3D Virtual Worlds." Paul Kirschner and Pedro De Bruyckere (2017, 135) added three important statements:

- Information-savvy digital natives do not exist.
- Learners multitask; they task switch which negatively impacts learning.
- Educational design assuming these myths hinders rather than helps to learn.

Digital literacy is not the same as digital fluency. Mitchel Resnick (2002) argued that digital literacy involves knowing how to construct things of significance with designated (multimedia) tools along with critical thinking, judgment, and cooperation. Gerard White argued that digital fluency required "the skills that are needed to successfully use digital technologies for learning e.g. critical thinking and collaboration" (White 2013).

Affordances

In "Why Gamers Don't Learn More: An Ecological Approach to Games as Learning Environments," Jonas Linderoth (2012) postulated that progression in games does not necessarily imply learning and that the unique ways in which game design facilitates progression might be rather unsuitable principles for learning. According to Linderoth, an affordance "offers the individual different ways of action, . . . is . . . always relative to an agent[, and] is not a property of the environment" (49).

In the paper "This Is Not a Door," Linderoth and Ulirika Bennerstedt (2007, 604) wrote, "In games you must discriminate between the parts of the game world that has something to do with the game mechanics and the parts of the world which [are] only 'decorations.' In many games there are doors, windows, mountains in a far distance etc. which are only there to add atmosphere and has nothing to do with the actual game . . . in order to make sense of this perceptual field the player must learn to make distinctions that make successful interaction possible."

Learning from Perceived Affordances

In *The Ecological Approach to Visual Perception,* James Gibson (2014, 138–39) defined an affordance as something provided to an animal by the environment: "An affordance is not bestowed upon an object by a need of an observer and his act of perceiving it. The object offers what it does because it is the object it is."

Unfortunately, the term has become used in many different if important ways. In human-computer interaction studies, the term gained popularity through the writings of Donald Norman (2008, 2018a, 2018b). Norman has previously worked with Gibson, but they disagreed on whether affordances were preexisting or perceived. Norman himself later said the term should be *signifiers,* not *affordances,* but the confusion has remained and the clarity of the definition and the effectiveness or usefulness of the theory has been questioned (Bærentsen and Trettvik 2002; Scarantino 2003).

Michael Hammond (2010, 205) found the idea useful and proffered a succinct definition of Gibson's concept of affordance: "An affordance, then, is a relation between an organism and an object with the object perceived in relation to the needs of the organism." Hammond summarized key differences of interpretations in the use of the term but arrived at his own definition (geared to ICT teaching) (2010, 207): "The perception of a possibility of action (in the broad sense of thought as well as physical activity) provided by properties of, in this case, the computer plus software. These possibilities are shaped by past experience and context, may be conceptually sophisticated and may need to be signposted by peers and teachers. . . . Perceptions of affordances can, and do, become habitual. Affordances arise because of real physical and symbolic properties of objects. Affordances provide both opportunities and constraints. Affordances are always relative to something."

Interpretations of these theories have been found occasionally in game studies and in VR papers. The paper "A Cognitivist Theory of Affordances for Games" by Rogelio E. Cardona-Rivera and Michael R. Young (2013, 1) posited three types of affordances: "1) real affordances, what actions are possible in a game, 2) perceived affordances, what actions players perceive possible in a game, and 3) feedback, perceptual information introduced in the game by its designers to advertise real affordances in the hopes of eliciting accurate perceived affordances."

They claimed there were two main works on affordances in game studies, by Treanor and Mateas (2009) and by Linderoth (2012). According to Cardona-Rivera and Young (2013, 3), Mateas posited that interactive narratives and games have two types of affordances: material affordances ("opportunities for action that are presented by the game to the player") and formal affordances ("[which] . . . provide the motivation to perform one particular action out of all actions that could potentially be available").

Cardona-Rivera and Young's theory describes affordances depending on an "underlying computational model" that might appeal to those interested more in cognitive science, but the combination of designed and perceived affordances are complicated, and there are also "real affordances" (which begs the question of what "real" means in a virtual environment). However, there are simpler models discussed, such as by Paul Rama and colleagues (2012) in "Affordances for Second Language Learning in World of Warcraft." Unfortunately, their use of affordances seems so generic that they could as easily be referred to as "generic features." The concept of affordance is extremely intriguing, but neither its definition nor its application seems to be agreed on by the majority of scholars.

Learning from Peopled Virtual Worlds

While some theorists have already described games as a type of narrative architecture, this is unfair to architecture. There are many spatial narratives in architectural form. Designers can provide virtual places that are evanescent, ephemeral, experientially immersive, and atmospheric. Architects could show our digital media colleagues the importance of key place concepts, such as interrelated and interstitial space, inhabitation-derived wear and tear, territoriality, kinesthetically learned narrative, proprioceptive feedback, phototropic signifiers, and head-tail spatial design.

However, we learn not only from material form but also from how the material form is designed to interact with both life-forms and the external environment. For example, Shadow of the Colossus (fig. 7.3) is a sophisticated and reflective explorative quest where the monsters are landscape puzzles. Luckily, we can learn and interpret from others, if the virtual place records their trails, paths, intentions, successes, and failures. To bring life back to virtual worlds for the enjoyment of the spectator, we require more understanding of communication design, specifically, interaction design as it relates directly to how people live in space and in time. This requires providing opportunities for meaningful participation for visitors to truly engage with an experience, not merely the superficial personalization or widespread destruction provided by commercial game worlds, but through employing games that are reflection friendly and not just trigger-happy.

Cultural presence exists via artifacts, objects that mediate communication between social agents (the creator and the recipient), even when the creator is not there. I have previously suggested the ability of an artifact to convey a sense of that creator's agency is a reflection of its "hermeneutic richness" (akin to the archaeological notion of the "trace"). However, a virtual environment can have hermeneutic richness in at least two ways, if it reveals the self in that world (not a common

Figure 7.3 *Shadow of the Colossus*, 2018, PS4. Copyright Sony, 2005, 2018. Erik Champion, screenshot.

attribute of computer games) or if it reveals the cultural presence of others (*Myst* went some way to providing a sense of the social presence of others, if not their cultural presence).

Cultural Learning

Cultural learning could be summarized as learning through observation, instruction, or trial and error. Therefore, there are two major ways of transmitting culture: through other social agents (through the language, actions, and reactions of other people) and through artifacts (the objects created and modified by people). The former seems necessary for understanding a culture natively (from the inside as vicarious experience), and the latter seems necessary for extending cultural knowledge or developing cultural awareness of alterity (from the outside as observation or as extrapolated experience).

Summary

The cultural geographer Yi-Fu Tuan (1975) has pointed out that the simple and taken-for-granted ways we interact with place are not so straightforward: "How do we recognize places and find our way among them? Are our movements guided by something like pictures in the head? What is the relationship between perception and the imaginative faculty that enables us to envisage places we have not directly experienced? How is it possible to give street directions to another person? How can the geography of strange lands be taught? If the questions sound naive, it may be because—like the blunt queries of precocious children—they are deep."

How do we learn about a place? As per a real environment, we learn through observation; through inhabitation; through embodiment and physical activity;

and through the action of others (platial roles and rituals). I suggested there are at least three relevant features: multimodality, sociability, and encultured physicality. I also suggested that through aspects of these features, we can experience a sense of place (placeness) in virtual environments. We also learn about a place through creative exploration and memorialization, not just by observing and responding to the actions, judgments, and behaviors of others.

Given the creative, additive, and agglutinative nature of place-making, I approach procedural rhetoric as warily as I approached gamification. Gamification shares key features with procedural rhetoric:

- The player has a goal in mind that the player works to achieve.
- The "game" has systematic or emergent rules.
- The game is considered a form of play or competition.

We may think gamification and procedural rhetoric can lead to interesting place design, but I suggest both are more likely to restrict agency and a sense of exploration. Adherence to the altar of procedural rhetoric, whether intended by Bogost or not, can lead to people thinking that the designer's idea of the game rules is what matters. Then we would have debates invoking the intentional fallacy and death-of-the-author arguments, only this time they would be over computer games, not literature.

Rhetoric involves the art of persuading, not necessarily the art of opening up games as vehicles of critical discourse (Chaplin 2011). And the power of procedural rhetoric begins to wane in the experiencing of richly interactive virtual places and virtual worlds. I suspect that gamification poses a similar risk to designing and learning from truly interactive places. Are they truly places, interactive places, if our experience of "place" is calculated and coerced? By extension, are we genuinely learning if we are guided every step of the way?

A return to how affordances are designed, perceived, and ignored seems to be a vital tool for creating successful virtual learning environments, but researchers seem to disagree on the term, what it describes, and how it should be employed. We can learn a great deal from studying the jumps and gaps between designed and perceived affordances and by observing people attempting to find their way or 'place' themselves. Unfortunately, learning from observing how other people navigate their surroundings is underplayed in much literature on affordances and perceived affordances.

Virtual people-watching is seldom a feature of serious games, while the powerful feedback that can be generated from collaborative learning and creative exploration within the virtual place is seldom an object of study. There are other issues with serious games: a confusion of terms, definitions, and applied methods and difficulty encountered when attempting to integrate procedural knowledge with prescriptive knowledge (how do we learn through doing things, and how can meaningful learning be reached through the free-ranging and often fantastical conventions of game-based entertainment)?

Learning with digital interfaces and related equipment should not focus on the technology but the experience and the quality and quantity of transferrable learning.

References

Ankowski, Amber A., Emily E. Thom, Catherine M. Sandhofer, and Aaron P. Blaisdell. 2012. "Spatial Language and Children's Spatial Landmark Use." *Child Development Research* 2012: 14. https://doi.org/10.1155/2012/427364.

Backhaus, Gary, and John Murungi. 2003. *Tensional Landscapes: The Dynamics of Boundaries and Placements*. Lanham, MD: Lexington Books.

Bærentsen, Klaus B., and Johan Trettvik. 2002. "An Activity Theory Approach to Affordance." In *Proceedings of the Second Nordic Conference on Human-Computer Interaction*, edited by S. Bødker, O. Bertelsen, and Karl Kuutti, 51–60. New York: ACM.

Balstrup, Sarah. 2013. "The Location of the Sacred: Methodological Reconsiderations of the Sacredness of Place." In *Journeys and Destinations: Studies in Travel, Identity, and Meaning*, edited by Alex Norman, 69–86. Newcastle upon Tyne, UK: Cambridge Scholars Publishing.

Bennett, Sue, Karl Maton, and Lisa Kervin. 2008. "The 'Digital Natives' Debate: A Critical Review of the Evidence." *British Journal of Educational Technology* 39 (5): 775–86. https://doi.org/10.1111/j.1467-8535.2007.00793.x.

Bogost, Ian. 2007. *Persuasive Games: The Expressive Power of Videogames*. Cambridge, MA: MIT Press.

———. 2011. "Gamification Is Bullshit." *The Atlantic*. Last Modified December 15, 2014. Accessed July 21, 2017. http://www.theatlantic.com/technology/archive/2011/08/gamification-is-bullshit/243338/.

Bowerman, Melissa, and Soonja Choi. 2003. "Space under Construction: Language-Specific Spatial Categorization in First Language Acquisition." *Language in Mind: Advances in the Study of Language and Thought*, edited by Dedre Gentner and Susan Goldin-Meadow, 387–428. Cambridge, MA: MIT Press.

Cardona-Rivera, Rogelio Enrique, and Robert Michael Young. 2013. "A Cognitivist Theory of Affordances for Games." In *DiGRA '13 - Proceedings of the 2013 DiGRA International Conference: DeFragging Game Studies*, edited by Celia Pearce, Helen Kennedy and John Sharp, 1–10. Atlanta, GA: DiGRA.

Champion, Erik. 2006. "Evaluating Cultural Learning in Virtual Environments." PhD diss., Department of Geomatics, Faculty of Engineering, University of Melbourne. https://www.researchgate.net/publication/43456139_Evaluating_Cultural_Learning_in_an_Online_Virtual_Environment.

———. 2016. *Critical Gaming: Interactive History and Virtual Heritage*. Edited by Marilyn Deegan, Lorna Hughes, Andrew Prescott, and Harold Short. Digital Research in the Arts and Humanities. Abingdon, UK: Routledge.

Champion, Erik, Ian Bishop, and Bharat Dave. 2012. "The Palenque Project: Evaluating Interaction in an Online Virtual Archaeology site." *Virtual Reality* 16 (2): 121–39.

Chaplin, Heather. 2011. "I Don't Want to Be a Superhero: Ditching Reality for a Game Isn't as Fun as It Sounds." *Slate*, March 29, 2011. Accessed March 6, 2017. https://slate.com/technology/2011/03/gamification-ditching-reality-for-a-game-isn-t-as-fun-as-it-sounds.html.

Charsky, Dennis. 2010. "From Edutainment to Serious Games: A Change in the Use of Game Characteristics." *Games and Culture* 5 (2): 177–98. https://doi.org/doi:10.1177/1555412009354727.

Choi, Soonja, Laraine McDonough, Melissa Bowerman, and Jean M. Mandler. 1999. "Early Sensitivity to Language: Specific Spatial Categories in English and Korean." *Cognitive Development* 14 (2): 241–68. https://doi.org/https://doi.org/10.1016/S0885-2014 (99)00004-0.

Cunha, Pedro, Jorge Brandão, José Vasconcelos, Filomena Soares, and Vítor Carvalho. 2016. "Augmented Reality for Cognitive and Social Skills Improvement in Children with ASD." Paper presented at the Thirteenth International Conference on Remote Engineering and Virtual Instrumentation (REV), Madrid, February 24–26, 2016.

Ducheneaut, Nicolas, Robert J. Moore, and Eric Nickell. 2007. "Virtual 'Third Places': A Case Study of Sociability in Massively Multiplayer Games." *Computer Supported Cooperative Work* 16 (1–2): 129–66.

Ducheneaut, Nicolas, Nick Yee, Eric Nickell, and Robert J. Moore. 2006. "Building an MMO with Mass Appeal." *Games and Culture* 1 (4): 281–317. https://doi.org /doi:10.1177/1555412006292613.

Duncan, Ishbel, Alan Miller, and Shangyi Jiang. 2012. "A Taxonomy of Virtual Worlds Usage in Education." *British Journal of Educational Technology* 43 (6): 949–64.

Egenfeldt-Nielsen, Simon. 2011. *Beyond Edutainment: Exploring the Educational Potential of Computer Games.* [Lulu]: Game-Research.com.

Flanagan, Mary. 2013. *Critical Play Radical Game Design.* Cambridge, MA: MIT Press.

Frazer, A., D. Argles, and G. Wills. 2008. "The Same, but Different: The Educational Affordances of Different Gaming Genres." Paper presented at the Eighth IEEE International Conference on Advanced Learning Technologies, Santander, July 1–5, 2008.

Gee, James Paul. 2003. *What Video Games Have to Teach Us about Learning and Literacy.* New York: Palgrave Macmillan.

Gelsomini, Mirko, Franca Garzotto, Vito Matarazzo, Nicolò Messina, and Daniele Occhiuto. 2017. "Creating Social Stories as Wearable Hyper-Immersive Virtual Reality Experiences for Children with Neurodevelopmental Disorders." In *Proceedings of the 2017 Conference on Interaction Design and Children*, edited by Paulo Blikstein and Dor Abrahamson, 431–37. New York: ACM.

Gibson, James J. 2014. *The Ecological Approach to Visual Perception: Classic Edition.* Sussex, UK: Psychology Press.

Hammond, Michael. 2010. "What Is an Affordance and Can It Help Us Understand the Use of ICT in Education?" *Education and Information Technologies* 15 (3): 205–17. https://link .springer.com/article/10.1007/s10639-009-9106-z.

Henrik, James. 2005. *The History and Theory of Rhetoric: An Introduction*, 3rd ed. Boston: Allyn and Beacon.

Hund, Alycia M., Lindsay J. Bianchi, Jayne F. Winner, and Matthew S. Hesson-McInnis. 2017. "Complex Spatial Language Improves from 3 to 5 Years: The Role of Prompting and Overhearing in Facilitating Direction Giving Using *Between* and *Middle*." *Cognitive Development* 43:170–81. https://doi.org/https://doi.org/10.1016/j.cogdev.2017.04.002.

Jewitt, Carey, Jeff Bezemer, and Kay O'Halloran. 2016. *Introducing Multimodality.* London: Routledge.

Jones, Chris, and Binhui Shao. 2011. "The Net Generation and Digital Natives: Implications for Higher Education." Higher Education Academy, York. Accessed May 4, 2021. http://oro.open.ac.uk/30014/.

Kalay, Yehuda, E., and John Marx. 2001. "The Role of Place in Cyberspace." In *Proceedings Seventh International Conference on Virtual Systems and Multimedia*, edited by Hal Thwaites and Lon Addison, 770–779. Los Alamitos, CA: IEEE Press.

Kirschner, Paul A., and Pedro De Bruyckere. 2017. "The Myths of the Digital Native and the Multitasker." *Teaching and Teacher Education* 67:135–42. https://doi.org/http://dx.doi .org/10.1016/j.tate.2017.06.001.

Koster, Raph. 2010. "Placeness Is a Feature, Not the Point." Raph Koster's Website. Last Modified February 24, 2010. Accessed August 2, 2017. https://www.raphkoster.com /2010/02/24/placeness-is-a-feature-not-the-point/.

———. n.d. "A Definition: Part One; The Play's the Thing." Raph Koster's Website. Accessed July 18, 2017. https://www.raphkoster.com/games/insubstantial-pageants/a-definition/.

Lepouras, George, and Costas Vassilakis. 2004. "Virtual Museums for All: Employing Game Technology for Edutainment." *Virtual Reality* 8 (2): 96–106. https://doi.org/10.1007 /s10055-004-0141-1.

Liarokapis, Fotis, Panagiotis Petridis, Daniel Andrews, and Sara de Freitas. 2017. "Multimodal Serious Games Technologies for Cultural Heritage." In *Mixed Reality and Gamification for Cultural Heritage*, edited by Marinos Ioannides, Nadia Magnenat-Thalmann, and George Papagiannakis, 371–392. Cham: Springer International.

Linderoth, Jonas. 2012. "Why Gamers Don't Learn More: An Ecological Approach to Games as Learning Environments." *Journal of Gaming and Virtual Worlds* 4 (1): 45–62.

Linderoth, Jonas, and Ulrika Bennerstedt. 2007. "This Is Not a Door: An Ecological Approach to Computer Games." Paper presented at the 2007 DiGRA International Conference, "Situated Play," Tokyo, September 24–28, 2007.

Molleindustria. 2019. "The McDonald's Videogame." Last Modified 2019. Accessed May 4, 2021. http://www.molleindustria.org/mcdonalds/.

Mon-Williams, Mark, and John P. Wann. 1998. "Binocular Virtual Reality Displays: When Problems Do and Don't Occur." *Human Factors* 40 (1): 42–49. https://doi.org/10.1518 /001872098779480622.

Moore, Robert, E. Hankinson Gathman, and Nicolas Ducheneaut. 2009. "From 3D Space to Third Place: The Social Life of Small Virtual Spaces." *Human Organization* 68 (2): 230–40.

Moreno, Roxana, and Richard Mayer. 2007. "Interactive Multimodal Learning Environments." Special issue on Interactive Learning Environments: Contemporary Issues and Trends, *Educational Psychology Review* 19 (3): 309–26. https://doi.org/10 .1007/s10648-007-9047-2.

Morrison, Ryan. 2017. "Virtual Reality in the Language Learning Classroom." *Morning Watch: Educational and Social Analysis* 44 (1–2): 1–9.

Murray, Janet H. 2001. *Hamlet on the Holodeck*. Cambridge, MA: MIT Press.

Newsgaming, and Gonzalo Frasca. 2021. "September 12th: A Toy World." [Online Flash game]. Newsgaming. Last Modified 2021. Accessed May 4, 2021. http://www .gamesforchange.org/game/september-12th-a-toy-world/.

Norman, Donald A. 2008. "The Way I See It: Signifiers, Not Affordances." *Interactions* 15 (6): 18–19. https://doi.org/10.1145/1409040.1409044.

———.. 2018a. "Affordances and Design." jnd.org. Last Modified December 3, 2018. Accessed May 4, 2021. https://jnd.org/affordances_and_design/

———. 2018b. "Signifiers, Not Affordances." jnd.org. Last Modified December 3, 2018. Accessed May 4, 2021. http://jnd.org/dn.mss/signifiers_not_affordances.html.

Paavilainen, Simo. 1982. *Nordic Classicism 1910–1930: Museum of Finnish Architecture*. Helsinki: Finlands arkitekturmuseum.

Pivec, Maja, Olga Dziabenko, and Irmgard Schinnerl. 2003. "Aspects of Game-Based Learning." Paper presented at the Third International Conference on Knowledge Management, Graz, August 2003.

Rama, Paul S., Rebecca W. Black, Elizabeth van Es, and Mark Warschauer. 2012. "Affordances for Second Language Learning in World of Warcraft." *ReCALL* 24 (3): 322–38. https://doi.org/10.1017/S0958344012000171.

Rapp, Christof. 2010. "Aristotle's Rhetoric" *Stanford Encyclopedia of Philosophy*. Stanford. Accessed July 21, 2017. https://plato.stanford.edu/archives/spr2010/entries/aristotle-rhetoric/.

Resnick, Mitchel. 2002. "Rethinking Learning in the Digital Age." In *The Global Information Technology Report: Readiness for the Networked World*, edited by Geoffrey Kirkman, Peter K. Cornelius, and Jeffrey D. Sachs, 32–37. Oxford: Oxford University Press.

Robinson, Andrew. 2011. "In Theory Bakhtin: Dialogism, Polyphony and Heteroglossia." *Ceasefire* Magazine. Last Modified March 6, 2017. Accessed August 3, 2017. https://ceasefiremagazine.co.uk/in-theory-bakhtin-1/.

Scarantino, Andrea 2003. "Affordances Explained." *Philosophy of Science* 70 (5): 949–61. https://doi.org/10.1086/377380.

Scoble, Robert. 2014. "Why Google Glass Is Doomed." *TNW* (blog). Accessed May 4, 2021. http://thenextweb.com/robertscoble/2014/01/02/google-glass-doomed/.

Senda, Mitsuru. 1992. *Design of Children's Play Environments*. New York: McGraw-Hill.

Shaffer, David Williamson. 2006. *How Computer Games Help Children Learn*. New York: Palgrave Macmillan.

Shrank, Brian, and Brian Gabor Jr. n.d. "Bust A Cup." Accessed May 4, 2021. https://shakethatbutton.com/bust-a-cup/.

Shusterman, Anna, and Peggy Li. 2016. "Frames of Reference in Spatial Language Acquisition." *Cognitive Psychology* 88:115–61.

Shute, Valerie, and Matthew Ventura. 2013. *Stealth Assessment: Measuring and Supporting Learning in Video Games*. Cambridge, MA: MIT Press.

Treanor, Mike, and Michael Mateas. 2009. "Newsgames: Procedural Rhetoric Meets Political Cartoons." In *Proceedings of the 2009 DiGRA International Conference: Breaking New Ground: Innovation in Games, Play, Practice and Theory*, edited by Tanya Krzywinska, Helen W. Kennedy, and Barry Atkins. London: Brunel University/DiGRA.

Tronstad, Ragnhild. 2010. "The Productive Paradox of Critical Play." *Game Studies: The International Journal of Computer Game Research* 10 (1). Accessed May 4, 2021. http://gamestudies.org/1001/articles/tronstad.

Tuan, Yi-Fu. 1975. "Images and Mental Maps." *Annals of the Association of American Geographers* 65 (2): 205–12. https://doi.org/10.1111/j.1467-8306.1975.tb01031.x.

Van Eck, Richard. 2006. "Digital Game-Based Learning: It's Not Just the Digital Natives Who Are Restless." *EDUCAUSE Review* 41 (2): 16.

Wann, John, and Mark Mon-Williams. 1996. "What Does Virtual Reality NEED? Human Factors Issues in the Design of Three-Dimensional Computer Environments." *International Journal of Human-Computer Studies* 44:829–47.

Wechselberger, Ulrich. 2009. "Teaching Me Softly: Experiences and Reflections on Informal Educational Game Design." *Transactions on Edutainment* 2:90–104.

White, Gerald K. 2013. "Digital Fluency: Skills Necessary for Learning in the Digital Age." Teaching and Learning and Leadership: Digital Learning Research. Australian Council for Educational Research ACERSearch, 1–13. Accessed May 5, 2021. https://research.acer.edu.au/digital_learning/6/.

Williams, Dmitri, Nicolas Ducheneaut, Li Xiong, Yuanyuan Zhang, Nick Yee, and Eric Nickell. 2006. "From Tree House to Barracks: The Social Life of Guilds in World of Warcraft." *Games and Culture* 1 (4): 338–61.

chapter eight

CULTURAL PLACES

Introduction

Many places depend on culture and vice versa, but cultural virtual places are rare. Why? Perhaps we only understand their pull on us when they are, ironically, uninhabited? For example, Tom Leddy wrote (2013), "There is the presence of the power of a people in the remains themselves . . . a magical presence. Ruins, unlike reconstructions, connect one to a past, to a past that went through a life and then a death . . . a past with a complete history, one that ends, of course, in tragedy. Ruins represent civilizations once alive and now dead . . . [and] speak of an earlier life for a culture, a thriving time that exists no more. The ruin contains within itself a ghost of former self."

Defining Culture

Culture is a widely used yet vaguely defined term (Bogdanovych et al. 2010). Michael Fischer (2006, 259) wrote, "Culture transcends material and behavioral contexts. Cultural solutions are instantiated in material and behavioral terms, but are based in large part on 'invented' symbolic constructions of the interaction space and its elements." For Fischer, culture is a dynamic system of representations that multi-agent modeling can simulate. He defined culture as "the system of activities and resources that support human social organization," but he neither detailed the social organization of multi-agents nor elaborated on how they would hold or convey values, beliefs, and attachments to material objects and intangible heritage.

While Fisher's article focused on extracting a notion of culture as systems of representation that can be algorithmically simulated, it did not address the role of the material in cultural heritage as being inextricably integrated with cultural heritage itself. Yet for philosophers such as Jeffrey Malpas (2008, 16), "the artwork is not reducible just to the materiality 'stuff' of which it is made and yet the artwork is what it is through its concrete spatio-temporal existence." Here lies a schism between those focused on the development of intelligent agents (such as Fischer) and those focused on how to explain and transmit the cultural significance of heritage sites, values, and objects (such as Malpas).

Cultural places can be organized into places that attempt to recapture a past culture, places that simulate contemporary culture, and places that communicate past or present cultural values or develop new ones. In addition to Malpas, other scholars place more emphasis on culture as the manifestation of values and beliefs over time. For architect Sverre Fehn, culture was the path that humans cut through nature, and therefore, culture is the resulting expression of the way the surroundings are comprehended by its inhabitants.

For Mike Crang (1998, 103), "spaces become places as they become 'time-thickened.'" Here culture is viewed as more a framework that places the worth of cultural objects and behaviors in a landscape. For Crang (1998), place is a cultural setting, it gives cultural interaction a specific time and a specific place. This is more clearly seen in UNESCO's (2015a) definition of cultural landscapes, in which land use is "associated in the minds of the communities with powerful beliefs and artistic and traditional customs."

However, cultural heritage is not merely sites, buildings, monuments, or landscapes. UNESCO (2015b) defines intangible heritage as "practices, representations, expressions, knowledge, skills—as well as the instruments, objects, artifacts, and cultural spaces associated therewith—that communities, groups and, in some cases, individuals recognize as part of their cultural heritage. . . . [It is] transmitted from generation to generation, is constantly recreated by communities and groups in response to their environment, their interaction with nature and their history, and provides them with a sense of identity and continuity."

Heritage sites are a complex amalgam of both tangible and intangible content *over time.*

Culture and Architecture

Architecture is not only about the artifacts we see built around us but also intimately connected to the *process* of designing and building, the way we are all embedded, and embodied, in the practice and praxis that is architecture. In a sense, people are not just physically embodied; they are also socially embedded. Their motives, intentions, and actions can be fully understood only in relation to a social perspective that makes sense of a specific physical environment.

Re-creating the objects that make up our society is not re-creating the society itself, as some of our cultural knowledge is neither ostensive nor directly tangible. For virtual worlds, cultural interaction can happen around them, but it is unproven as to how much cultural interaction happens through them. Uniqueness is essential, or the location where cultural interaction could happen and could be performed and could be recalled is experientially irrelevant.

Cumulative Culture

An important distinction between culture and society is the cumulative nature of human culture, which separates us from animals (Vale, Flynn, and Kendal 2012).

According to biologists (Claidière et al. 2014, 1), "a wide range of other animals have culture too, but often in a limited form that does not complexify through the gradual accumulation of innovations." Humans accumulate culture; they modify cultural knowledge (culture managed by infrastructure or institution) using past knowledge from previous generations. Culture is also an assortment of objects and rituals that frame and express a communally shared idealized future. In these dual functions culture extends beyond society: a social environment can exist where shared understandings are never preserved beyond the life experiences of the group. Yet the cultural heritage of a real-world society outlives specific individuals. For example, in archaeology, we can draw interpretations of past societies in terms of their cultural heritage.

This does not mean that developing a social virtual environment is necessarily the same as developing a cultural virtual environment. Imagine meeting people in an airport lounge and socializing with them; one is not likely to be partaking in a shared culture as the social exchanges will not become part of a cultural framework. Likewise, meeting people in a social online world does not require that the social online world is a cultural online world.

While virtual heritage is typically orientated toward UNESCO and ICO-MOS definitions and criteria (Addison 2001, 2008), many papers discussing social agents or cultural agents still conflate culture and society or culture and art. In research into telepresence (virtual presence), culture is also often placed alongside society, or the terms are used interchangeably but without clear distinctions or definitions (Riva and Mantovani 2000; Riva et al. 2002).

Cultural Presence

For virtual places designed to communicate the importance of cultural heritage content, I suggest they should convey the unique significance of the simulated culture, which requires an attempt to understand how the original site was experienced and understood by its original inhabitants. I previously defined cultural presence as "the feeling of being in the presence of a similar or distinctly different cultural belief system" (Champion 2011, 179).

This may help us evaluate how closely culture can be observed, appreciated, or understood through virtual environments. This does not mean we must build virtual environments for thousands of people; after all, we can experience *some* sense of cultural presence in an otherwise empty museum. Unlike social presence, which requires other people to appear to be in the same real or virtual environment, we can experience cultural presence without (necessarily) having to meet or hear other people. However, it does require a feeling of layered history as a situated palimpsest, and it does raise the issue of what sort of interaction would best allow us to understand the mindset of other distant or exotic societies.

Various digital heritage infrastructures have adopted this or similar definitions (v-must: Virtual Museum Transnational Network 2011; UPF Barcelona n.d.), unfortunately, providing for this experience is no easy exercise (Rizzo and Mignosa 2013). Recognizing semblances of culture independently of living people is possible because that is what cultural heritage specialists attempt to uncover (Jacobson and Holden 2007) through the analysis of signs of inhabitation (Champion 2011, 49). But that does not mean the culture is still extant, only that it can be *interpreted* via place. Cultural presence requires understanding the social agency behind the cultural landscape; it is very difficult when we have artifacts left but no idea as to how they were used.

Hermeneutic Richness

Proponents of hermeneutics (Gadamer 1976) argue that we must grasp the world of the interpreter as well as the world of the interpreted to gain the meaning of the text or artwork. The inherent nature of digital or new media invites the redefinition of the viewer as an active participant in such interpretative practices because it enables both dynamic interactions with content and participative interaction with other viewers. The hermeneutic environment, as I defined, the third type of virtual environment, allows visitors to these virtual environments to gain an idea of indigenous social and cultural beliefs of past and present inhabitants (the visitors are the "others"), or it allows visitors to inscribe the environment with the results of their own interaction with it (so there are two subcategories of the hermeneutic).

Being able to observe a distinct cultural presence does not necessarily indicate a great amount of cultural learning has taken place. To evaluate the effectiveness of cultural learning there needs to be a measure of the cultural "immersivity" of a virtual environment. For want of a better term, I suggest hermeneutic richness: the depth and vividness of a medium that allows for interpretation of different cultural and social perspectives as judged from an emic or etic viewpoint.

Hermeneutic richness does not mean photorealism or social presence. If cultural presence is a measure of how markedly a cultural force is perceived to imprint or ingrain itself on its surroundings; hermeneutic richness is the depth of affordance that a virtual environment gives to the interpretation of a natively residing culture in that virtual environment. The ability of an artifact to convey a sense of that cultural agency is a reflection of its collective "hermeneutic richness" (akin to the archaeological notion of the "trace"). The perceived sense of that culture through an artifact is itself cultural agency. For an artifact is itself a cipher, a mark of cultural agency.[1]

To evoke cultural learning of a historic nature, this passive hermeneutic richness is an elusive and intangible quality. Hermeneutic richness also exists in two distinct ways. On the one hand, this type of virtual environment might act as a symbolically projected identity, dynamically customized by us as the visitor to reflect our social and individual values and outlook. On the other hand, a virtual environment might be hermeneutic when it affords meaningful interpretations of its shareholders (clients and subjects) to those that visit it, be it a virtual museum, flight simulation level, online world, or serious game.

Specific Issues in Modeling Culture

How do we model culture if we are unsure about what it is? Real-world culture is often learned via observation, ritual practices (which take time), or by instruction. Agents might appear to provide for learning by observing their actions or being guided by their instruction, but they lack granularity of expression, individuality, or rich and expressive responses. Rituals are especially hard to simulate; in virtual environments, there is no social judgment that will teach people right from wrong and ensure they keep to cultural protocols when visiting and interacting with these virtual environments (Champion 2009).

East-West Distinctions: Museumization

Current notions of place in Western literature may be ignorant of other cultural perceptions of place as opposed to space (Suzuki 1997), and other ethnicities may be underrepresented or stereotyped (Kolko, Nakamura, and Rodman 2000). Real-world cultural perceptions can also be found to affect interaction in virtual worlds (Nakamura 2008; Jackson et al. 2009; Waddell et al. 2014), yet I am still not convinced that we have captured culture *inside* the virtual worlds. For instance, some critics have claimed virtual worlds (cyberspace) are the erasure or deliberate ignorance of non-Western histories (Sardar 1996). Z. Sardar (1996) wrote, "In the postmodern world where things have systematically become monuments, nature has been transformed into 'reserve', and knowledge is giving way to information and data, it is only a matter of time before Other people and their cultures become 'models', so many zeros and ones in cyberspace, exotic examples for scholars, voyeurs and other interested parties to load on their machines and look at. Cyberspace is a giant step forward towards museumization of the world: for anything remotely different from Western culture will exist only in digital form."

In a chapter for *The Oxford Handbook of Virtuality* (Champion 2014), I criticized the view that non-Western cultures are not interested in virtual heritage; that is not the case, and there are historical accounts of two Babylonian kings who were archaeologists, Nebuchadnezzar II and Nabonidus (Grassi 2014). Apart from the attack on the West (and a conflation between preserving other cultures and subsuming them), there are indeed serious problems of cultural appropriation, ownership of virtual heritage equipment, data, and overall intellectual property (Skeates 2000). And while it is debatable that the sterility of virtual environments is purely due to Western mindsets, Sardar's overall criticism is valid: meaningful *situated* interaction is missing in virtual world design.

I don't know if Sardar later suggested answers to these challenges, but one possibility is to critique the essence of virtual reality (VR) technology as purely instrumental; it is instrumental insofar as we use it primarily as a form of control. The technical limitations of VR can be thematically incorporated as cultural constraints, myths can become (virtually) physical laws, and differences and debates can be transformed into the conflicting intentions and desires of virtual world characters: homogeneity, immediate usability, familiarity, consistency, and certainty do *not* have to be the goals of digital simulations. An alternative option is to give the tools and techniques to the shareholders themselves so they can fashion their stories for each other. And a third option is to explore how intangible heritage (oral history and so on) can be transmitted with VR (and other) technology.

Virtual environments can be culturally constrained, or they can be multiperspectival; there is no *inherent necessity* for metanarratives or Western-biased viewpoints. Interaction can, in fact, be employed to cause participants to reexamine ideology and question fixed viewpoints. Virtual environments can also be abstracted, challenging, and dynamic. Participants can choose their preferred form of presentation, interface, navigation, feedback, reward system, avatar, narration, and goal. Virtual environments can contain more than objects, and they can do more than offer sensory feedback; they can also force us to be constrained by the social roles and rituals residing in the environment that has been digitally simulated.

Technology can "throw" us into specific situations far beyond the power of museum exhibits. However, the major issue restricting engagement, in the opinion of many people, is suitable contextual interaction (Gillings 2002; Adams 2004). Any technology (such as virtual reality modeling language) or platform (such as Adobe Atmosphere or Google Lively) that does not provide intuitive social interaction soon becomes moribund. And so far, even the commercially successful world-building communities in cyberspace have struggled to afford presence, ritual, and community. There are enthusiastic social groups and displaced clusters that meet online, but their social transactions do not fully happen inside the virtual worlds themselves.

Computer games are not (yet) genuine worlds. Rich social interaction is usually *around* rather than *inside* computer games, and individuals and cultural roles cannot be deciphered from the *traces* of the participants. We can understand and extrapolate more about Mesopotamian tax evaders from five-thousand-year-old tablets than we can from traces left by modern massive multiplayer online role-playing game (RPG) players in giant commercial game worlds such as *World of Warcraft*.

Cultural Transmission

The mind and the body are our interfaces to place; through them, we learn the spatial and platial nature of our culture. But culture is not simply a product; it is a process, and it takes form and space in the real world. Place and culture are inseparably joined; a culture is a form of knowledge framework. We learn through a place, not just about a place.

To give an example of cultural transmission, using a metaphor that both describes itself and probably does not exist, a place is memetic.[2] It is not a meme exactly, but it helps to both store and spread aspects of cultural knowledge and cultural value. A place can be considered an inhabited meme or an inhabited colony of memes.

Places are not so much meme objects as they are meme carriers or meme transmitters. A place is an inhabited meme where the meme is more of a process than a material or a conceptual object. Places are cultural, real-world environments that contain their own paradata and their own building blocks. Virtual worlds' paradata has vanished, with no traces, smears, or smudges arising from construction and use.

Culture is interactive, but as a process, it is missing from virtual places. Culture as a process is also not always evident to the public when visiting real-world cultural heritage sites. For example, Peter Howard (2003, 50) wrote, "Heritage always has been about people, but the challenge today is to make it relevant to a much wider section of people, and that emphasis will not necessarily be on the conservation of concrete objects."

Games as Cultural Places

Cultural learning is a highly interactive process. Despite being instruments, virtual-world tools are not objective and could be realigned to reflect a particularly culturally constrained way of moving, viewing, and acting. Reflecting on specific tools to acquire them as "ready-to-hand" persuades the participant to understand how they are to be used in a culturally performative context.

With better camera tracking and improved physical computing interfaces, participants can indulge in chat, learn by observation and mimicry, or select different versions of history. They might be required to select the culturally appropriate or historically correct objects or appearance to move about the "world" or to trade cultural goods, or to advance social roles over a period of time. Tasks could involve an understanding of local scale, landscape or climate changes, or the need to decipher codices. Game engines can also afford collaborative storytelling (via in-world role-playing and filmmaking through machinima tools).

It is a serious design challenge to blend experiential journeys with historically accurate stage sets, but virtual *cultural* places also require designing rituals that use, are circumscribed by, and help identify place; transit places providing passage between profane and sacred spaces and between social classes and states of mind; some way of conveying ergodic feedback through place; alterity in embodiment; thematic cultural constraints expressed spatially; place as civic space; and ways of accumulating socially meshed affordances through the landscape.

Technology is not necessarily the problem; rather, it is the issue of how digital media can help afford cultural learning and learning via place. Virtual environments can be abstracted, challenging, and dynamic. They can choose their own form of presentation, interface, navigation, narration, and goal. Virtual environments can contain more than objects, and they can do more than offer sensory feedback; they can also force us to be constrained by the social roles and rituals residing in the environment that has been digitally simulated. Perhaps they can also allow more localization and personalization by incorporating more of our own sense of embodiment and more thematically appropriate integration of our own interactive behavior.

Virtual Worlds

World is a vague and misused concept. It is not just space: users navigate through space, but they explore places and their relationship to each other "inside" virtual worlds. Their exploration is thematic, cognitive, and motivated; their interaction directly shapes their experience. A world is not just the collection of a single user's phenomenological experiences. The famous American architect Louis Kahn once defined the city as a place a boy can explore until he knows what he wants to do for the rest of his life. A city is a collection and *intersection* of places, it is a miniature yet engaging collection of life worlds.

Likewise, virtual worlds can involve spatial, historical, counterfactual, or objectively chronological exploration or exploration of a character's potential future or past. A virtual world may require visitors to learn how to translate, disseminate, modify, and create the language and material value systems of real or digitally simulated inhabitants. Participation would hinge on how well culturally appropriate information can be learned and developed by the participant and passed on to others.

The Term Lacks Clarity

Kim Nevelsteen (2015) has decried the lack of clear definitions of virtual worlds and offered one of his own: "a simulated environment where many (one or more) agents can virtually interact with each other, act and react to things, phenomena and the environment; agents can be zero (exactly zero) or many human(s), each represented by many (a virtual self is not required to be unique herein) entities called a 'virtual self' (an avatar), or many software agents; all action/reaction/interaction must happen in a real-time shared spatiotemporal non-pausable virtual environment; the environment may consist of many data spaces, but the collection of data spaces should constitute a shared data space, one (one and only one) persistent shard."

Unfortunately, many seem to believe that merely the addition of others (participants, players) creates a culture. When does a social world become a cultural world? Douglas Thomas and John Seely Brown (2009) seem to have followed this perilous simplification when they quoted, "The embodiment of the player in the form of an avatar has the ability to transform the space of a virtual world into a sense of place. In doing so, it grounds the experience of the player in a sense of presence with others, allowing for, as we have argued earlier, an opportunity to truly engage in the 'play of imagination'" (Brown and Thomas 2007, 147).

Like other writers, they chose metaphors of physical embodiment for actions we don't actually perform when visiting virtual worlds: "The element of imagination that most significantly distinguishes virtual worlds from other online media and communities is our ability to step into them, bringing many of our physical world attitudes, dispositions, and beliefs into the virtual space, while leaving others behind."

Later in the article, Thomas and Brown suggested criteria by which one could talk about culture in virtual worlds: it is "both strange and familiar . . . a space inhabited by others" (with physical distribution of the players' bodies yet a feeling of copresence), but I don't see how these criteria provide "the basis for constructing the world they each inhabit."

For Thomas and Brown, these digital three-dimensional spaces that become places because they are "culturally imagined; the practices of the participants, their actions, conversations, movements, and exchanges come to define the world and continually infuse it with new meanings." Only, they don't clearly show how this happens. "This sense of coordinated interaction with others produces much more than just social interaction or conversation. It allows for a deep sense of presence that is akin to what Michael Polanyi . . . called 'indwelling,' a tacit understanding and construction of the world, people, and practices that define experience and embodiment."

Nowadays virtual worlds have a wide range of applications almost everywhere: organizations, education, entertainment, training, virtual communities, e-commerce, scientific research, etc. There is no unique, widely accepted classification of virtual worlds. Based on Porter's paper (2004), Paul Messinger, Eleni Stroulia, and Kelly Lyons (2008) proposed a set of criteria for establishing a virtual world typology: purpose, place, platform, population, and profit. However, place only means colocation or geographical dispersion and common features of interaction. Their typology allows for persistence of the virtual world, but *not* dynamic cultural interaction.

The vagueness of the term *world* is prevalent throughout even academic literature (Champion 2009). *World* has been used as if it is self-explanatory in scholarly publications (Darken and Sibert 1996; Okada et al. 2001; Celentano and Nodari 2004; Ondrejka 2006). PC Mag (2015) defined a virtual world as "a 3D computer environment in which users are represented on screen as themselves or as made-up characters and interact in real time with other users," but this does not describe a world, only a virtual environment that provides for social interaction.

Definitions of a "virtual world" in recent textbooks (Grimshaw 2014) also seem to focus on the simulation of the real world (particularly social interaction and community identification) but not any cultural practice. Even in his book *Designing Virtual Worlds*, Richard Bartle (2003) avoided a detailed definition of what exactly is a "virtual world" and L. Klastrup (2003) also pointed out how difficult it was to reach a clear definition.

I have previously described experiencing virtual worlds in terms of environmental presence, social presence, and cultural presence (Champion 2009). Society defines who we are, how we communicate, and the values that we strive toward. It is the acceptance or condemnation of other people in a society that separates social behavior from individual habits. Stranded on a desert island, a human who was once part of society would endeavor to live according to his or her social upbringing, perhaps because these behaviors are so fully ingrained, or perhaps in case they hoped to be eventually rescued and reunited with human society.

Quickly bored with automatic feedback mechanisms, humans desire regular but also varied degrees of social affirmation. In computer games, there are reward systems that reflect medals, awards, and social respect, but in single-player computer games, we typically cannot gain the social recognition of others. Deliberately or subconsciously moderating one's external behavior in response or anticipation of the opinions or actions of others while in a computer game is a sign that a game is functioning as a social world. However, without social recognition, a single-player game is less likely to bind the player to social rules or laws, as players do not have social affirmation or condemnation to guide their social behavior. We could also argue that a single-player game is less likely to compel a rich, expansive, and creative experiencing of cultural learning and behavior, as there is no sentient audience to act as cultural arbiters.

Worlds are not only physical and social but also cultural. I have written about this definition before (Champion 2011), but it bears repeating: "Culture consists of patterns, explicit and implicit, of and for behavior acquired and transmitted by symbols, constituting the distinctive achievement of human groups, including their embodiment in artefacts [artifacts]; the essential core of culture consists of traditional (i.e. historically derived and selected) ideas and especially their attached values; culture systems may on the one hand, be considered as products of action, on the other as conditioning elements of further action" (Kroeber and Kluckhohn 1952, 357).

Culture is not simply passive; it is also a storehouse of values, aspirations, and identities. Culture can be viewed as a material embodiment of social structure, mediating the relation between the individual and the community and expressing (as well as protecting) the sacred from the profane. Culture provides instructions on how habits can become intrinsically meaningful and socially ordered through the practice of ritual (Dornan 2007). Rituals and cultural role-playing is curatorial: we choose which aspects of culture are worth keeping and the rest we discard.

In the real world, past inhabitations could have left cultural traces of their "micro-histories" (to paraphrase Ruth Tringham 2015) life worlds in the real world, but is this replicated in virtual worlds? I doubt it. Virtual worlds typically lack the ability to record micro-scale life worlds. For example, many fantasy RPGs portray previous cultures or cultural beliefs, real or imaginary. The games may feature named characters, treasure, three-dimensional objects, goals, and so forth, but they often lack distinctly cultural places, there are few, if any, identifiers of how to behave in another culture and few, if any, identifiers to the passing of unique or specifically imaginable individuals. When roles, group behavior, and places are easily interchangeable, inhabitation may be experienced at a personal level, but it can never be deeply cultural.

Conversely, any premise that visitors require other real people in the virtual environment to feel cultural presence is not, at least in my opinion, necessary. People are needed to create culture but culture can continue to exist in some material form (and to some extent) without the creators. I suggest that we can gain a *sense* of cultural presence without experiencing explicit social presence. To quote J. Agnew (1999, 93), "All people live in cultural worlds that are made and re-made through their everyday activities."

I defined cultural presence as a visitor's overall subjective impression when visiting a virtual environment that people with a different cultural perspective occupy or have occupied as a "place." Such a definition suggests cultural presence is not just a feeling of "being there" but of being in a "there and then," not the cultural rules of the "here and now." Cultural presence, albeit in a weakened form, is possible in the absence of social presence. This is important for designers who wish to convey a sense of past inhabitation, and here place is essential.

However, the sense in which these virtual environments move beyond "cyberspace" toward "place" is not clear to many (Johnson 2005). To edge a virtual world closer to being perceived and remembered as a place rather than as a space, I propose three criteria: it must provide different ways to do things, it must allow for ways to record and memorialize what has been done, and it must provide for social mobility, social competition, and social progression.

1. A virtual world may be viewed as a *possibility space*.[3] The digital environment allows for different ways of *doing* a multitude of things; it is interactively rich and layered, and it has *worldfulness*. For example, Steven Johnson (2005) and Constance Steinkuehler (2006) have argued that current massive multiplayer game environments are often a mixture of vague and clear objectives. In these environments, people immerse themselves, not just spatially by navigating from point A to point B but also existentially by exploring the environment as a shifting world of interactive possibilities. In other words, they navigate not only the physical geography but also the possible experiences.

2. A virtual world of a computer game may involve learning how to translate and disseminate, and the simulation may also modify or create the language or material value systems of real or digitally simulated inhabitants. In this situation, the game play hinges on how well culturally appropriate information can be learned and developed by the player or passed

on to others. I had earlier described this capacity, as *worldfilledness*, to what hermeneutical extent the virtual environment or game can store, display, and retrieve information on the encounters of people in places.

3. A virtual world could afford *worldliness* in terms of its social aspects: the skillful cunning and strategic experience by which players can choose social roles to improve their standing and success in a virtual world. The player may decide (or be compelled) to choose between a range of self-identifying livelihoods and positions that allow them to develop and maintain social skills and status (Herold 2006). In a virtual world that provides for this social role–based competition, the players could be rewarded or punished depending on how well they interact with other players or imitate appropriate social behavior.

I now wish to change these terms; they are clumsy, grating, and not memorable. I confuse and forget both worldfulness and worldfilledness, while worldliness is defined by László Ropolyi (Damer and Hinrichs 2013), although his definition differs from mine. It might be more useful to suggest that a virtual world features and affords platial richness, an engaging collection and intersection of places full of interactive possibilities (worldfulness); hermeneutic richness, a rich source of interpretation and creativity (worldfilledness); and social embeddedness, influential, identify-forming, but potentially flexible social roles (worldliness).

Roles and Cultural Learning[4]

Roles and rituals are essential for creating, situating, and maintaining cultural practices. Computer role-playing games (CRPGs) and virtual online worlds that appear to simulate different cultures are well known and highly popular (Champion 2016). It might appear that the roles and rituals of traditional cultures are easily ported to computer games. However, I contend that the meaning behind worlds, rituals, and roles are not fully explored in these digital games and virtual worlds and more needs to be done to create worldfulness, emotionally moving rituals, and role enrichment.

Role-playing is both an important part of cultural learning (Hallford and Hallford 2001, 231–36) and an important genre in computer games (Tychsen 2006). Roles are intrinsically related to the notion of social worlds, yet the mechanics of this relationship is not clear in the academic literature. There are few grounded theories in computer game studies on how role-playing works in sustaining and augmenting a thematic world. There are few clear descriptions of what "world" means in this context and how roles, worlds, and rituals are interrelated, and distinctions between social and cultural dimensions are seldom discussed in any great detail.

For historical simulations and virtual heritage projects, the cultural and social dimensions of both real-world and virtual-world playing are important, and commercial CRPGs seem to offer more opportunities to support deeper cultural

Figure 8.1 *Assassin's Creed: Origins.* Copyright Ubisoft, 2017. Erik Champion, screenshot.

aspects of role-playing. Can "deeper" notions of culture be conveyed through a deeper understanding of worlds, roles, and rituals?

Computer games can be studied to determine how people learn through interaction, how different types of knowledge can be presented and learned, and how to engage people with digital media. Unfortunately, those games that supposedly present historical content, such as the *Assassin's Creed* series (Ubisoft, 2007–18), are highly successful in terms of entertainment but have been criticized as misleading and impoverished social and cultural worlds (Reparaz 2011; Chapman 2012) even if we can forgive them for historical inaccuracies. Their attraction is at least in part due to their richly detailed yet still engagingly interactive game worlds (fig. 8.1), but the contrast between their ludic quality and their educational value may deter educators from employing games to teach heritage and historical content.

My concern in regards to CRPGs is that the character is too often merely a graphically drawn avatar whose unique relationship to the world can be merely cosmetic. Their role fades into nothingness, as most computer games do not involve genuine role-playing (Tychsen 2006). The missing quality in CRPGs that appears to exist in live role-playing has been observed by Michael Hitchens and Anders Drachen (2008), who proposed that an RPG requires a combination of factors: a (sandboxed) game world ("a role-playing game is a game set in an imaginary world"), participants, characters, a game master, a wide range of interaction, and narrative. As real-world role-playing allows roles to be transfigured, expanded, overtaken, or replaced, so too should virtual RPG worlds also afford these possibilities.

Then what are the features and dimensions of real-world roles and role-playing? Hitchens and Drachen (2008) have already remarked on differences between live role-playing and digital RPGs. If we take a dictionary definition (Dictionary.com n.d.) of roles as "the modifying of a person's behavior to accord with a desired personal image, as to impress others or conform to a particular environment" or as "psychology: The unconscious acting out of a particular role in accordance with the perceived expectations of society" (Lexico.com. 2021), the intersocial dimension of role-playing is more obvious.

I suggest that social roles in our real world do more than distinguish individuals, provide an individual purpose in life, or divide up responsibilities according to capabilities and political acumen. Roles are purposeful and goal-based. They create and demarcate social identities (Fein 2015), but they also have a component of cultural curation (preserving and transmitting elements of social mores and values) while allowing for evolution and personalization.

In *Critical Gaming: Interactive History and Virtual Heritage* (Champion 2015c), I wrote for some length on role-playing. I will just note here the main points. First, RPGs allow people to explore spatially or aesthetically (viewing the elements of the game), strategically (understanding the game system), and psychologically (delving into their own identity, values, or inner conflicts). A virtual world, even one not specifically designed for role-playing, should allow players to explore different roles. Second, a virtual world should be able to adjust according to the way the role is performed and the way it affects other roles. Third, role-playing is curatorial. As I wrote in *Critical Gaming* (Champion 2015c), "we choose which aspects of culture are worth keeping and the rest of the information we discard."

The problem for computer games is we don't know if roles are conducted appropriately and attentively, and this is also problematic for rituals. Rituals are framed by specific places, exacting actions and behaviors, certain times, and select audiences; roles often are too (Kilmer 1977; Roskams et al. 2013). Rituals may allow us to see through the eyes of the original inhabitants or at least feel that this place once belonged to someone else.

One type of framework or event-based system that helps demarcate roles but also displays information about how people can *be moved* (inspired) and *move* beyond (transcend) their current role is the ritual. Rituals are not often described in any great detail in computer game literature, at least not in a way that parallels discussions in anthropology. (Although there are anthropologists who have influenced game studies, the concept of rituals in game studies is not as detailed as in more anthropological fields.) This is particularly significant for RPGs, but even what *role-playing* means is seldom clarified.

This framework is much simpler than but potentially congruent with Mark Wolf's (2014) criteria for imaginary worlds. However, the virtual worlds that I have in mind are not the secondary worlds (imaginary worlds that are separate from our real world), as exemplified by J. R. R. Tolkien's *Lord of the Rings* and discussed by Wolf. *Lord of the Rings* was not only fantasy; it was also reconstituted mythology, a conjectural reassembly of past themes and narratives but with a post–world war allegory. If they are to be more than static models, archaeological

176

Rethinking Virtual Places

simulations must be simulations of the past through present remains, contemporary scholastic imagination, and evidence-based hypotheses. But this is not only a feature of archaeological simulations; it is also a feature of cultural representation in general. Culture is a recollection but also a teleological and conjectural process. These virtual worlds are thus *conjectural* worlds. As they combine historical situations, conflict, social agents, and cultural beliefs, these conjectural worlds require their own ethical dimensions and attention paid to how their story can be told while engaging the player and contextualizing their actions.

Contested Places

Fede Peñate Domínguez claimed the historian does not capture information from raw historical sources but derives information from a process of interpretation and generate a discourse that seeks to explain the events of the past. Neither the Civil War nor Pompeii makes any sense if we do not know why they occurred or the consequences that arose from them. As the past is always framed via the present, Domínguez (2017) concludes "history is very different from the past because, firstly, the sources are partial and incomplete and, on the other hand, it is a past that conforms to the needs and concerns of the present." History is not objective and the writer must both respect the sources and avoid the temptation of claiming this historical account is the only one or completely accurate.

Archaeological and anthropological virtual environments can show the process and systematic differences between our world and another world (of past perception). Imagine putting on a virtual medieval suit of armor. The weight and discomfort would shock most people today. To a knight seven centuries ago it may have been such a badge of honor and a functionally superior life-saving device that it seems to weigh less. Plus, they will have spent years lifting it as a squire and wearing it, so after years of training, they were balls of bone and muscle. Should the simulated weight be the weight you would experience or the weight that a trained knight would experience? I argue it should alternate between both.

Heritage and Care

Genius loci, heritage, and a sense of place seem linked, and caring for the spirit of a place is a vanishing concern but of central importance to heritage. For instance, the ICOMOS Ename Charter (2007) recognized several notions of place: "Cultural Heritage Site refers to a *place*, locality, natural landscape, settlement area, architectural complex, archaeological site, or standing structure that is recognized and often legally protected as a *place* of historical and cultural significance" (emphasis added).

In a virtual heritage environment (VHE), protection can perhaps be taken for granted (as that was the point of the simulation). But who protects the virtual world or the digital world of the computer game? What is missing here is care. While gossip and, conversely, a need for privacy can be seen as elements of successful, rich social virtual worlds, few academics talk about care and talk about care of a specific place. Care requires investment and awareness of local and impending phenomenon (a careful gardener considers soil, weather, pests, *and climate*). Long-term care is not only dedication but also awareness and attention. In the real world, we are quick to note someone who does not care.

In most virtual worlds, there are no mechanisms to care for things, and there are no social mechanisms to view and judge others who do not care enough about their surroundings. This is also a problem with games: the reincarnation of our avatars means we can explore freely and fully, but it also means players risk the digital avatars without thought and don't exhibit or worry about any duty of care.

Presence and Role-Playing

With environmental presence, the individual affects and is affected by the outside world. If there is any social presence then we affect others in a virtual world. If there is cultural presence, we should be able to detect a distinctly situated sense of inhabitation, of social values and behaviors preserved and transmitted through ritual, artifact, and inscription.

Social presence does not necessarily require multiple players (although single-player social presence is much more difficult) and cultural presence does not have to be alive (active). One thing that is required is hermeneutic richness, the depth of interpretation available to self-understanding or understanding others through artifacts and other cultural remains. Here ritual plays an important part, if it does not become too tiresome, if observing and performing it provides in-game benefits, and as long as it does not seem labored or "cheesy."

However, socially enriched roles are also vital; they help us develop our own identity in relation to our society. Long-term development of these roles results in an attitude of care and compassion and installs respect for other people or players in similar positions. Roles also allow us to play out different aspects of our selves; they provide a framework for future plans.

Place and Place Agents

This section is related to a journal article called "Defining Cultural Agents for Virtual Heritage Environments" (Champion 2015a) but focuses instead on explaining the functional relationship between roles and agents, particularly agents that are both pedagogical (Moreno and Mayer 2007) and cultural agents. How do we distinguish between social agents and cultural agents? Can cultural agents meet these specific heritage objectives?

Earlier in this book, I mentioned that proponents of virtual worlds advocated intelligent agents and other avatars to overcome a lack of "life" in online digital worlds but a simple directive to "populate" a virtual environment with intelligent agents masquerading as walk-on characters will not necessarily communicate cultural significance (Bogdanovych et al. 2009). Communicating cultural significance is an objective of VHEs and not necessarily a requirement of all virtual places, but even if it is not a requirement of all virtual environments, providing a way of communicating the individual and shared meaning and significance of a place is likely to be of interest to virtual world designers.

VHEs should, by definition, provide the best example of cultural agents. Despite criticism of virtual heritage projects as being sterile and lifeless, there are various examples of projects that feature intelligent agents. Perhaps the most common examples are of guides (Roussou 2001; Lim, Aylett, and Jones 2005) and route planners (Song et al. 2004; Papagiannakis and Magnenat-Thalmann 2007; Costantini et al. 2008). In other projects, intelligent agents are employed to create a sense of inhabitation and enact crowd simulations (Bogdanovych et al. 2009; Lim et al. 2013; Sequeira and Morgado 2013; Sequeira, Morgado, and Pires 2014). However, they are not cultural agents.

More sophisticated examples exist, such as belief-desire-intention agents that perform social roles, as in the City of Uruk project (Bogdanovych, Ijaz, and Simoff 2012). There are storytelling agents (Ibanez, Aylett, and Ruiz-Rodarte 2003) and virtual augmented characters who reenact dramatic events. In other examples, agents are employed to create a sense of inhabitation and enact crowd simulations. In a few of these examples, such as the Roma Nova project, agents are employed to improve learning about historical simulations (Vourvopoulos, Liarokapis, and Petridis 2012).

One major distinction between VHEs and computer games is that the latter typically place more emphasis on challenge and competition than on expressive intelligent agents. There are sophisticated commercial games where agents as NPCs (nonplaying characters) are used, but these are few. For example, in the commercial game *Elder Scrolls V: Skyrim* (Champion 2015b), NPCs can complete requests from players, such as carry or find specific objects, and provide limited social feedback on the player's action back to the player.

In most virtual heritage projects, intelligent agents are primarily used as guides (Bogdanovych et al. 2009), leading players to important landmarks, or they are specifically historical guides (perhaps even revealing past events and situationally appropriate behavior). This is particularly important for larger environments or where navigation (orientating and wayfinding) is difficult, as intelligent agents can provide a sense of scale and inhabitation. However, these intelligent agents are usually designed for limited forms of conversation and typically help convey social presence rather than cultural presence.

When digitally simulated sites require a sense of inhabited place, engaging narrative-related elements, or embodiment, the field of virtual heritage should develop and test the following concept of cultural agents who help provide a sense of cultural presence. A cultural agent recognizes, adds to, or transmits physically embedded and embodied aspects of culture. Either the cultural agents interpret cultural cues, or their interaction with the human visitor/player leads to a situated interpretation of cultural cues and wider cultural frameworks. These cues could be contested or contradictory or even fragmented, but they are required to convey a situated understanding of resources, monuments, environmental events, and behaviors in a way that both engages and educates participants.

Cultural agents are not merely conversational agents, for they should be able to

1. Automatically select correct cultural behaviors given specific events or situations;
2. Recognize/correct cultural behaviors given specific events, locations, or situations;
3. Transmit cultural knowledge; and
4. Modify, create, or command artifacts that become cultural knowledge.

To fulfill these features as criteria, cultural agents are culturally constrained. They are not just socially constrained; they are dependent on role, space, and time. They can understand and point out right from wrong in terms of culturally specific behavior, and they understand the history and possibly also the future trajectory of specific cultural movements. We could distinguish at least three types of cultural agents: agents as impostors; agents acting in culturally staged settings; and agents who can influence aspects of history.

Imagine the aim is to convey cultural knowledge through an impostor-style game where the player has to adapt, steal, or change (via a spell) their appearance and attempt to infiltrate a local community through effectively imitating certain professions, races, or individuals. The player must disguise himself or herself as an NPC or take over an NPC's role in society and see how long he or she can escape detection. Unfortunately, most contemporary games and virtual environments do not clearly and consistently distinguish between NPCs in terms of race, locality, profession, or voice, and it would require more spatial awareness to allow for a rich role-playing experience.

The second option is that the agents are only social agents, but situations could be "staged" in such a way that their behaviors and detection techniques are triggered, affected, and modified by culturally specific events and settings. A similar scenario is played out in the *SpyParty* game ("SpyParty" n.d.) in which a sniper is situated outside a party with a single bullet and inside is a spy among a crowd of partygoers. The goal is to detect the spy and shoot that player or convince the sniper to shoot someone else; therefore, while it does involve aspects of mimesis, it is a social scene, not a cultural one.

A third scenario suggested here is providing cultural learning by directing or otherwise persuading cultural agents to perform certain actions that affect and modify historical events. Cultural artifacts could also be collected and used to train agents. By opening in-world books to specific pages, certain events or other forms of knowledge could be communicated to the NPCs. Some existing moddable games (such as *Elder Scrolls V: Skyrim*) have more NPC options, including the ability to collect followers. One great benefit of incorporating the training of NPCs by players is that an external person can judge how effectively a player has learned the content by how accurately he or she conveys information in the training of NPCs (learning by teaching).

Agents could be persuaded according to the correct timing and information provided by the human player. Like the second scenario, this puts more responsibility on the human player to observe, experiment, and act according to local customs and beliefs. For a very complicated simulation, perhaps the detection of appropriate, correct, or logically reasonable decisions in history require human experts, or perhaps agents can incorporate some form of distributed historical consciousness that allows them to predict the historical likelihood or cultural authenticity of human player decisions.

In all three of these scenarios, the human player becomes an active participant, a social actor who is culturally constrained and to some extent socially judged by the cultural agents. As the human participant becomes focused on achieving the appropriate task, and as some form of narrative or game play depends on the responses of the cultural agents, these scenarios differ from environments where the human player merely observes the behaviors of artificial characters (intelligent agents). And this may also mean the agents' apparent authenticity and ability to engage the human players is easier to achieve.

Summary

Virtual worlds should be more than virtual places (for example, how virtual places connect is an aspect of the world rather than just the place), but they share common features; they are more than spaces, but they are still missing culture as a process rather than as a product. Culture is not just the social. It is not only knowledge handed down from generation to generation; its boundaries and visions are made manifest, in material and immaterial form. Culture is somehow transmitted; how, we are not yet sure.

Ritual-making is also an underresearched area of investigation, and I have suggested three components of role-play that need to be incorporated into a rich RPG as well as three aspects of virtual worlds that may help enhance role-playing:

- A virtual world should enable freedom of choice and individuality but also a complex fate. An important part of role-playing is role selection and a world rich in such affordances would allow a multitude of possible paths.
- A virtual world allows its inhabitants to act as curators of tradition, for role-playing allows society to carry forward its goals, values, structure, and messages.
- A virtual world has the capacity to afford the social jockeying of position as roles are socially defined, shifting, and often challenged by other social agents.

I mentioned the terms *worldfulness, worldfilledness,* and *worldliness* are clumsy and difficult to remember. A clearer way of expressing this might be to say that a world needs to have elastic mutability; it needs memetic but entropic ways of communication and memorialization, and it must have malleable but impactful modes of social identity and responsibility.

1. Elastic mutability: every action and interaction ripples through the environment as part of a physical ecosystem.
2. Memetic and entropic cultural communication: communication and individual agency are corrupted and fade, erode, or dissolve (individual actions become social records).
3. Malleable but impactful modes of social identity and responsibility: roles and rituals affect people and in turn, the way we enact and represent and transform them affects how we see each other in relation to our society.

I also suggested three dimensions of presence that all help virtual worlds afford a sense of role-playing. These are physical presence, environmental presence, and cultural presence. Unfortunately, RPGs are not fully developed cultural worlds; players do not hermeneutically interpret the virtual world, nor are their actions hermeneutically interpreted. One may argue the limitations that I discussed are the inevitable consequences of single-player computer games. I counter that CRPGs could be further developed as both social and cultural worlds, and I provided some design ideas to help us improve these CRPGs.

Cultural presence, world, place, and interaction are all interrelated in the real world; it is up to designers to interpret and transfer their power and potential to virtual environments. In doing so, we should be more critical of the superficial use and application of these key terms for they are critically important. VHEs have special needs that create more criteria than those required by mainstream digital environments (Tost and Champion 2007); while too many cultural virtual places have not communicated the significance and value of the heritage content, due to their focus on perfecting technology per se. In their attempt to create more engagement, virtual environment researchers and designers have conflated social presence with cultural presence (Flynn 2007; Champion 2011).

A solution is to reconsider the role of rituals and develop agents who help interpret cultural cues and transmit to the human participant a sense of situated cultural presence and awareness through place- and time-specific interaction of the local cultural significance of the simulated sites, artifacts, and events. Such agents would be cultural agents, not merely social agents, as they would convey accumulated and place-specific cultural knowledge that would outlast or extend beyond their own individual "lives."

Another problem is our understanding of the potential of virtual worlds. As a concept, virtual worlds are not something new (Munoz and Chalegre 2012). They already existed long before *Second Life,* and even before the first computers, they existed in literature. Despite their long history, I have not found a great deal of recent literature about *place* in virtual worlds (apart from place defined as locating things). Nor, in the abstract world of theory, have I found much of direct use in the design and understanding of place in virtual worlds.

I have found more interesting information in discussion revolving around computer games, for games are fundamentally concerned with challenging but engaging interaction. And both place and culture are fundamentally interactive mediums. Computer games are not always cultural places, but they reveal interaction that can help understanding about culture as a process.

While virtual worlds are more than past definitions, they have a culture, not just an algorithm, unfortunately, that culture is typically outside the virtual world. In general, virtual worlds aren't greatly inspiring in terms of interaction, their designers are more concerned about numbers, and the problem of culture isn't directly addressed. I suggest this is a mistake.

Notes

1. I am fascinated and intrigued by how archaeologists can separate understanding of a culture as opposed to an individual artist from an artwork. How could this play out with the future uncovering of past virtual worlds?

2. A meme is a popular self-serving cultural concept with no single owner, a cognitive equivalent to Richard Dawkin's description of the "selfish gene." See Aunger (2000, 2001).

3. I had earlier described this as *worldfilledness*; however, the term is too clumsy and easy to forget!

4. For more details, refer Champion (2016).

References

Adams, Ernest. 2004. "The Philosophical Roots of Computer Game Design." Accessed April 28, 2021. http://www.designersnotebook.com/Lectures/Roots/roots.htm.

Addison, Alonzo C. 2001. "Virtual Heritage: Technology in the Service of Culture." Paper presented at the Proceedings of the 2001 Conference on Virtual Reality, Archeology, and Cultural Heritage, Athens, Greece, 2001.

———. 2008. "The Vanishing Virtual: Safeguarding Heritage's Endangered Digital Record." In *New Heritage: New Media and Cultural Heritage*, edited by Yehuda Kalay, Thomas Kvan and Janice Affleck, 27–39. Oxford: Routledge.

Agnew, J. 1999. "Place and Politics in Post-war Italy." In *Cultural Geographies*, edited by K. Anderson and F. Gale, 71–93. South Melbourne: Addison Wesley.

Aunger, Robert. 2000. *The Status of Memetics as a Science*. New York: Oxford University Press

———. 2001. *Darwinizing Culture: The Status of Memetics as a Science*. Oxford: Oxford University Press.

Bartle, Richard. 2003. *Designing Virtual Worlds*. Indianapolis: New Riders.

Bogdanovych, Anton, Kiran Ijaz, and Simeon Simoff. 2012. "The City of Uruk: Teaching Ancient History in a Virtual World." Paper presented at the Intelligent Virtual Agents Twelfth International Conference, Santa Cruz, CA, September 12–14, 2012.

Bogdanovych, Anton, Juan A. Rodriguez-Aguilar, Simeon Simoff, and Alex Cohen. 2009. "Virtual Agents and 3D Virtual Worlds for Preserving and Simulating Cultures." Paper presented at the Intelligent Virtual Agents, Eleventh International Conference, IVA 2011, Reykjavik, Iceland, September 15–17, 2009.

———. 2010. "Authentic Interactive Reenactment of Cultural Heritage with 3D Virtual Worlds and Artificial Intelligence." *Applied Artificial Intelligence* 24 (6): 617–47.

Brown, John Seely, and Douglas Thomas. 2007. "The Play of Imagination: Beyond the Literary Mind." *Games and Culture* 2:149–72.

Celentano, A., and M. Nodari. 2004. "Adaptive Interaction in Web3d Virtual Worlds." In *Web3d '04: Proceedings of the Ninth International Conference on 3d Web Technology*, edited by Don Brutzman, 41–50. New York: ACM.

Champion, Erik. 2009. "Roles and Worlds in the Hybrid Game of Oblivion." *International Journal of Role-Playing* 1 (1): 37–52.

———. 2011. *Playing with the Past*. London: Springer.

———. 2014. "History and Cultural Heritage in Virtual Environments." In *The Oxford Handbook of Virtuality*, edited by Mark Grimshaw, 269–83. Oxford: Oxford University Press.

———. 2015a. "Defining Cultural Agents for Virtual Heritage Environments." Special issue on "Immersive and Living Virtual Heritage: Agents and Enhanced Environments," *Presence: Teleoperators and Virtual Environments* 24 (3): 179–86. http://www .mitpressjournals.org/toc/pres/24/3.

———. 2015b. "Roleplaying and Rituals for Heritage-Oriented Games." Paper presented at the 2015 DiGRA Digital Games Research Conference, Lüneburg, May 14–17, 2015.

———2015c. *Critical Gaming: Interactive History and Virtual Heritage*. Surrey, UK: Ashgate.

———. 2016. "Worldfulness, Role-Enrichment & Moving Rituals: Design Ideas for CRPGs." *Transactions of the Digital Games Research Association* 2 (3): 1–27.

Chapman, Adam. 2012. "Privileging Form over Content: Analysing Historical Videogames." *Journal of Digital Humanities* 1 (2): 1–2.

Claidière, Nicolas, Kenny Smith, Simon Kirby, and Joël Fagot. 2014. "Cultural Eevolution of Systematically Structured Behaviour in a Non-human Primate." *Proceedings of the Royal Society of London B: Biological Sciences* 281 (1797): 1–9.

Costantini, Stefania, Leonardo Mostarda, Arianna Tocchio, and Panagiota Tsintza. 2008. "DALICA: Agent-Based Ambient Intelligence for Cultural-Heritage Scenarios." *Intelligent Systems, IEEE* 23 (2): 34–41.

Crang, Mike. 1998. *Cultural Geography*. London: Routledge.

Damer, Bruce, and Randy Hinrichs. 2013. "The Virtuality and Reality of Avatar Cyberspace." In *The Oxford Handbook of Virtuality*, edited by Mark Grimshaw, 17–41. Oxford: Oxford University Press.

Darken, R. P., and J. L. Sibert. 1996. "Wayfinding Strategies and Behaviors in Large Virtual Worlds." In *Proceedings of the Sigchi Conference on Human Factors in Computing Systems: Common Ground*, 142–49. Vancouver: ACM.

Dictionary.com. n.d. "Role-playing." In *Dictionary.com*. Random House, Inc.

Domínguez, Fede Peñate. 2017. "La verosimilitud de la Historia en el videojuego histórico." *Presura* (blog), March 21, 2017. Accessed July 11, 2020. http://www.presura.es/2017/03 /21/la-verosimilitud-videojuego-historico/.

Dornan, J. 2007. "Us Being Human." *TerraNova* (blog). Last Modified July 22, 2007. Accessed April 27, 2021. http://terranova.blogs.com/terra_nova/2007/02/us_being_human .html#more.

Ename Charter. 2007. *The ICOMOS Charter for the Interpretation and Presentation of Cultural Heritage Sites*. ENAME (Quebec). https://www.icomos.org/charters/interpretation _e.pdf.

Fein, Elizabeth. 2015. "Making Meaningful Worlds: Role-Playing Subcultures and the Autism Spectrum." *Culture, Medicine, and Psychiatry* 39:299–321. https://doi.org/10.1007/s11013-015-9443-x.

Fischer, Michael D. 2006. "Cultural Agents: A Community of Minds." In *Engineering Societies in the Agents World VI*, 259–274. Berlin: Springer.E

Flynn, Bernadette Mary. 2007. "Digital Knowledge as Archaeological Spatial Praxis." Paper presented at the Online Proceedings of the13th International Conference on Virtual Systems and Multimedia: Exchange and experience in space and place, Brisbane, September 23–26, 2007.

Gadamer, H.-G. 1976. *Philosophical Hermeneutics*. Berkeley: University of California Press.

Gillings, M. 2002. "Virtual Archaeologies and the Hyper-Real." In *Virtual Reality in Geography*, edited by P. Fisher and D. Unwin, 17–32. London: Taylor & Francis.

Grassi, Giulia Francesca. 2014. "Nabonidus, King of Babylon." *Middle East-Topics & Arguments* 3:125–35.

Grimshaw, Mark, ed. 2014. *The Oxford Handbook of Virtuality*. Oxford: Oxford University Press.

Hallford, N., and J. Hallford. 2001. *Swords & Circuitry: A Designer's Guide to Computer Role Playing Games*. Roseville, CA: Prima Tech.

Herold, Charles. 2006. "So Many Rackets, So Little Time." *New York Times*, April 20, 2006. Last Modified July 22, 2007. Accessed May 15, 2020. http://www.nytimes.com/2006/04/20/technology/20game.html?ex=1185076800&en=82f426956ef91ac1&ei=5070.

Hitchens, Michael, and Anders Drachen. 2008. "The Many Faces of Role-Playing Games." *International Journal of Role-Playing* 1 (1): 3–21.

Howard, Peter. 2003. *Heritage: Management, Interpretation, Identity*. London: Continuum.

Ibanez, Jesús, Ruth Aylett, and Rocio Ruiz-Rodarte. 2003. "Storytelling in Virtual Environments from a Virtual Guide Perspective." *Virtual Reality* 7 (1): 30–42.

Jackson, Linda A., Yong Zhao, Edward A. Witt, Hiram E. Fitzgerald, and Alexander von Eye. 2009. "Gender, Race and Morality in the Virtual World and Its Relationship to Morality in the Real World." *Sex Roles* 60: 859–69. https://doi.org/10.1007/s11199-009-9589-5.

Jacobson, Jeffrey, and Lynn Holden. 2007. "Virtual Heritage." *Techné: Research in Philosophy and Technology* 10 (3): 55–61.

Johnson, Steven. 2005. *Everything Bad Is Good for You: How Popular Culture Is Making Us Smarter*. London: Allen Lane.

Kilmer, Scott. 1977. "Sport as Ritual: A Theoretical Approach." In *The Study of Play: Problems and Prospects; Proceedings of the First Annual Meeting of the Association for the Anthropological Study of Play*, edited by David F. Lancy and B. Allan Tindall, 44–49. New York: Leisure Press.

Klastrup, Lisbeth. 2003. "A Poetics of Virtual Worlds." In *Digital Arts and Culture Conference*, edited by Adrian Miles, 100–109. Melbourne: RMIT.

Kolko, Beth E., Lisa Nakamura, and Gilbert B. Rodman, eds. 2000. *Race in Cyberspace*. New York: Routledge.

Kroeber, A., and C. Kluckhohn. 1952. *Culture: A Critical Review of Concepts and Definitions*. New York: Vintage Books.

Leddy, Tom. 2013. "Aesthetics Today." *Aesthetics Today* (blog), September 4, 2013. Accessed April 29, 2021. http://aestheticstoday.blogspot.com.au/2013/09/is-there-asthetics-of-ruins.html.

Lexico.com. 2021. "Role Playing." Oxford University Press. Accessed April 29, 2021. https://www.lexico.com/definition/role_playing.

Lim, Chen-Kim, Marie-Paule Cani, Quentin Galvane, Julien Pettre, and Talib Abdullah Zawawi. 2013. "Simulation of Past Life: Controlling Agent Behaviors from the Interactions between Ethnic Groups." Paper presented at the Digital Heritage International Congress 2013, Marseille, October 28–November 1, 2013.

Lim, Mei Yii, Ruth Aylett, and Christian Martyn Jones. 2005. "Affective Guide with Attitude." In *First International Conference, ACII 2005, Beijing, China, October 22–24, 2005, Proceedings*, edited by Jinahua Tan, Tieniu Tan and Rosalind Picard, In Lecture Notes in Computer Science, 772–79. Berlin: Springer.

Malpas, Jeff. 2008. "Cultural Heritage in the Age of New Media." In *New Heritage: New Media and Cultural Heritage*, edited by Yehuda Kalay, Thomas Kvan, and Janice Affleck, 13–26. Oxford: Routledge.

Messinger, Paul R., Eleni Stroulia, and Kelly Lyons. 2008. "A Typology of Virtual Worlds: Historical Overview and Future directions." *Journal for Virtual Worlds Research* 1 (1): 1–18. https://doi.org/10.4101/jvwr.v1i1.291.

Moreno, Roxana, and Richard Mayer. 2007. "Interactive Multimodal Learning Environments." Special issue on Interactive Learning Environments: Contemporary Issues and Trends, *Educational Psychology Review* 19 (3): 309–26. https://doi.org/10.1007/s10648-007-9047-2.

Munoz, R., and V. Chalegre. 2012. "Defining Virtual Worlds Usability Heuristics." In *2012 Ninth International Conference on Information Technology - New Generations*, 690–695. https://doi.org/10.1109/ITNG.2012.138.

Nakamura, Lisa. 2008. "Neoliberal Space and Race in Virtual Worlds." *The Velvet Light Trap* 62:72–73. https://doi.org/10.1353/vlt.0.0016.

Nevelsteen, Kim J. L. 2015. "Virtual World, a Definition Incorporating Distributed Computing and Instances." In *Encyclopedia of Computer Graphics and Games*, edited by Newton Lee, 1–11. Cham: Springer International Publishing.

Okada, M., H. Tarumi, Yoshimura T. Tetsuhiko, and Moriya. K. 2001. "Collaborative Environmental Education Using Distributed Virtual Environment Accessible from Real and Virtual Worlds." *SIGAPP Applied Computing Review* 9 (1): 15–21. http://doi.Acm.Org/10.1145/570142.570147.

Ondrejka, Cory. 2006. "Finding Common Ground in New Worlds." *Games and Culture* 1 (1): 111–15. http://gac.sagepub.com/cgi/reprint/1/1/111.

Papagiannakis, G., and N. Magnenat-Thalmann. 2007. "Mobile Augmented Heritage: Enabling Human Life in Ancient Pompeii." *International Journal of Architectural Computing* 5 (2): 396–415.

PC Mag. 2015. "Encyclopedia: Virtual World." Accessed December 30, 2019. http://www.pcmag.com/encyclopedia/term/59269/virtual-world.

Porter, Constance Elise. 2004. "A Typology of Virtual Communities: A Multi-Disciplinary Foundation for Future Research." Journal of Computer-Mediated Communication 10 (1). https://doi.org/10.1111/j.1083-6101.2004.tb00228.x.

Reparaz, Mikel. 2011. "The Top 7… Historically Inaccurate Historical Games." *Gamesradar* 2015 (22 January). Accessed January 22, 2015. http://www.gamesradar.com/top-7-historically-inaccurate-historical-games/.

Riva, G., G. Castelnuovo, A. Gaggioli, and F. Mantovani. 2002. "Towards a Cultural Approach to Presence." Paper presented at the Proceedings of the Fifth Annual International Workshop PRESENCE, Porto Portugal, October 9–11, 2002.

Riva, Giuseppe, and Giuseppe Mantovani. 2000. "The Need for a Socio-cultural Perspective in the Implementation of Virtual Environments." *Virtual Reality* 5 (1): 32–38.

Rizzo, Ilde, and Anna Mignosa. 2013. *Handbook on the Economics of Cultural Heritage.* Cheltenham, PA: Edward Elgar.

Roskams, Steve, Cath Neal, Jane Richardson, and Ruth Leary. 2013. "A Late Roman Well at Heslington East, York: Ritual or Routine Practices?" *Internet Archaeology* 34 (34). https://doi.org/10.11141/ia.34.5.

Roussou, Maria. 2001. "The Interplay between Form, Story, and History: The Use of Narrative in Cultural and Educational Virtual Reality." Paper presented at Virtual Storytelling Using Virtual Reality Technologies for Storytelling, Avignon, September 27–28, 2001.

Sardar, Z. 1996. "alt.civilizations.faq: Cyberspace as the Darker Side of the West." In *Cyberfutures: Culture and Politics on the Information Superhighway*, edited by Z. Sardar and J. Ravetz, 14–41. London: Pluto Press.

Sequeira, Luís Miguel, and Leonel Caseiro Morgado. 2013. "Virtual Archaeology in Second Life and Opensimulator." *Journal for Virtual Worlds Research* 6 (1). https://doi.org/10.4101/jvwr.v6i1.7047.

Sequeira, Luís Miguel, Leonel Morgado, and E. J. Pires. 2014. "Simplifying Crowd Automation in the Virtual Laboratory of Archaeology." *Procedia Technology* 13:56–65.

Skeates, R. 2000. *Debating the Archaeological Heritage.* London: Duckworth.

Song, M., T. Elias, I. Martinovic, W. Mueller-Wittig, and T. K-Y. Chan. 2004. "Digital Heritage Application as an Edutainment Tool." Paper presented at the International Conference on Virtual Reality Continuum and Its Applications in Industry (2004 ACM SIGGRAPH), Singapore, June 18–18, 2004.

"Spyparty." n.d. Accessed April 28, 2021. http://www.spyparty.com/.

Steinkuehler, Constance A. 2006. "Why Game (Culture) Studies Now?" *Games and Culture* 1 (1): 97–102. https://doi.org/10.1177/1555412005281911.

Suzuki, H. 1997. Introduction to *The Virtual Architecture: The Difference between the Possible and the Impossible*, edited by Ken Sakamura and Hiroyuki hen Suzuki. Tokyo: Yonsei University.

Thomas, Douglas, and John Seely Brown. 2009. "Why Virtual Worlds Can Matter." *International Journal of Learning and Media* 1 (1): 37–49. https://doi.org/10.1162/ijlm.2009.0008.

Tost, Laia Pujol, and Erik Malcolm Champion. 2007. "A Critical Examination of Presence Applied to Cultural Heritage." Paper presented at the Tenth Annual International Workshop on Presence, Barcelona, Spain, October 25–27, 2010.

Tringham, Ruth. 2015. "Creating Narratives of the Past as Recombinant Histories." In *Subjects and Narratives in Archaeology*, edited by Ruth M. Van Dyke and Reinhard Bernbeck, 227–54. Boulder: University Press of Colorado.

Tychsen, Anders. 2006. "Role Playing Games: Comparative Analysis across Two Media Platforms." Proceedings of the Third Australasian Conference on Interactive Entertainment (IE '06), Perth, ACM Press, December 4–6, 2006.

UNESCO. 2015a. "Cultural Landscapes." UNESCO. Accessed July 12, 2020. http://whc.unesco.org/en/culturallandscape/.

———. 2015b. "Text of the Convention for the Safeguarding of the Intangible Cultural Heritage." Accessed July 12, 2020. http://www.unesco.org/culture/ich/index.php?lg=en&pg=00006.

UPF (Universitat Pompeu Fabra) Barcelona. n.d. "[LEAP] LEarning of Archaeology through Presence." UPF. Accessed July 15 2020. https://www.upf.edu/leap/.

Vale, Gillian L., Emma G. Flynn, and Rachel L. Kendal. 2012. "Cumulative Culture and Future Thinking: Is Mental Time Travel a Prerequisite to Cumulative Cultural Evolution?" *Learning and Motivation* 43 (4): 220–30.

v-must: Virtual Museum Transnational Network. 2011. "Cultural Presence." v-must-Virtual Museum Transnational Network. Last Modified 2011. Accessed April 29, 2021. http://www.v-must.net/virtual-museums/glossary/cultural-presence.

Vourvopoulos, Athanasios, Fotis Liarokapis, and Panagiotis Petridis. 2012. "Brain-Controlled Serious Games for Cultural Heritage." Paper presented at the Eighteenth International Conference on Virtual Systems and Multimedia (VSMM), Milan, September 2–5, 2012.

Waddell, T. Franklin, James D. Ivory, Rommelyn Conde, Courtney Long, and Rachel McDonnell. 2014. "White Man's Virtual World: A Systematic Content Analysis of Gender and Race in Massively Multiplayer Online Games." *Journal of Virtual Worlds Research* 7 (2). https://doi.org/10.4101/jvwr.v7i2.7096.

Wolf, Mark J. P. 2014. *Building Imaginary Worlds: The Theory and History of Subcreation.* Hoboken, NJ: Taylor and Francis.

chapter nine

EVALUATING SENSE OF PLACE, VIRTUAL PLACES, AND VIRTUAL WORLDS

Introduction: What Do We Want?

What do we want to show using digital technology, for what purpose, and for which audience? How will we know when we have succeeded? Throughout my research career, I have suggested that rather than concentrate on the technology first, content experts should focus on articulating the problems, ideal solutions, and the expected audience. Technology experts would create far better solutions if they had a clearer idea of what is required, what is needed, and what sort of evidence is required to show the application does the job it is meant to.

In the preceding chapters, I have argued that the generic definitions of place and place criteria for virtual environments that both I and others have described in the past, is ready for revision. The scale, scope, and potential of virtual reality has changed focus, research into both the mind and body has changed some of our preconceptions. The scope for exploring exciting new interactive virtual places has exploded with emerging displays, new computer peripherals, more robust and pleasing design technologies, and new markets more open to game-like interaction. More sustained thinking on the components, techniques, and impacts of game design has created new fuel for thinking about the design of virtual places. All this while educational courses based around online environments, blended environments, and virtual environments have been called into question. Yet still, there is the vague, fuzzy, and puzzling notion of the "sense of place." How can it be evaluated? Is "sense of place" meaningful and relevant to the discussion?

Perhaps the designer only wishes to communicate or otherwise highlight certain decorative features or impressive spatial attributes or evaluate the effect of participation in the virtual place with certain activities, based on user preference or task performance. Perhaps their overall aim is to encourage a certain activity, preserve a place in digital form, or capture the essence of a place through digital simulation. Yet how can we evaluate interaction in a place if we don't know what *place* means?

Solutions Looking for Problems

In the original 2004 version of *3D User Interfaces Theory and Practice*, Doug Bowman and colleagues argued that extrapolating guidelines from the two-dimensional world of human-computer interaction (HCI) heuristics to virtual environments may obscure the distinctive characteristics of virtual environments. They wrote, "3D UIs are still often a 'solution looking for a problem.' Because of this, the target user population or interaction technique to be evaluated may not be known or well understood. . . . Presence is another example of a measure often required in VE evaluations that has no analogue in traditional UI evaluation" (2004, 363).

This book was completed sixteen years after the first edition of the afore-mentioned book, and there are still calls for improved and standardized evaluation methods; however, now the calls are for specialized subfields, such as augmented reality (Radu 2014; Billinghurst, Clark, and Lee 2015) and gesture-based games (Simor et al. 2016). In 2017, *3D User Interfaces Theory and Practice* was published as a second edition, with a new statement on the cover: "An essential guide for anyone developing interfaces for Virtual and Augmented Reality gaming experiences." The explosion of virtual and augmented reality (VR and AR) technology and content is a boon and a challenge for usability, usefulness, and performance studies, but will the swiftly changing devices, creation tools, and platforms allow us to design and share useful, effective and robust tools and methods of evaluation?

For most HCI research is geared toward the two dimensional. Despite the recent proliferation in three-dimensional usability publications, we lack significant and applicable evaluation of virtual places per se or even research on virtual worlds beyond their sociability characteristics. For example, in "The Scientific Research Potential of Virtual World," William Bainbridge (2007) suggested that virtual worlds had great promise in "observational ethnography, and quantitative analysis of economic markets or social networks." Yet research on target groups with specific needs, such as the elderly (Cook and Winkler 2016), lacks suitable evaluation methods or background research, and there is also a gap between the development of virtual environments and suitable learning activities and tasks (Minocha and Hardy 2016). Where are the methods for evaluating virtual places for specific audiences? Or are virtual places and virtual worlds merely graphically pleasant social networks?

Despite their potential, there are several recurring problems or simplifications in the study and evaluation of virtual places. For example, before we even get to the issue of how to evaluate a virtual place, we need to have a grasp of the definition and the parameters of its meaning.

Virtual Learning Environments Are Not Worlds

Pierre Dillenbourg, Daniel Schneider, and Paraskevi Synteta (2002) reviewed the concept of virtual learning environments (VLEs). They suggested defining parameters and stated their potential contribution to learning if certain risks are avoided. Their requirements for a VLE included that it is a "designed information space," a social space (where educational interactions occur in the environment, "turning spaces into places"), an explicitly represented space (but can be two-dimensional text or three dimensional), and a space where students are "not only active but also actors: they co-construct the virtual space."

As I wrote earlier, I am not convinced virtual worlds can be text-only, nor am I convinced that I understand from this publication how space is turned into places, there is little detail to explain how it is or could be done. Dillenbourg, Schneider, and Synteta did stress the importance of the participants being actors and coconstructing the space. However, how do virtual environments, or VLEs differ from virtual places? Are actor-active, coconstructed spaces merely desirable features for VLEs, not essential features?

Third Places and Sociability Not Enough

Leveraging Ray Oldenburg's notion of "third places," places in which sociable association tend to take place, Nicolas Ducheneaut, Robert J. Moore, and Eric Nickell (2007) explored the sociability ("the sheer pleasure of the company of others") of the massively multiplayer online game (MMOG) *Star Wars Galaxies* (*SWG*). Their paper concludes that real-world architecture when copied slavishly can adversely affect sociability and that while the appearance of social space in, say, the *SWG* cantina may depict relaxation and informality, it does not help and, in fact, hinders sociability in games. Its location and setting are at odds with where players would want to socialize, and the three-dimensional depiction of an informal place in no way prevents businesslike activities from being forced on locals. The digital simulation does not provide for localization and personalization (Ducheneaut, Moore and Nickell 2007, 158): "Yet for all its visual richness, the cantina remains a surprisingly impoverished communication space. Indeed, the entire building is managed as a single conversational space: any utterance typed in the 'spatial' channel can be heard by anyone in the cantina, whether they are at the bar, in one [of the] side alcoves, or in the offices at the back."

The authors have hit on an important gap in the evaluation of sociable online spaces without realizing it: social spaces are important but not as important as the community spaces. For instance, they noted (2007, 131), "Game designers want to promote interactions among their players since they recognize that these encounters are essential to the success of their virtual worlds: in the words of one player, 'it's the people that are addictive, not the game.'"

As Ducheneaut, Moore, and Nickell observed, MMOG players are not just competitive; many of them enjoy shared experiences and the collaborative nature of many activities, "and, most importantly, the reward of being socialized into a community of gamers and acquiring a reputation within it" (2007, 131).

We can agree that "multiplayer games heavily rely on space (virtual space, but space nonetheless) to create and maintain a sense of community among their players" (Ducheneaut, Moore, and Nickell 2007, 131), but space itself is not place, because the sense of community does not constantly change the virtual space. This sense of community may be helped by the sensation of social presence, but the space is not persistently a community place; the community hovers around it and is not embedded in the activity itself.

Proposed Distinctions between Virtual Environments, Places, Worlds

Virtual environments are often seen as being equivalent to virtual worlds, but some writers have added necessary criteria for the latter, such as they must have multiple players, avatars, and persistence (the environment will still be there if you return to it some days later). However, some still see virtual worlds as only mimetic representations of real-world places. In her doctoral dissertation in geography, Susan Bergeron (Bergeron, 2011, 107) wrote:

> Despite optimism that experiencing place through a spatial experience engine is potentially very rewarding, further research is clearly necessary in order to assess the effectiveness of the system in specific domain areas.
>
> We can use the term "virtual world" to describe an electronic environment that visually mimics complex physical spaces, where people can interact with each other and with virtual objects, and where people are represented by animated characters.

Are virtual worlds merely representational simulations of real-world locations? Here *virtual world* seems to mean a digital environment that mimics a part of the real world. Or are virtual worlds "communit[ies] of choice" (Hill et al. 1995)? Both definitions do not fully address the potential of virtual worlds. Bergeron's notion only describes a digital space with social communication; Hill's description does not clarify whether a community of choice allows its participants to see their decisions and actions reflected *in* the virtual world.

One of the most cited papers on defining virtual worlds is entitled "Toward a Definition of 'Virtual Worlds'" and written by Mark Bell (2008). Bell said his definition was an extension of definitions by Edward Castronova, Raph Koster, and Richard Bartle. They share similar ideas on the requirements of a virtual world to be a virtual *world*, but their definitions differ in significant and interesting ways.

Edward Castronova is an academic famous for writing about the economy of online worlds (and other matters), his definition of virtual worlds was "crafted places inside computers that are designed to accommodate large numbers of people" (Castronova 2001), but he has also stated that virtual worlds have interactivity, physicality ("an interface that simulates a first-person physical environment on their computer screen; the environment is generally ruled by the natural laws of Earth and is characterized by scarcity of resources"), and persistence ("the program continues to run whether anyone is using it or not; it remembers the location of people and things, as well as the ownership of objects").

As I mentioned earlier, Raph Koster, who worked on *Ultima Online* and *Star Wars Galaxies* (and wrote a book on game design, *A Theory of Fun*), also led his own virtual place company, Metaplace (Takahashi 2009). Koster's definition included notions of persistence and numerous people, and one online blog post on his website seems to capture the important elements of his definition: that it is a spatial representation, an avatar representation (within that space), and a sandbox where activities have some form of persistence. But in Koster's definition, the avatars seem to be at most stand-in props, 3D icons, not representatives of inhabitants *to* inhabitants.

Perhaps the lack of spatiality is because early multiuser adventure computer games were often text based. For example, MUD (multiuser dungeon), which originated in 1978 and inspired numerous other games and virtual worlds, was originally text based. Even today, the most cited book on virtual worlds is possibly *Designing Virtual Worlds* by MUD's coinventor, Richard Bartle.

I noted earlier that Bartle (2004) defined a virtual world as "an environment that its inhabitants regard as being self-contained. It doesn't have to mean an entire planet: It's used in the same sense as 'the Roman world' or 'the world of high finance.'" I have already questioned such a simple definition, but now when we are selecting an evaluation method for virtual places, we may need to compare the features of virtual places to virtual worlds. Perhaps Bell's definition combined the best of the three former definitions? Bell's definition was "a synchronous, persistent network of people, represented as avatars, facilitated by networked computers." Given Bell's definition included a notion of technology while Bartle's definition includes the opinion of the "inhabitants" (players), do either offer enough for evaluation purposes? No, I don't believe so. A virtual environment may be persistent (it is the same when you later return to it) and may be considered "self-contained" by its "inhabitants," but that does not mean it is a virtual place, let alone a virtual world.

While Bell's definition includes both the concept of persistence and the requirement of a sizeable group of people who need to be represented and engaged as a (social) network, he ignored Castronova's interesting but problematic requirement for a virtual world to be "crafted." This is a problematic requirement because while Castronova's definition does remind us a virtual world is designed and that virtual worlds can be "taken care of" (in the real world we see everywhere signs of both care and neglect), it leaves open the question of who designs the virtual world. Could a single author–designed virtual world hinder individual creativity?

A more useful evaluation might be to determine what constitutes an inhabitant, but surely being seen as an inhabitant (or not) is a better indicator of a virtual world as opposed to a virtual place. If everyone is automatically considered an inhabitant (a digital local), can the digital environment be considered a rich collection of virtual places? For places in the real world block us from entering and keep out others but also welcome and include or protect us.

Here we come face to face with a pervading problem that an observant reader may have noticed throughout this book: *virtual place* and *virtual world* seem to be synonyms. I agree; this was a deliberate move on my part. This equivalence has been accepted before; in most academic papers, these terms seem to be treated as synonyms. So why should we now distinguish them? I have two major reasons: in the real world we distinguish them, and a virtual world implies a greater deal of complexity, multiplicity, and scale than a virtual place. Unfortunately, in the design and marketing of virtual worlds, this potential distinction is lost.

Perhaps virtual worlds are a combination of reality and imagination? Bartle (2004, 1) has also offered a second definition for virtual worlds: "Virtual worlds are places where the imaginary meets the real." This doesn't help us work out evaluation, and it seems to be predicated on the notion that presence is constant. If what is real is that which is, and imaginary is that which isn't, how can a virtual world, in Bartle's words, be "that which isn't, having the form or effect of that which is (?)" After all, Bartle defined the virtual as being between the real and the imaginary, not a subset of the imaginary. And surely I can enter a three-dimensional digital environment, supported by VR technology yet not feel that I am part of an imaginary world?

Bartle explicitly separated virtual worlds from VR: "Virtual reality is primarily concerned with the mechanisms by which human beings can interact with computer simulations; it is not especially bothered by the nature of the simulations themselves." While I agree that technology does not necessitate subjective feelings of immersion and that focusing on the technology and only using content to support the technology is short-sighted, I cannot agree that people exploring VR are not interested in the content. For example, members of the International Society for Presence Research (ISPR) are interested in studying presence, formerly known as telepresence, where technology blurs into the background. They define presence in this way: "Presence, short for telepresence, happens when people use technology and overlook at least part of its role in the experience."

Addressing Place Evaluation with Sense of Place

Sense of place has been defined by I. Ghani, A. Rafi, and P. Woods (2016, 1) as "the unique human experience, bonding, and emotion towards a particular place." They argued that phenomenology, as an "interpretative study of human experience," is required in architecture to "safeguard the spirit of the place or the genius loci, to avoid the loss of place" (2016, 1). However, they equate a sense of place to studies of presence in virtual environments. While presence has been defined as "being there," or being in a "place," and sometimes questions have related to the experience of "spatial presence," presence studies have arguably not focused in the main on the sensation of being in a place, nor have they focused on evaluating what creates a specific sense of place in virtual environments.

In their work on place-based learning for science education, Steven Semken and colleagues (2009, 136) defined *sense of place* as follows: "Sense of place encompasses the meanings that a given place holds for people and the attachments that people develop for that place." Semken's paper went further, adding a requirement of authentic evidence of place-based learning, helping us acquire (2009, 136) "locally situated knowledge and skills, but also enrichment of the sense of place." They also stated that valid and reliable studies have already been conducted in measuring sense of place.

The proposal that a sense of place can be measured reliably is interesting because their definition of sense of place was inspired by the phenomenologist and cultural geographer Yi-Fu Tuan: "Place is defined as any locality or space that has become imbued with meaning by human experience in it" (Semken et al. 2009, 136–37). For Semken and colleagues, a place develops many scientific and humanistic meanings, reflecting all the ways diverse groups and individuals experience it, including strong emotional attachments, and they mention Ed Relph's 1976 framework, encompassing a range: alienation, personal sense of place, and belonging (Relph 1976). They appear to follow earlier geographers in claiming the sense of place is the (Semken et al. 2009, 136) "combined set of the place meanings and place attachments that a person or a group develop for a place."

They cite approvingly a Relph-inspired seven-point empirical intensity scale for place undertaken by Shmuel Shamai (1991). Kaltenborn (1998) used the scale to characterize place attachment among inhabitants of the Svalbard archipelago (with "two geographically and culturally distinct groups"). Semken and colleagues also recommended a place attachment survey by Daniel Williams and Jerry Vaske (2003) and the two-dimensional theoretical model it was based on. This theoretical model was summarized by Semken's paper as "place dependence, the capacity or potential of a place to support an individual's needs, goals, or activities . . . [and] . . . place identity, an individual's various affective relationships to a place" (Semken et al. 2009, 139).

While this appears to be an effective and popular measure of places already well known to visitors, how would this scale work for virtual environments, especially ones simulating places inaccessible or inhabited by different cultures to those of the participants?

For example, if you view the place attachment instrument of Williams and Vaske (2003, 6), it becomes clear that all the criteria are for familiar places:

- I feel (place name) is a part of me.
- (Place name) is the best place for what I like to do.
- (Place name) is very special to me.
- No other place can compare to (place name).
- I identify strongly with (place name).
- I get more satisfaction out of visiting (place name) than any other place.
- I am very attached to (place name).

- Doing what I do at (place name) is more important to me than doing it in any other place.
- Visiting (place name) says a lot about who I am.
- I wouldn't substitute any other area for doing the types of things I do at (place name).
- (Place name) means a lot to me.
- The things I do at (place name) I would enjoy doing just as much at a similar site.

This emphasis is apparent in other place-based evaluations, such as the study of an indigenous shellfish harvesting community in Puget Sound, Washington, undertaken by Jamie Donatuto and Melissa Poe (2015). They emphasized the strength of place attachment and identity for inhabitants based on duration, activity, and requirements for physical survival. Community territories are linked to a shared culturally defined sense of place, property, and investment in the place-related activity; there are no felt boundaries between members, and many of the inhabitants' activities are communal and social in nature. Donatuto and Poe argued that social relationships affected place-based activities and psychological aspects of a place. Interestingly, the sense of smell "seemed to be one of the more powerful ways that participants connected their experiences to sense of place and way of life" (35–36).

Familiarity increases a sense of place identity and attachment, which seems logical. However, each study also emphasized the importance of physical activity and the interactions of society and place. Interestingly, Ed Relph's thoughts in *Place and Placelessness* (Relph 1976) have inspired several surveys and evaluation scales of place or placelessness, and he has referred to some of these surveys and evaluation tools in a blog post titled "Sense of Place: An Overview" (2015). However, an article Relph (2007) wrote on virtual places, "Spirit of Place and Sense of Place in Virtual Realities," has not had anywhere near the same amount of influence on evaluation metrics in virtual places. Perhaps this is because in that online publication, he raised a serious phenomenological challenge:

> Real places are existential phenomena, the meaningful and rather messy contexts of everyday life. This cannot be true for virtual places, which are not at all fundamental to our being and are not even necessary to the functioning of the Web. I find it difficult to conceive that existential feelings of rootedness and belonging to a place are in any way transferable except perhaps as a type of psychosis or addiction accompanying perfect presence. And in its precise, sacred sense genius loci cannot be simulated in virtual worlds any more than it can be created in real ones, because humans do not create gods and spirits.

The phrase that we do not create gods and spirits seems to have been echoed in the second edition of *On the Internet* by Hubert Dreyfus (2008). I presume the statement here proclaims that we need to be in the presence of an externally omniscient and omnipotent force with the power of life and death over us to force us to believe in and commit to every situation. This is a big claim.

Relph also argued that authenticity cannot be applied to virtual places, because they are not real. For Relph, authentic places:

1. "simultaneously reveal and respond to the qualities of spirit of place and reflect the existential realities of being";
2. are "original, not a fake or copy"; and
3. cannot be considered to be inauthentic places, "those that have no relationship to context or offer the pretense that they are somewhere else."

With premise 1, I suspect Relph was channeling the writing of Martin Heidegger. With premise 2 he was perhaps referring to the problem of authenticity in the mechanic (and electronic) age, as foreshadowed by Walter Benjamin. With premise 3, I am reminded again of Heidegger (Malpas and Wrathall 2000) but also of Ed Casey's (1997, 247–248) reading of Heidegger. Despite their reference to earlier, famous texts, these three premises or criteria for authenticity are hard to evaluate. They are also demanding criteria, insisting on the requirement of authenticity for virtual places to be real-world places.

The capacity to reflect on "the existential realities of being" is rather vague, and it is not even clear if and how all real-world places manage this (or if they need to reflect this concept to even be considered real-world places). Additionally, there may exist many real-world places that are copies, yet the inhabitants are oblivious to this fact or are often so engrossed in place-making activities that it no longer registers. The third premise could be two premises: virtual places lack context or convey a pretense (illusion?) that they are somewhere else, somewhere other than where they are.

It is a common occurrence to see buildings, homes, banks, and restaurants designed to appear as if they are fragments of foreign cities, distant or historical architectural masterpieces, famous but mythical settings, or glamorous overseas destinations. Places are often "parasitic" on other places. Many more architectural forms are planned and placed independently of their locale or deliberately despite their surroundings (such as the Pompidou Art Museum, Paris). They are still real. I would argue they are no less authentic, or at least they are still capable of fostering authentic place memories and attachments. Perhaps architects, city planners, and art historians could argue their style does not fit in with their cultural or historical surroundings. The issue of authenticity, as Relph acknowledged, is not clear-cut.

And even if we grant that real-world places need to fulfill the above criteria (premises), is it impossible for virtual environments to provide a sense of placelessness? Heidegger has granted "Being-in-the-world" gets distracted and fragmented; it needs to be revived regularly. And (virtual) presence researchers are beginning to argue that presence is also a flickering, not explicitly binary phenomenon. Surely the sense of authenticity or the moments of complete (or near complete?) engagement and commitment inside a virtual environment may also lead to moments or memories that participants believe is authentic?

The elderly are another group of people who typically cannot explore their surroundings with the full physical embodiment and freedom of others, but who do seem to value "cyberspace" attachments and who appear to have "rich tales of other places" via digital technology (Wiles et al. 2009). Their computer-based travel and conversations with family and friends across the world appear to be rich, meaningful, memorable, and significant to them. Are their diminished mobility and shrinking "personal geography" a total impediment to the experiencing of other places?[1]

If it is hard to determine how to create a sense of authenticity regards virtual places, it is even harder to determine a sense of authenticity if the place simulated is foreign and of symbolic importance to a distant or foreign culture. And yet this is surely the goal of cultural heritage projects, to convey the historically and culturally situated significance of the historic objects being digitally simulated.

Even if authenticity is not a required criterion for all experiences of virtual worlds, we have an even more immediate problem, how do we convey the significance of the place to people who have never visited that place and are now visiting it thanks to a virtual environment? And here we have a bifurcation, to experience a virtual environment as a place for oneself or as a place as experienced by others.

Luckily, there have been investigations into developing a sense of virtual place measures. Vipin Arora and Deepak Khazanchi (2014) recently developed a measure for the sense of virtual place (SOVP). Their definition of place is as follows: "In essence, a place is made up of not just the physical environment but also the activities, and the social interactions among the people who occupy the place. . . . We define a virtual place as 'a virtual setting along with the activities, and human social and psychological processes rooted in the setting'" (2017). As for their definition of an SOVP, it is "an individual's perception of the capability of a virtual place to actively engage the individual by supporting a set of well-defined place-specific functional and socio-emotional needs of the individual." I have a few queries about this definition. Do the individuals need to be actively conscious they are in a virtual place to judge its capability to "actively engage the individual by supporting a set of well-defined place-specific functional and socio-emotional needs of the individual"? For virtual places to be places, do they have to be actively engaging and supporting of place-specific functional and "socio-emotional needs"? Despite the word *socio-emotional*, I am also not sure whether or how social relationships are related to the sense of place in this definition. Social relationships appear to be key to the forming of place attachments and place identity in the real world. No doubt individuals can form place attachments without other people, but it seems to be harder to maintain, and "socio-emotional needs" in the previous definition is vaguely formulated.

Arora and Khazanchi (2014) also produced a table to demonstrate place attributes as they relate to "virtual world affordances," but please note there is no enriched cultural affordance listed in the typology shown in table 9.1. The

Table 9.1. Arora and Khazanchi's 2017 Schema: Three Elements of Place in Virtual Worlds

Place Attributes	Virtual World Affordances
Physical characteristics	Simulate characteristics of real-world places. Example: A co-located setting designed in a synthetic environment that provides artifacts and a social context for remote participants where they can work together on shared artifacts.
Social interaction	Synchronous interaction between users personified as avatars. Example: Real-time text or voice chat supported by an embodied avatar.
Afforded activities	Shared viewing, creation, and manipulation of artifacts. Example: Virtual experiments, design teamwork, group projects, roleplaying, etc.

typology does have three dimensions to virtual place: virtual place identity, virtual place dependence, and virtual place attachment.

However, I am not convinced by some of the paper's definitions. The paper seems to have a heavy focus on defining place as subservient to the clear needs of the users. No doubt many places are indeed seen in terms of their functional utility, but not all. However, the third dimension, virtual place attachment, is interesting, as it is based on emotional bonds built up over time. Despite this dimension, inhabitation is not mentioned; can people never inhabit a virtual world?

In Arora and Khazanchi's evaluation of ninety-seven students who assessed eleven criteria for a sense of virtual place, using a simulation of a laboratory in *Second Life*, students were given fifteen minutes for learning about the virtual environment, they were guided to the evaluation test area of the *Second Life* environment, and then they had ten minutes to explore. Whether the overall time for the experience was half an hour or fifty minutes, it is unclear to me how participants could form strong place attachments. The issue of minimum duration and exposure and what determines a sense of inhabitation has not been addressed. Indeed, how participants could develop virtual place identity, virtual place dependence, and virtual place attachment for a laboratory in *Second Life*, within an hour, is not clear to me. And the refined eleven items of the SOVP are not mentioned in the 2017 paper; what are they?

Evaluation Methodology and Problems

The aforementioned surveys and scales may prove useful, but they appear to be overlooking an important conceptual distinction between virtual places and virtual environments. I distinguished between virtual environments, virtual places, and virtual worlds to stress their differences, but they overlap in many cases (table 9.2). I can consider virtual places and virtual worlds to be virtual

Table 9.2. Virtual Environments, Virtual Places, and Virtual Worlds

	Virtual Environment	Virtual Places	Virtual Worlds
Space	Spatial but not necessarily platial visualization	Single place	Combination or range of various places that distinctively or memorably differ from each other
Scale	Typically one overall scale but size may vary	Typically smaller in scale	Supposedly large with a large range of simulated detail
Areas	Can feature any amount of internal areas but typically focuses on one overall area	Singular and discrete overall area	Transition areas and thresholds and other intermediate and interstitial spaces *between* virtual places
Themes	Theme not necessary	Unified theme	Combination and juxtaposition of themes
Persistency	Can be persistent	Persistent	Persistent
Inhabitation	Not necessarily populated but more likely to be successful if populated	At least signs of potential inhabitation	Designed for large numbers of people, typically represented by avatars
Interactivity	Usually some level of interactivity	Arguably must have some level of dynamic processes and interactivity	Arguably must have some level of dynamic processes and interactivity
Localization and personalization	Not necessary	Possible or simulated	Possible or simulated
Uniqueness and memorability	Not essential	Essential	Essential

environments, but the reverse is not necessarily true. And if we can separate these types of phenomena in terms of desired features, it will be easier to develop evaluation guidelines that address their desired features.

For example, virtual worlds and virtual places differ mostly in terms of scale and scope but can differ markedly from (non–virtual place and non–virtual world) virtual environments. The latter does not necessarily have to worry about uniqueness; memorability; ability to evoke, trigger, or record specific emotions; afford personalization; or be distinctive yet unified in terms of design and content. Quantitative data may be enough for the evaluation of virtual environments, but virtual places and virtual worlds probably require qualitative data exploring their abilities to evoke, trigger, and record unique and memorable experiences and memories.

Figure 9.1 Juan Hiriart's Anglo-Saxon serious game, Cologne 2018. Erik Champion.

A Paucity of Metrics and Guidelines

Despite the increasing amount of papers in HCI studies, and the development of interaction design communities and academic publishing outlets (see for example the relatively recent academic conference https://chiplay.acm.org), there are still very few serious evaluations of interaction and cognitive learning styles in cultural heritage (Raptis, Fidas, and Avouris 2017). One notable exception is Juan Hiriart's doctoral dissertation and serious games project (Hiriart 2017, 2018) developing a serious game about Anglo-Saxon history for children (eight to eleven years old) in Key Stage 2 school classrooms in the United Kingdom (fig. 9.1).

Metrics can be useful for educating future colleagues but also to provide simple but useful parameters for application and design. I'll summarize two surveys here to explain common mistakes in serious games and digital heritage research, but many more could have been mentioned.

Jennifer Vogel and colleagues (2006) created criteria drawn from a metastudy on serious games. The most common methodological flaw they contained was an absence of a control group (and therefore no evidence of the significance of the intervention); however other flaws included a lack of evidence showing how the new method differed from traditional teaching methods, and many provided no statistical data or left out "important demographic details." A further flaw they mention, which I also often encounter in academic publications, is insufficient detail provided on the nature, context, and settings of the tasks and activities that were meant to be the subject of the evaluation. If readers do not know what participants did, how can they either believe in the veracity of the findings or redo the experiments themselves?

The second example focused on the evaluation of digital heritage evaluation. In a 2017 paper entitled "Empirical Evaluations of Interactive Systems in Cultural Heritage: A Review," Panayiotis Koutsabasis (2017) surveyed and found wanting empirical evaluation methods employed in fifty-three papers in (digital) cultural heritage research over the 2012–16 period. What sort of empirical evaluation methods can be used? He lists as examples "observation (strategies), interview (strategies), focus groups, user testing (with respective protocols), field testing, field studies, questionnaires, . . . surveys, diary studies, and probes" (2).

Koutsabasis claims that the following are important components of empirical evaluations:

1. The dimensions of the evaluation (factors).
2. The participants (users).
3. The purpose of the evaluation, (exploratory: evaluate prototypes and proof of concepts, formative: to yield recommendations, or summative: reach conclusions about the quality of the user experience).
4. The data (evidence) of the qualitative evaluation (observations, notes, comments, user reactions), or quantitative data ("task success, time to task, errors (and types of), responses in scaled statements (questionnaires)."
5. The place of evaluation (the computer lab, the field, online).
6. The time of evaluation (system use: before, during, or after system use, or during phases of the design process).
7. Whether the evaluation is comparative or not.

These seven factors appear to be useful ones, and I note here many systems, especially in digital heritage environments, are not tested in locations or with audiences that the system was initially intended for. How test participants are selected to foreshadow expected users is a difficult part of many evaluations; ensuring the system is ready for testing but the evaluation is early enough in the design phase to effectively respond to bugs caught or important user requests is also challenging. Another major issue is knowing how and when to combine qualitative data with quantitative data.

Koutsabasis uncovered major problems in his evaluation of the evaluation undertaken of interactive digital heritage environments. He noted, "In general, usability involves both 'objective' and 'subjective' measures: the former are related to effectiveness and efficiency of use and the latter are about user satisfaction. . . . What seems to be missing in these 'lenses' of empirical evaluations is whether some kind of 'cultural value' is conveyed to the visitors." This was my point in chapter 7: ironically, many digital heritage projects don't specifically mention how cultural knowledge and knowledge of what is culturally valuable and meaningful are conveyed effectively by the projects to the audience.

Other issues he discovered in his metareview included missing data: many papers did not mention the specific questions asked in questionnaires, and some did not even report on the number of participants. I would add, from my knowledge of some of the papers he examined, that not all appeared to use sequencing when required (the order of test conditions experienced may affect results, due to tiredness, increased skill, or increasing boredom), and others did not explain how they resolved missing or incomplete data from participants who did not finish the evaluations or view and complete all tasks. The technical specifications and in-the-field performance of computers used for evaluations (and how or if they would differ from end user computers) are seldom adequately described in evaluation studies in (digital) cultural heritage.

However, there is also an important conceptual issue in this meta-review. While Koutsabasis approvingly quotes Nikolas Papadimitriou's concern that many projects have a strict and limited idea of interaction, a concern I have with his paper (of direct relevance to the topic of interest in this book) is that place and space seem to be interchangeable terms. Yet if a place is not just space but also *meaningful* space, and conveying cultural meaning is an important part of digital cultural heritage, then conveying place is surely also important.

Specific Evaluation Issues

What are the major evaluation issues we have uncovered? Not only are *virtual worlds, virtual places,* and *virtual environments* often used as interchangeable terms, but it also is not always clear in the evaluations of these types of digital environments what elements are being evaluated and the purpose for which they are being evaluated.

Can individual responses to specific virtual place situations be compared? Why aren't places created and evaluated in the virtual worlds' community? Because there is no one virtual worlds community. Perhaps virtual world communities could set their own standards and tools for evaluation? This is related to a problem I mentioned earlier and corroborated (at least in the area of digital cultural heritage) by Koutsabasis (2017): a lack of virtual place data and case studies to work from also leads to designers re-creating similar problems without leveraging the work of others and without furthering standards and agreed-on guidelines.

Some academic publications may confuse "methodology" with "method" and not provide clear reasons for why certain methods were chosen and others excluded. For example, there are two famous examples of presence research defining presence and immersion (Witmer et al. 1996; Slater 1999), but they quite obviously disagree with each other. Furthermore, while they are well known to presence researchers, it is not clear if they are well known to researchers in other fields.

The attraction of creating dramatic or overly realistic correspondences between real-world and virtual-world places can also lead to this question: Are the situations in the virtual environment designed to be realistic or are they designed to provoke powerful responses indicating if and when the virtual response was equivalent to real-world responses? This is not necessarily the same thing and it leads to the next problem: the potential interference of the designer. A related problem, particularly in some virtual heritage projects is that designers, being human, tend toward creating the most aesthetically pleasing and comprehensive virtual environments possible, even if this supererogatory effort risks undermining attempts at realism, the degree of similarity to real-world environments, or the suitability of the environment for evaluation.

The opposite problem is of course designing a virtual environment (a place or world) more for a laboratory experiment than for a genuine need or attempting to extrapolate from specific set conditions to universal applicability. If the evaluation will not produce results that could improve future iterations for the wider public, or if the design will never influence future designs, is the evaluation or the designed virtual environment of value to the general public?

Virtual places may be designed to simulate a wide range of interactive possibilities, but they may also be designed for more specific ends, such as to trigger specific responses. So analogies between real-world places (especially architectural places) and virtual-world places can lead one to confuse cause with effect. To evoke significant and observable responses, the designers may create extraordinary events in virtual worlds to trigger real-world reactions: What should the evaluator do in this specific situation? And could overdramatization of cause and effect desensitize the participants or condition them to only respond to exaggerated triggers, dilemmas, or calamitous situations?

This may sound like a hypothetical situation, but I have listened to a keynote speaker explaining that in his virtual reality research lab the designers specifically did just that: creating a huge phobic trigger (a hole in the second virtual room visited) to create discernible responses and stimulate the participants to treat every virtual reality situation as real.

Using verifiable hypotheses for the evaluation is usually recommended, but without past exemplars, it can be difficult for new researchers to select a tightly focused but potentially significant and illuminating area of investigation. Hence, pilot studies, focus groups, and inviting domain experts to give early feedback are generally preferable to one giant evaluation right at the end of the design.

Although quantitative evaluation can provide clear and explicit data for analysis, calculation, and comparison, scientists have warned against scientism, appropriating scientific evaluations without a careful study of the content, understanding demographic factors, or extrapolating conclusions not specifically substantiated by the experiment. Place-related research provides a future minefield of an issue to the last risk, extrapolating a conclusion based on the absence of one or more sensory fields without considering the gestalt-like nature of the place.

For example, Russ Bradley Jr. (1970) took the architect and academic Amos Rapoport to task for all of these previously noted flaws, but of particular relevance to the topic of virtual places, he criticizes the architect's discussion of sensory deprivation studies conducted in the 1940s and 1950s. The McGill University experiment created a test condition of total sensory deprivation, but

Amos Rapoport and Robert E. Kantor (Rapoport and Kantor 1967) discussed the importance of visual deprivation.

For virtual place–related research in particular, where virtual place involves developing a sense of place and a sense of inhabitation, how much time is required? People who have visited and lived in certain places which are simulated by say virtual reality, will almost certainly have stronger feelings of attachment and identity or aversion to those who have never lived in the places being simulated.

Time may be required to provide them with adequate skills and knowledge to understand and interact with the virtual place. How long must they experience the simulated environments to develop a sense of an inhabited place or some other aspect of a sense of place? If the point of the project is to engender a sense of care, to induce people to want to care for the environment or specific place to be preserved, not only is the time required for the experience indeterminate, but a specific minimum duration will differ according to the individual.

From a phenomenological viewpoint, the "dwelling" of a test participant in a virtual environment for it to be sensed as a place is a particularly interesting problem. How can phenomenological responses be evoked, articulated, and summarized in academic publications?

In previous chapters, I raised the issue of educational theory not keeping up with changes in related research areas of neuroscience and cognitive psychology and diminishing confidence in the concept of cognitive maps (for navigation). Both issues highlight a persistent danger: underlying theories used to evaluate virtual environments may become refuted or modified by either emerging research or by new technology, unbeknownst at the time to the virtual place evaluators.

Another issue arises when the evaluator wishes to measure task performance between different demographic groups and also collate the personal preferences of the participants. If there are two test groups, a test group, and an experimental group, how can they be asked which condition they prefer? Inability to compare across test groups is a frequent problem and exacerbated when evaluators confuse cardinal scales with numerical ones or average Likert-type scaled responses (Strongly disagree; Disagree; Neither agree nor disagree; Agree; Strongly agree), which are easy to abuse and difficult if not impossible to aggregate (Jamieson 2004).

Likert scales can record individual responses to specific phenomena, but for novel technologies and applications, they pose challenges, especially when evaluating particular and personal responses to evocations of place, which may or may not be experienced in the same way or same order by test participants in dynamic, changing, interactively rich, and complex virtual environments.

Summary: Considerations for Evaluating People Visiting Virtual Places

The evaluation of place, and especially the evaluation of virtual place, is difficult and challenging. I have perhaps only increased questions and concerns in the evaluation of virtual places, but there are also more generic decisions that need to be made when evaluating virtual environments, virtual places, and virtual worlds that may help their overall design and eventual success.

1. Determining the target market: Given the potential online and highly interactive possibilities of virtual places and virtual worlds, can we determine who will be the participants? Do they reflect the expected target audience? How does one compare or filter experienced participants with participants without experience?

2. Scalable and applicable results: Is it more important to assess task performance or individual preference, and how can these results be meaningfully collated and analyzed? Can the results be verified independently? How dependent on technology is the experience (and therefore the evaluation results)?

3. Setting and conditions: Should evaluations be done in the laboratory or the real-world environment? What is the minimum duration of experience required to gain a necessary understanding of the virtual place? What maximum duration should be allowed? Given many interactive environments can be experienced in different ways, over different playing times, how does the duration of the experience compare across the group or groups?

4. Analysis: How can qualitative experiences be recorded and analyzed? Can ethnographic or phenomenological methods provide useful analysis? This is a real problem for the design of virtual places. Is the designed experience supposed to provide an experience of a specific place or a general, universally recognizable place? If the latter, how can it be a fully experiential, significant, and evocative place?

5. Reflection and dissemination: Why was this evaluation carried out? What were the expectations? What flaws and discoveries were uncovered? How does this relate to humanities areas? How are they evaluated? By their peers, by impact, or by engagement? What implications are there for humanities, is place-making of secondary importance for them?

6. Storage: Are the responses stored, in durable formats, and quickly retrievable? Do they link to easily accessible and well-stored archives or repositories? Are the intentions and methods and related paradata also stored and easily retrievable? Are the conditions in which they were created and maintained recorded? Are any specific requirements for privacy or distribution associated with the stored evaluation data? If research data, paradata, and publications are listed separately (in white papers, reports, or academic papers), does the data stored link to these documents?

Note

1. Virtual travel is particularly pertinent during the Coronavirus pandemic, a time where much of the world has been locked.

References

Arora, Vipin, and Deepak Khazanchi. 2014. "Towards Developing a Measure for Sense of Virtual Place." Paper presented at the Twentieth America's Conference on Information Systems (AMCIS 2014), "Smart Sustainability: The Information Systems Opportunity," Savannah, Georgia, August 7–9, 2014.

———. 2017. "Sense of Virtual Place (SOVP): Conceptual Exploration and Initial Empirical Validation." Paper presented at the Twenty-Third Americas Conference on Information Systems, Boston, MA, August 10–12, 2017.

Bainbridge, William Sims. 2007. "The Scientific Research Potential of Virtual Worlds." *Science* 317 (5837): 472–76.

Bartle, Richard A. 2004. *Designing Virtual Worlds*. Indianapolis: New Riders.

Bell, Mark W. 2008. "Toward a Definition of 'Virtual Worlds'. 'Virtual Worlds Research: Past, Present & Future'." *Journal For Virtual Worlds Research* 1 (1). Accessed July 17, 2017. https://journals.tdl.org/jvwr/index.php/jvwr/article/viewFile/283/237.

Billinghurst, Mark, Adrian Clark, and Gun Lee. 2015. "A Survey of Augmented Reality." *Foundations and Trends® in Human-Computer Interaction* 8 (2–3): 73–272.

Bowman, Doug A., Ernst Kruijff, Joseph J. LaViola Jr., and Ivan Poupyrev. 2004. *3D User Interfaces: Theory and Practice*. Redwood City, CA: Addison-Wesley.

Bradley, Russ V. V., Jr. 1970. "A Critical Analysis of the Writings of Amos Rapoport." *Journal of Architectural Education* 24 (2–3): 16–25.

Bergeron, Susan J. 2011. "Engaging the Virtual Landscape: Toward an Experiential Approach to Exploring Place through a Spatial Experience Engine." PhD diss., West Virginia University. https://researchrepository.wvu.edu/etd/4696.

Casey, Edward S. 1997. *The Fate of Place: A Philosophical History*. Berkeley: University of California Press.

Castronova, Edward. 2001. "Virtual Worlds: A First-Hand Account of Market and Society on the Cyberian Frontier." *EconPapers* 618:1–41. Accessed July 18, 2017. https://ideas.repec.org/p/ces/ceswps/_618.html.

Cook, Nicole, and Sandra L. Winkler. 2016. "Acceptance, Usability and Health Applications of Virtual Worlds by Older Adults: A Feasibility Study." [In English]. *JMIR Research Protocols* 5 (2): 1–9. https://doi.org/10.2196/resprot.5423.

Dillenbourg, Pierre, Daniel Schneider, and Paraskevi Synteta. 2002. "Virtual Learning Environments." In *Proceedings of the 3rd Hellenic Conference "Information & Communication Technologies in Education"*, edited by A. Dimitracopoulou, 3–18. Rhodes, Greece: Kastaniotis Editions.

Donatuto, Jamie, and Melissa R. Poe. 2015. "Evaluating Sense of Place as a Domain of Human Well-Being for Puget Sound Restoration." University of Washing Puget Sound Institute. Accessed April 27, 2021. https://www.eopugetsound.org/articles/evaluating-sense-place-domain-human-well-being-puget-sound-restoration.

Dreyfus, Hubert L. 2008. *On the Internet*. 2nd ed. London: Routledge.

Ducheneaut, Nicolas, Robert J. Moore, and Eric Nickell. 2007. "Virtual 'Third Places': A Case Study of Sociability in Massively Multiplayer Games." *Computer Supported Cooperative Work (CSCW)* 16 (1–2): 129–66.

Ghani, Izham, Ahmad Rafi, and Peter Woods. 2016. "Sense of Place in Immersive Architectural Virtual Heritage Environment." In *22nd International Conference on Virtual System & Multimedia (VSMM)*, 1–8. Sunway University, Kuala Lumpur: IEEE.

Hill, Will, Larry Stead, Mark Rosenstein, and George Furnas. 1995. "Recommending and Evaluating Choices in a Virtual Community of Use." In *Proceedings of the Sigchi*

Conference on Human Factors in Computing Systems, edited by Irvin R. Katz, Mack Robert, Linn Marks, Mary Beth Rosson, and Jakob Nielsen, 194–201. Denver, CO: ACM/Addison-Wesley.

Hiriart, Juan. 2017. "Designing and Using Digital Games as Historical Learning Contexts for Primary School Classrooms." Paper presented at the Historia Ludens: One day conference on history and gaming, University of Huddersfield, Huddersfield, UK. Accessed June 12, 2021. https://www.researchgate.net/publication/319879666 _Designing_and_Using_Digital_Games_as_Historical_Learning_Contexts_for _Primary_School_Classrooms.

———. 2018. "The Game of Making an Archaeology Game: Proposing a Design Framework for Historical Game Design." Paper presented at the Computer Applications and Quantitative Methods in Archaeology (CAA) International Conference, Tübingen, DEU, March 19–23, 2018.

Jamieson, Susan. 2004. "Likert Scales: How to (Ab)use Them." *Medical Education* 38 (12): 1217–18. https://doi.org/10.1111/j.1365-2929.2004.02012.x.

Kaltenborn, Bjørn P. 1998. "Effects of Sense of Place on Responses to Environmental Impacts: A Study among Residents in Svalbard in the Norwegian High Arctic." *Applied Geography* 18 (2): 169–89.

Koster, Raph. n.d. "A Definition: Part One; The Play's the Thing." Raph Koster's Website. Accessed July 18, 2017. https://www.raphkoster.com/games/insubstantial-pageants/a -definition/.

Koutsabasis, Panayiotis. 2017. "Empirical Evaluations of Interactive Systems in Cultural Heritage: A Review." *International Journal of Computational Methods in Heritage Science* 1 (1): 100–122.

Malpas, Jeff, and Mark A. Wrathall. 2000. *Heidegger, Coping, and Cognitive Science: Essays in Honor of Hubert L. Dreyfus*. Vol. 1. Cambridge, MA: MIT Press.

Minocha, Shailey, and Christopher Hardy. 2016. "Navigation and Wayfinding in Learning Spaces in 3D Virtual Worlds." In *Learning in Virtual Worlds: Research and Applications*, edited by Sue Gregory, Mark J. W. Lee, Barney Dalgarno, and Belinda Tynan, 3–41. Issues in Distance Education. Athabasca: Athabasca University Press.

Radu, Iulian. 2014. "Augmented Reality in Education: A Meta-Review and Cross-Media Analysis." *Personal and Ubiquitous Computing* 18 (6): 1533–43. https://link.springer.com /article/10.1007/s00779-013-0747-y.

Raptis, George E., Christos Fidas, and Nikolaos Avouris. 2017. "Cultural Heritage Gaming: Effects of Human Cognitive Styles on Players' Performance and Visual Behavior." UMAP '17, Adjunct Publication of the Twenty-Fifth Conference on User Modeling, Adaptation and Personalization, Bratislava, SVK, July 9–12. Accessed April 27, 2021. http://dl.acm.org/citation.cfm?id=3099023.3099090.

Rapoport, Amos, and Robert E. Kantor. 1967. "Complexity and Ambiguity in Environmental Design." *Journal of the American Institute of Planners* 33 (4): 210–21. https://doi.org/10 .1080/01944366708977922.

Relph, Edward C. 1976. *Place and Placelessness*. London: Pion.

———. 2007. "Spirit of Place and Sense of Place in Virtual Realities." *Techné: Research in Philosophy and Technology* 10 (3): 17–25.

———. 2015. "Sense of Place: an Overview." *Placeness, Place, Placelessness* (blog), July 19. Accessed April 27, 2021. http://www.placeness.com/sense-of-place-an-overview/.

Semken, Steven, Carol Butler Freeman, Nievita Bueno Watts, Jennifer J. Neakrase, Rebecca Escobar Dial, and Dale R. Baker. 2009. "Factors That Influence Sense of Place as a

Learning Outcome and Assessment Measure of Place-Based Geoscience Teaching." *Electronic Journal of Science Education* 13 (2): 136–59.

Shamai, Shmuel. 1991. "Sense of Place: An Empirical Measurement." *Geoforum* 22 (3): 347–58. http://www.sciencedirect.com/science/article/pii/001671859190017K.

Simor, Fernando Winckler, Manoela Rogofski Brum, Jaison Dairon Ebertz Schmidt, Rafael Rieder, and Ana Carolina Bertoletti De Marchi. 2016. "Usability Evaluation Methods for Gesture-Based Games: A Systematic Review." *JMIR Serious Games* 4 (2): e17. https://doi.org/10.2196/games.5860.

Slater, Mel. 1999. "Measuring Presence: A Response to the Witmer and Singer Presence Questionnaire." *Presence: Teleoperators and Virtual Environments* 8 (5): 560–65. https://doi.org/10.1162/105474699566477.

Takahashi, Dean. 2009. "Metaplace to Shut Down Its Site for Thousands of Virtual Worlds." Venturebeat. Last Modified December 21, 2009. Accessed July 18, 2017. https://venturebeat.com/2009/12/21/metaplace-to-shut-down-its-site-for-thousands-of-virtual-worlds/.

Vogel, Jennifer J., David S. Vogel, Jan Cannon-Bowers, Clint A. Bowers, Kathryn Muse, and Michelle Wright. 2006. "Computer Gaming and Interactive Simulations for Learning: A Meta-Analysis." *Journal of Educational Computing Research* 34 (3): 229–43.

Wiles, Janine L., Ruth E. S. Allen, Anthea J. Palmer, Karen J. Hayman, Sally Keeling, and Ngaire Kerse. 2009. "Older People and Their Social Spaces: A Study of Well-Being and Attachment to Place in Aotearoa New Zealand." *Social Science & Medicine* 68 (4): 664–71. https://doi.org/10.1016/j.socscimed.2008.11.030.

Williams, Daniel R., and Jerry J. Vaske. 2003. "The Measurement of Place Attachment: Validity and Generalizability of a Psychometric Approach." *Forest Science* 49 (6): 830–40.

Witmer, Bob G., John H. Bailey, Bruce W. Knerr, and Kimberly C. Parsons. 1996. "Virtual Spaces and Real World Places: Transfer of Route Knowledge." *International Journal of Human-Computer Studies* 45 (4): 413–28.

chapter ten

PLACE-MAKING INTERFACES AND PLATFORMS

Introduction

Virtual places are not just made; they are hosted and preserved. Their success and longevity rely on platforms, markets and new opportunities, software, file formats, and related repositories. Are these platforms and associated technologies converging, and should they be? How are they endangered by perceived obsolescence and designed obsolescence?

Place Platforms

Virtual Reality

In "Virtual Reality: Is This Really How We Will All Watch TV in Years to Come?," Stuart Dredge (2017) interviewed industry experts who believe the future is interactivity, game engines, or character-led theater. There is also a battle looming between Facebook (Oculus) and Google (Daydream) because they are not only selling head-mounted display (HMD) systems but also attempting to build walled-garden product ecosystems that compel consumers to choose one product over the other. Their battle with each other is keeping costs competitive, especially in the area known as mobile virtual reality (VR) or smartphone VR (Sag 2017).

Augmented and Mixed Reality

In 2004, Ron Azuma published a survey on augmented reality (AR), contrasting it with virtual environments and VR. In that paper, Azuma declared that unlike VR, AR supplements the real world, superimposing virtual objects on the real world, or compositing virtual objects on the real world.

Many of today's AR phone applications do not qualify as AR because they do not use computer vision to merge three-dimensional data, instead simply relying on the GPS tracking of the camera, while many others just rotate 360-degree panoramas (fig. 10.1). Even with this less sophisticated and less spatially immersive

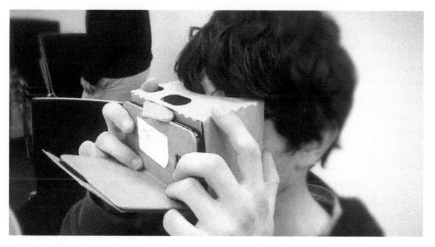

Figure 10.1 Google Cardboard VR. Erik Champion.

technology, the potential for accessible virtual heritage is obvious (Billinghurst, Clark, and Lee 2015; Chung, Han, and Joun 2015; Jung et al. 2016). In particular, new sensory devices can greatly expand the experiential dimensions of virtual environments: "We are at a turning point in development and thought about multi-sensorial engagement using digital mediation. From Oculus Rift VR goggles, Google Cardboard, noise-reducing headphones, vibrating-haptic simulating gloves, smell generators, and virtual treadmills, every week a new technology or software emerges that can be used to virtualise, augment or diminish our reality, across all of our senses. In many cases these technologies have been used by archaeologists or museum professionals to didactically present or reconstruct archaeological sites or artefacts [artifacts]. However, Mixed Reality [MR] is rarely used to actively explore or analyze archaeological sites."

In the same article, Stuart Eve (2017) suggested we are at a sensory-device turning point in digital archaeology. AR does not have to create or re-create an entire scene; it can now be carried on consumers' mobile phones because it does not require the same graphic rendering as a full VR environment, and it can range in complexity from augmented avatars that appear on your phone or HMD to text labels on the screen of a phone camera, appearing to float above real-world objects (Dredge 2011). There are even research projects examining how AR can integrate with museum collections (Kraemer and Kanter 2014) and community-based projects (Speiginer et al. 2015).

The recent craze of *Pokémon Go* (Moskowitz 2016) may have also convinced serious game and virtual place designers and professionals of a huge potential education and cultural tourism market. Phone-based AR is accessible and collaborative. Apple CEO Tim Cook favors AR over other technologies (perhaps he is alluding to VR development by Facebook via Oculus). Cook declared, "I think it's something that doesn't isolate people. We can use it to enhance our discussion, not substitute it for human connection, which I've always deeply worried about in some of the other technologies" (Graham 2020).

Although there are potentially fascinating uses for such technology (Bonus et al. 2017), there are ethical and safety concerns that go along with them (Serino et al. 2016). What are the required ethics for alternative reality games, and should bystanders be actively involved in pervasive games (Greenspan 2015; Davies 2017)?

Due to fast-moving changes in AR technology, there are also preservation issues (Serino et al. 2016): the field is still developing in the commercial arena far faster than in many educational ones (Noh, Sunar, and Pan 2009). In "5 Ways Virtual and Augmented Reality Is Changing Our Lives," Brian Pene (2016) (director of Emerging Technology, Autodesk) lists five major areas for AR: entertainment, architecture, automotive design, training, and education. But tourism offers further opportunities (Kounavis, Kasimati, and Zamani 2012).

Popular augmented reality software (at the time of writing) include Vuforia, Wikitude, and HP Reveal (formerly Aurasma), ARKit 2 (Apple), and ARCore (Google). Sadly, many AR software companies appear to have disappeared already, such as Metaio (acquired by Apple), Junaio (disappeared in 2015), instantAR (free AR software developed for a research project but no longer maintained), and Layar (currently insolvent). AR technology, particularly platforms that save data only to the cloud in proprietary software and formats, can cause serious preservation and ownership issues down the line.

Obscure formats, hidden files, incompatible version updates—these are all common risks when taking up new software, but the hype cycle of new technology can be seductive and disarming (Gilbert 2015; Gaudiosi 2016). But not being able to access the data created by the user? This was a failure of infrastructure.

At the time of writing, there is a great deal of hype over recent and emerging technology like Apple's ARKit and Google ARCore. Even the Smithsonian was moved to write an article titled "How Augmented Reality Will Change How You Buy Furniture" (Rieland 2016). The online press predicted a future where AR made screens vanish in the real world (Chapman 2016), but it seems that the AR products, or even AR companies, are the ones doing the vanishing (Miller-Kipp and Constine 2015; Vincent 2018; Meisenzahl 2019).

Many designers create AR content to augment real places and store it in the cloud. When the software changes or the company goes bankrupt or is sold to an even larger company, they may lose their project as well as the digital media assets that made up that project. It is always desirable to acquire software (from a proven, reliable company) that allows the user to store the project and assets offline, provides and accepts standard formats, can be linked to other media and other referencing systems, and can export in different formats. But as Henry Ogden (2015) noted, commercial AR products are walled gardens, with little in the way of shared standards.

Haptics, Wearables, and Alternative Sensory Input

As I noted previously, Eve (2017) has predicted a combination of MR and haptics, but he has also developed olfactory reality—AR with smell. Haptics and olfactory interaction is a fascinating area for virtual place design. The sense of smell is closely linked to memory (Gaines Lewis 2015). As Alan Chalmers noted (Chalmers 2014), this has not been an intensive part of virtual reality research and development. However, coupled with wearable computing, and three-dimensional sensing technology (becoming more and more accessible thanks to both entertainment computing and AR devices), as well as the Internet of Things, physical interfaces, and biofeedback, alternative sensing devices may help develop richer and more personalized place experiences (Side, Gang, and O'Neill 2014; Barfield 2015; Bostanci, Kanwal, and Clark 2015).

I may be wrong about the revival of biofeedback; it has been predicted before. Richard Leadbetter (2011) wrote about how major game design and software company Valve predicted an upturn in biofeedback computer gaming, but Nintendo's failed interface may have dampened spirits. There has however been recent interest in brain-computer interfaces (Friedman 2017; Gurkok, Nijholt, and Poel 2017). And there have been very interesting recent experiments in wearable emotive interfaces (Sanjeev 2018) and speech interfaces (Alexander and Chambers 2017). By 2020, the hype had moved to camera-based hand tracking, with consumer-level HMDs, such as the Oculus Quest, available that include controller-free hand-tracking software development kits.

Place-Making Software

Prototyping Tools

Despite the increasing range of game design courses (Schreiber 2009), books (Fullerton 2014), and presentations (Lewis-Evans 2012) on game design prototyping, there is still a paucity of useful design and review articles (Gray et al. 2005), available game design prototype tools (Manker 2012; Neil 2015, 2016), and venues for noncommercial developers, academics, and related experts to present, pitch, play test, and perform their game prototypes, especially for serious games and virtual place-making (Ardito et al. 2009; Unver and Taylor 2012; Ardito, Desolda, and Lanzilotti 2013).

Potential tools include game play cards, game prototyping mechanisms, scenes or videos from a three-dimensional editor or game editor (Unity, Unreal, Blender), board games as prototypes, playing cards, physical artifacts that are role-played by the presenter, illustrations, slideshows, game editors (like the SIMS) used to make films (machinima), role-playing videos, flowcharts, or online interactive fiction software.

Computer-Aided Design, Geographic Information Systems (GIS), and GIS Engines

Despite originating as practical aides for the design of real-world architecture, computer-aided design and drafting (CAD or CADD) software initially encountered a great deal of resistance, in part because of their initial expense and apparent technical complexity but also because they were seen as blunt tools, crude instrumentation inadequate for the artistic expression of place. Recent developments in interactive technology offer new and exciting ways of conveying lived and experientially deepened notions of architectural place-making.

Yet there are trade-offs. For example, are traditional devices and technologies for designing, experiencing, and reflecting on a place in danger of being lost in this digital era? Have recent developments in virtual places and their related interfaces fully explored the usability and power of traditional place-seeking devices (such as maps and compasses)? Have we fully explored how these external cognitive devices can help us discover, explore, and absorb place experiences? Should we transfer them as representationally realistic as possible, or do they work on cognitive processes that are better catered for with new interactive metaphors? Do we see any of these new ideas in existing and emerging displays or peripherals? Are there potential issues (health, safety, sociability) or other limitations to next-generation technology, peripherals, place-making design software, or digital consumer infrastructures?

Preservation, Three-Dimensional Repositories, GIS, and GPS Repositories

Storing the components of virtual places is still problematic.[1] Models are hard to find, impossible to download and edit, and are in unusual, unwieldy, or obsolete formats. Many of the freely available models are stand-alone three-dimensional meshes with no accompanying metadata or information on the acquisition of the data. Few inform users how the models can be shared (or if they are editable). Fewer still quantify the accuracy of the scanning or modeling process or make available the scholarly documents, field reports, photographs, and site plans that allowed the designers to extract enough information for their models. Where there are suitable models in standard formats that are available from repositories, such as Sketchfab, TurboSquid, and cultural institutions like ARIADNE EU, 3D-ICONS EU, and the Europeana library portal (Europeana Network Association Members Council 2020), they are likely to be in unwieldy three-dimensional formats.

Dr. Hafizur Rahaman and I recently published a paper on how accessible and prevalent three-dimensional models in digital heritage publications are (Champion and Rahaman 2019). We collated a group of 1,483 conference papers from major digital heritage–related conferences: Virtual Systems and Multimedia (VSMM) 2015–17; Computer Applications and Quantitive Methods in Archaeology (CAA) 2013–16; the International Committee for Documentation of Cultural Heritage (CIPA) 2013, 2015, and 2017; EuroMed 2013 and 2015; and Digital Heritage Congress 2013 and 2015. Of these 1,483 papers we found only 264 papers (17.8%) referred and contained images of three-dimensional assets or three-dimensional digital models (table 10.1).

Table 10.1. Three-Dimensional Heritage Conference Papers

Conference	2017	2016	2015	2014	2013	2012	Total Papers
VSMM	55	65	53	—	—	—	173
CAA	—	—	117	73	50	—	240
CIPA	111	—	82	—	112	—	305
EuroMed	—	105	—	84	—	95	284
Digital Heritage	—	—	270	—	211	—	481
TOTAL	166	170	522	157	373	95	1,483

Contrary to our initial expectations, accessible three-dimensional assets or three-dimensional models were found in only 9 papers (3.4%). Of the 264 selected articles, 12 contained external web links to video content (4.6%), and 33 articles (12.5%) provided external links for other accessible visual material, including VR models, photographs, and images of three-dimensional models (table 10.2). Only 19 articles had external web links to three-dimensional models and *none of them were working!*

Of the nine articles that provided external links to accessible three-dimensional assets, they all shared four common locations and repositories (Champion and Rahaman 2019). While there are commercial, US, and European repositories for three-dimensional models, they are not designed for research and teaching, and academic publications in the field of virtual heritage (as well as related fields) do not seem to make much use of them! We need incentives for model creators to upload their models and ensure they are more accessible and retrievable.

Virtual Places as Digital Three-Dimensional Models

According to Kelly Greenop and Justin Barton (2014), "the reliability of 3D data for long-term preservation is an ongoing issue." Formats are another issue (McHenry and Bajcsy 2008). In the field of computer games, researchers have even preserved entire original games by wrapping them as an executable inside another program (Carroll 2012). Sven Havemann (2012) went so far as to complain, "The file format problem is maybe today the most annoying obstacle for a further spread of 3D technology. Most of the aforementioned sophisticated shape representations can simply not be stored due to a lack of a common file format. The menace of file format degradation makes sustainable 3D only an illusion."

I agree. A serious technical obstacle is the absence of a shared, secure, feature-rich format for three-dimensional models (Koller, Frischer, and Humphreys 2009). Although there are at least 140 file formats for three-dimensional models (McHenry and Bajcsy 2008), almost all have major issues in terms of access,

Table 10.2. Total Articles Containing References to Three-Dimensional Models and Heritage Assets

Conference	Total Papers	Papers Mentioning 3D Assets	%
VSMM 2015–17	173	31	17.9
CAA 2013–15	240	38	15.8
CIPA 2013, 2015, 2017	305	79	25.9
EuroMed 2012, 2014, 2016	284	61	21.5
Digital Heritage Congress 2013, 2015	481	55	11.4
TOTAL	1483	264	17.8

reliability, longevity, or range of features (Koller, Frischer, and Humphreys 2009). Which three-dimensional format holds the most promise for virtual places? Determining a format that is robust, durable, well supported, free, highly interactive, cross-platform, and easy to create or export to or from is a serious challenge.

Particularly for virtual places, we need to distinguish between a format to store models in an archive and a format that allows people to immerse themselves in an online browser-based virtual environment. For example, .x3d (related to and a successor of virtual reality modeling language) offers a stable environment, is truly cross-platform, works well on the internet, and is free; however, its functionality is limited and it still has relatively few exemplars and showcases.

To make interactive three-dimensional models available via the internet, various commercial and open-source game engines provide a range of features, three-dimensional model libraries, examples, and shortcuts to avoid extensive programming. Major common game engines that feature accessible editing and modding for communities include Unity, CryENGINE, and Unreal. Most of these game engines can run as standalone applications, as web plugins, and across a range of devices (desktop and surround computers, specialized stereoscopic surround display screens, smartphones, and game consoles).

Despite the power of the computer game engines associated with them, a proprietary three-dimensional format is best avoided. If a game engine (a real-time rendering engine) is required, then one solution would be to have the game engine or application add the components (assets) dynamically, requiring the model to be broken up into subcomponents, and then the computer would stream and connect to these subcomponents (packages) at runtime. There may also be a compromise solution that allows both a robust but limited three-dimensional format for archived models and a more interactive format available either via a browser or as a downloadable application.

Planned or Perceived Obsolescence

An aspect of VR systems and multimedia equipment that can fly under the radar is the potential for obsolescence, including planned (designed) obsolescence and perceived obsolescence. While high-level VR systems a decade or more ago could be abandoned due to lowering costs and increasing processors, difficult code, or inability to find skilled programmers and audience-attracting content, the new, more mobile VR and even phone-based systems coerce consumers to constantly upgrade based on new styles (lifestyle fashion), increased portability, and more impressive yet hardly necessary technical features.

Software that scales to suit older and slower computing systems along with open source community-backed platforms controlled by users is one way to ensure there is some level of control on accidental or deliberate obsolescence. There is however at least one more option: government intervention. In 2015, France became the first country to pass legislation designed to curb the practice of planned obsolescence (Prindle 2015). Manufacturers will have to tell their vendors "how long spare parts for a given product will be produced." Community pressure and government legislation are increasingly important factors in ensuring widespread usage.

VR and Repositories

Three major thematic issues could prove to be of great importance to a virtual place repository. First, VR equipment is moving toward the consumer level, based on the notion of a component-based system where your smartphone is both the stereoscopic viewer and the computer (such as in the case of the Samsung Gear). Such consumer technology frameworks will help VR technology and related content become far more accessible.

Second, there are research groups, particularly in digital humanities, so concerned about the silo mentality and preservation challenges of digital models that they develop solutions to allow people to create their content using free and open-source technology, or they provide technical exemplars via free software that others can download, modify, and learn from.

Third, journals are beginning to provide technology that allows authors to add three-dimensional models inside or next to text-based articles. So far, the main research field appears to be archaeology, but this will hopefully spread to other disciplines.

The Mobile Internet of Things (Wearables, Augmentables, Trackables, and Recordables)

The rise of mobile phones, tablets, and phablets has indeed been breathtaking, but what is of even more interest is what can be done with these devices and with the increasingly accessible surround displays. For example, the GLAM (galleries, libraries, archives, and museums) sector has been exploring how web-based and locative media can connect physical holdings with international audiences, and provide more personalized and filtered content to visitors (Giridharadas 2014).

Three-dimensional printing and the makerspace revolution have thrived due to these and other technological innovations, allowing people to even print commercially viable three-dimensional cars (Kirkland). The promise of HMDs such as Google Glass, Samsung Gear VR, and the Oculus Rift to provide more accessible, economic, and immersive experiences have been seized on by companies such as Facebook for hitherto unbelievable figures (Dingman 2014; Miller 2014). So technological innovation does seem to be creating radical changes in web-based companies (Parkin 2014).

Convergence

The computer paradigm is giving way to the mobile internet paradigm (Gartner 2014; Lunden 2014a, 2014b). Always on, always connected, always linked, always beeping, and always being triggered. Increased mobility suggests lighter and yet more powerful devices, greater contextualization, and improved personalization. Unfortunately, in my area of research, virtual heritage (games and VR applied in the services of cultural heritage), the *development* of technology for the transmission of cultural knowledge in a virtual world is arguably still at a primitive stage. Ideally, digital cultural innovation in this field develops in parallel with technological innovation, but projects and commercial applications so far show either a lack of technical flexibility or a paucity of rich cultural interaction and thematic appropriateness.

It is however possible that crowd-sourcing, popular culture trends, and walled gardens of technological ecosystems, will improve the field of virtual places. In his book *Convergence Culture*, Henry Jenkins (2006) argued that fan culture was equivalent to collective intelligence; that mainstream popular media is a good example of participatory media; that there will be no one black box through which all media will have to flow; and that old media never dies. If he was correct, this would be great news for the development of platforms for virtual places.

In Jenkins's (2006, 2, 282) introduction and glossary, *convergence* is "a word that describes technological, industrial, cultural, and social changes in the ways media circulates within our culture . . . the flow of content across multiple media platforms, the cooperation between multiple media industries, the search for new structures of media financing . . . the migratory behavior of media audiences who would go almost anywhere in search of the kind of entertainment experiences they want."

Yet convergence culture is introduced as "a shift in the logic by which culture operates, emphasizing the flow of content across media channels" (Jenkins 2006, 283–84). And even more surprisingly, divergence is "part of the same process of media change" as convergence, at least according to Pool Ithiel de Sola (1983). I won't here try to determine what exactly convergence culture is, but I will raise the question of whether we have reached the point of truly converged media. In his blog post "The Digital Humanities Is About Breaking Stuff," Jesse Stommel (2013) wrote that we have reached this point: we now combine film and media. ("Our apparatuses for media-consumption juxtapose digital media, literature, and film:

Now, we watch Ridley Scott's *Alien* in a window alongside Twitter and Facebook. Film no longer exists as a medium distinct from these other media.") This certainly happens, but one may question whether this happens successfully across all media equally or easily.

A second major theme in Jenkins's book is participatory culture: "Rather than talking about media producers and consumers as occupying separate roles, we might now see them as participants who interact with each other according to a new set of rules that none of us fully understands" (2006, 2).

So even if the relationship can be unequal, for Jenkins convergence is not via media appliances—not even, perhaps, via corporations—but "within the brains of individual consumers and through their social interactions with others." Does this happen as a democratic, collaborative, and creative process? Could such an idealistic dream be possible?

Others, such as Bruce Sterling, have declared that old media has been superseded, but writers have also suggested that the future involves all content controlled through a single proprietary device or network franchise. For Jenkins, it is a fallacy to think there will be a black box, "the nexus through which all future media content will flow." Is the black box metaphorical, is it hardware, or could it be a corporate franchise?

At least three global giants, Facebook, Apple, and Samsung, already deploy walled gardens (Bajarin 2013; Grubb 2013). The walled garden phenomenon also applies to games. Matt Geraldi (2012) wrote, "Because of the strict ownership rules set in place by the various digital-only retail services, such as Valve Corporation's Steam for computer games and Microsoft's Xbox Live Arcade on the Xbox 360, preservationists have very few legal options when it comes to duplicating and distributing modern games for research purposes." So even if there is no universal black box, there are certainly attempts by large corporations to restrict people to one device or one delivery service (Higa 2008).

Jenkins claimed that old media never die; the tools and the delivery services that we use to access the media content may die, but this is *not* the same thing as the media itself. I have to disagree here. When we use media, we employ both our declarative memory and our procedural memory. Procedural memory is not something that we can just call on; it guides how we act, but it has to be triggered. We may not be aware of it or able to express exactly how we know what to do, but we can perform routine activities merely by having access to it (Schermer 2014). However, procedural learning often relies on tools, and our tools are external cognitive artifacts; they are physical objects that augment our memory, such as calendars, diaries, and maps, but also activity-dedicated spaces. Here lies a contradiction: we use tools as part of the culture, but we also in a sense become our tools. We cannot just retrieve the content independently of the tool, space, or the delivery service. The way we perform with media means that if we are to preserve media, then we need to preserve the environment along with the media itself.

Ironically, it is the development of walled gardens and black box franchises that prevent our interaction with *historical* new media, at least in the area of game design. As Henry Lowood remarked, "Download-only distribution, copyright law, and end-user license agreements—those lengthy contracts users agree to but seldom read when installing a new computer program—are the biggest hurdles facing video game preservation at the moment" (Gerardi 2012). In the online article "How Will Historians Study Video Games?," Ilya Zarembsky (2013) interviewed the same Henry Lowood, who warned against seeing game preservation as merely being about retaining working software; it is "rather a historically specific site of shared experience." To preserve games and various types of new media, we must preserve not only the technology but also the cultural practices.

The third major theme in Jenkins's book is collective intelligence, a term coined by Pierre Lévy (1997). Jenkins (2006, 4) argues that via collective intelligence, "we can put the pieces together if we pool our resources and combine our skills . . . an alternative source of media power." Jenkins seems to think that collective intelligence is exemplified by the TV series *Survivor* fan base (a "group of active consumers who pool their knowledge to try to unearth the series' many secrets before they are revealed on air"), the 2004 US elections, and the "narrative activism" attempts of the *Big Brother* TV show fans. The most detailed example that Jenkins provides for collective intelligence is *The Matrix* franchise across the three films, games, and website. I cannot see this. Jenkins's definition of transmedia story is that it "unfolds across multiple media platforms, with each new text making a distinctive and valuable contribution to the whole." Even if we grant that *The Matrix* franchise provides cultural attractors and cultural activators à la French philosopher Pierre Lévy; the media creation seems to be all one way. It is not collaboratively shaped and created by leveraging the fan base community's knowledge and expertise.

The Matrix franchise was directed by two brothers; it is still authorial. Here the media as a superset is not collective knowledge, which Jenkins defined as "the sum total of information held individually by the members of a knowledge community that can be accessed in response to a specific question." The directors themselves said no one will ever understand all the clues.

Are these media experiments making us more intelligent? Jenkins doesn't directly suggest the above question, but it is surely an indication of successful collective intelligence. Is popular media making us smarter, or is it constraining our imagination? In the book *Everything Bad Is Good for You*, Steven Johnson (2005) goes out of his way to argue that the media outputs of modern popular culture (particularly commercial games and television), despite their apparent banal and frivolous content, are improving our cognitive abilities.

While some of Johnson's observations are pertinent and interesting (particularly about the increasingly complex "multiple threading" narratives of television shows like those on *The Sopranos* and the mental telescoping required for computer games), Johnson has been correctly criticized by Stephen Poole (2005) for confusing correlation with causation. Johnson's case that television and games are increasing in complexity seems reasonable, but his claim that we are performing better and better in IQ tests because of these increasingly complex narratives is not so convincing.

Innovation

Both Jenkins and Johnson have written fluid, provocative, but ultimately only partially substantiated books on the popular culture of television, the internet, and computer games. This is understandable; both writers began their books with caveats that they wanted to be provocative, but the field is so quickly changing that any final critical pronouncement would be premature. Still, there are some gaps in their monographs that we could help address, particularly in defining the key term *innovation* and how we can understand and judge the relationship of culture and technology in this new internet age.

The dictionary definitions of *innovation* seem fairly straightforward: the introduction of something new, or a new idea, method, or device (*Merriam-Webster* n.d.). A method for classifying innovations was provided by Rosanna Garcia and Roger Calantone (2002). The duo suggested that radical innovation is seldom discussed because it involves "innovations that embody a new technology that results in a new market infrastructure." They went further, stating, "Radical innovation results in the creative destruction or envelopment and suppression of the existing infrastructure. Examples include the steam engine, the World Wide Web, and the Bessemer steel manufacturing process." Unfortunately, their well-researched paper focused on market innovation per se, not community innovation.

Community and culture are not always explained by bureaucratic definitions of innovation. The notion of convergent cultural innovation would not be covered by the official Organisation for Economic Co-operation and Development (OECD) definition, as quoted by Luise Langergaard and Anne Hansen (2013, 1): "the implementation of a new or significantly improved product (good or service), or process, a new marketing method, or a new organizational method in business practices, workplace organization or external relations." Langergaard and Hansen argued against the generic OECD definition by stating that "innovation is renewal, but always something that strives for creating something new and better. Creating and renewing for something better can only be done within a certain context or domain."

However, this view creates a problem for defining innovation in the nexus of culture and technology: What would be "better"? Indeed, what is the content? According to an older and more generic definition in an engineering academic thesis by Jan Mentz (1999), innovation requires people to generate or realize a new idea; develop this idea into reality or a product; and then diffuse, implement, and market this new idea. If we take Joel Hruska's (2014) definition of *innovation* as involving invention, (product) realization, and implementation, then the development of mobile computing (including augmented reality, location-based services, and smartphones) appears to be highly innovative. I suggest this definition may be relevant to our discussion due to its open-endedness and its relevance to the mobile internet.

Who Are We Designing For? Pedagogical Issues

I argued earlier in this book that *digital natives* is a misleading term. If we follow Jenkins, the youth of today do not need to be experts: they only need to be open to collective intelligence via participatory media. Some may also argue that digital media culture is converging and, positively, that media is being increasingly consumed, filtered, and reorganized by participatory culture and a collective conscience (Jenkins 2013). There are without a doubt various critics of convergence culture (Conley 2013; Maher n.d.), but even if the evidence for convergence culture is open to debate, convergence culture would be highly inspiring for designers of e-learning, social games, and virtual worlds.

Gamification

A widely discussed, if controversial, development has been gamification. Gamification appears to exemplify convergent culture, but many in the gaming industry and many game design academics seem opposed to it (Bogost 2011; Deterding et al. 2011). Gamification can be explained as the addition to websites and learning environments of quantifiable actions that can be ranked and processed (and the information from which then stored), with immediate and vastly exaggerated feedback and graphically designed in the idiom of well-known computer games. Task performance can be graphically rewarded and socially shared, and some advocates will even argue that gamification can provide deeper, richer, and more engaging learning (Betts, Bal, and Betts 2013; Schoech et al. 2013; Hamari, Koivisto, and Sarsa 2014).

Gamification might be viewed as a convergent practice, but generally, there is no socially shared environment of play, no cultural creation and preservation of related space, little fantasy and imagination required, and no shared ergodic dimension (you don't see the work of other players as it happens). Any claims to gamification being an example of participatory media and collective intelligence seems weak: the framework and content are generally authored and directed, there is little if any shared knowledge and collaboratively creative input required, and players can complete on their own.

However, it is amusing to read the outrage of some academics as computer games themselves do not seem to have a clear and agreed-on definition or essence. One distinction might be the level of agency; in games, it is fun to explore, test, and challenge the apparent rules, and in gamification, this option is seldom available. On the other hand, if gamification can provide enjoyment, deep narratives, and rich learning experiences, I question whether they are not simply successful games with a learning component.

Digital Humanities and Community

I have suggested in my critique of Jenkins's discussion of reality TV series and *The Matrix* franchise that there is little clear evidence of collective intelligence and truly participatory media. There is even less evidence of long-term significant *specific* cultural change arising from these developments in virtual worlds and online games. However, one trend has shown promise, the move from humanities computing to digital humanities. This is arguably not just a change of name. An innovative aspect of digital humanities has been the development and integration of communities of humanities scholars with their audience via flexible and real-time digital technology.

Tools such as Neatline and Commons in a Box aim to bring the power of data-driven maps, journal-driven reprogrammable visualizations, and community-friendly website design for less technically experienced scholars. Community portals such as HASTAC (http://www.hastac.org/) collate news, issues, and methods. Open Editions (http://www.openeditions.com/) and Scalar (http://scalar.usc.edu/scalar/) promise new types of publishing platforms. DHnow (http://digitalhumanitiesnow.org) attempts to aggregate and filter leading hot-off-the-press articles (Barfield 2015). Many in the field of digital humanities hope to create an ecosystem where tools, papers, projects, and researchers are shared and dynamically updated (Wright and Richards 2018; Sewell et al. 2019; Uzwyshyn 2019).

In other publications, I have suggested objectives to combat these issues for virtual heritage, but these suggestions apply to virtual places in general (Champion 2017). I have recommended a scholarly ecosystem for virtual heritage where both the media assets involved and the communities (of scholars, shareholders, and the general public) are all active participants in the experience of the virtual places and the judgment of those virtual places and their related digital assets and paradata.

I realized a scholarly ecosystem is of vital importance when presenting a paper titled "Researchers as Infrastructure" at the 2013 Digital Humanities Congress in Sheffield, UK (Champion 2014). The audience questions centered mostly on the issue of people; they did not ask about equipment. One of the questions asked was "How do we keep our programmers?" A huge resource (in terms of people skills and experience) is lost when skilled information and communications technology (ICT) people leave the university for the higher-paying commercial world. ICT people are typically not well recognized academically and would be more likely to stay if their creative and intellectual input was appreciated and they were given time to work on self-directed projects that could feed back into the overall center. This would be similar to the one day a week option at Google, where workers were given "time off to innovate" (Baldwin 2017).

In Europe and across the world, too many university departments are given money to buy equipment but not the staff (to not just maintain the equipment and ensure it stays relevant, but also to support and train scholars on how to use that same new and complex equipment). Infrastructure is required equipment used by people for certain goals, and it is modified in turn. Given this cyclical nature, we could say that a genuine infrastructure is the ecosystem of resources added to people (and their goals) and a feedback system (otherwise the infrastructure atrophies because people and their needs change over time). I have argued that Jenkins's arguments forgot the importance of culture as space, but I fully support his attempts to explore and justify the importance of people and communities. I believe this is the great promise of digital humanities.

New Media and New Heritage

As I wrote in the edited collection *New Heritage: New Media and Cultural Heritage* (Champion 2008), one problem with new media theory (as with many aesthetic definitions) is that it often uses individual and unique cases or tries to create a complete theory from the entanglement of complicated literary criticism rather than consider typical publicly available examples that we might find in the wider world. Another problem with definitions of new media is that there are continually new definitions of new media. How can such hybrid practices, definitions, and media hope to have essentialist criteria that focus and provoke rather than constrain? The phrase confuses as much as it clarifies; we need to understand new media and its relation to this new convergence culture.

Given there are books entitled *New Media, 1740–1915* (Gitelman and Pingree 2003), to define new media as *new* media seems laughable. It is possible to define new media as the continual search for new forms, for new technologies, for new media. New media can also be defined as recent multimedia, genres, or products that provide interactive digital entertainment, or the distribution of digital content. However, digital media is fast becoming a conventional and pervasive medium.

In the *New Heritage* collection (Champion 2008), I suggested that one overriding of new media is the development of user-centered, personalizable data, not constrained by one type of hardware device. Users navigate through space, but they explore worlds. Their exploration is thematic, cognitive, and motivated; their interaction directly shapes their experience. So, for the sake of simplicity, I define new media as *the act of reshaping the user experience through the innovative use of digital media.*

Summary

I have briefly discussed four claims by Jenkins on the related role of digital entertainment platforms: fan culture examples show evidence of collective intelligence; mainstream popular media is a good example of participatory media; there will be no one black box through which all media will have to flow; and old media does not die. While he was speaking in particular of fan culture, it is interesting to apply these claims to virtual places. Unfortunately, there are few examples of successful collective intelligence in fan culture–related virtual places (*Second Life? Active-Worlds?*).[2] Popular media has problems with collaboration and meaningful interaction. Universal standards and protocols are some way off. And old virtual places (environments, games) definitely do die!

But do these trends, visions, and hopes tally with the promise of convergence? Not yet, for current software and hardware and services don't seem to parallel hopes of increasing collective intelligence. I have also argued that convergence culture is not suitable to describe the interaction of culture and technology, at least in the domain of virtual places. It might be of use in understanding more traditional media such as film and television, but even in these areas, it seems to have trouble separating what is happening (the spread of digital popular media) from potential claims that what is happening is good or even desirable. A relatively simple example would be reality television. Yes, these shows are run in parallel with other digital media, but many have criticized either their contribution to culture (Maher n.d.) or their ability to showcase and exemplify collective intelligence (Tripp 2008; Conley 2013).

Jenkins's claim that media will not be controlled by a single black box is debatable: the essential question is whether media infrastructures are narrowing our options and restricting potential creative freedom or improving and strengthening media content, media technology, media audiences, and media infrastructures. Yet quasi-monopolies in national and international media have not seen an improvement in creativity or exhibited innovation in any particularly obvious and significant way. Media infrastructures have improved and benefited other aspects of humanity, but it is an interesting question as to whether media audiences learn, think, and communicate more efficiently or more expressively, and whether new developments in technology have seen a corresponding influx of innovative cultural practice.

This subsection on convergence has suggested two solutions: agreeing on a shared format and reconnecting the making of visualization and virtual place design with the interests and abilities of communities. Recent technological developments in providing cheaper, lighter, more flexible, more accurate, and more powerful equipment are key, but another essential factor is the development of community-supported information networks and participatory toolsets and frameworks, as evidenced by the fledging digital humanities communities.

Virtual places are too important to be locked away in proprietary, unsupported file formats. As designers, practitioners, and educators, we need to provide both public access and robust preservation infrastructures to support them. Technology is only one part of the solution; we must also develop incentives, guidelines, and frameworks.

It is difficult to evaluate "place" in virtual realms, but this is at least in part due to the preservation of the research data and 3D models. To solve this, we require a systematic pipeline featuring open-source software, a well-organized online archive of three-dimensional models in a robust open format, and globally accepted metadata. But it also requires a community that reviews, critiques, augments, and maintains suitable content. In short, a digital ecosystem for scholars and community participants.

Technical issues may appear to be the central problem to resolve, but if there is no public involvement, understanding, and appreciation, virtual places will disappear, despite any technical brilliance or infrastructure support. An infrastructure that is not used is not infrastructure; it is merely equipment. Previous writers have written convincingly about the importance of archives (Limp et al. 2013), but there is another important step, ensuring the archive is effectively used. As Vicky Garnett and Jennifer Edmond (2014; Edmond and Garnett 2015) have declared, there are many issues with APIs, but one critical issue is how to get enough people to use them.

To design infrastructure for virtual place technology, we need cheaper, lighter, more flexible, more accurate, and more powerful hardware, software, and sensors, but we also need to develop community-supported information networks, participatory tool sets and frameworks, and robust yet flexible shared three-dimensional formats, protocols, and ways to link assets, degradable design, and free or freemium tools (Grayburn et al. 2019; Europeana Network Association Members Council 2020).

A good start would be to agree on a shared format, work on ways to strengthen the scholarly and practitioner-based ecosystem of place design and thinking, and reconnect the making of culture with the community. At present, the people who design-build and critique elements and concepts underpinning virtual places are too scattered.

In this new age of digital communication, the three-dimensional model must be recognized as a key scholarly resource (Di Benedetto et al. 2014). As a core part of a scholarly ecosystem, the three-dimensional model should be traceable, it should link to previous works and related scholarly information.

I suggest that the model should be component-based so that parts can be directly linked and updated. Web models could be dynamically created at runtime. The model should be engaging; thus, extensive play testing and evaluation will be required to ensure that it does engage its intended audience.

As part of the scholarly infrastructure, the three-dimensional model format (and all related data formats) should be easy to find and reliable. It should not require huge files to download, or it should at least provide users with enough information to decide whether and what to download. Metadata can also help record the completeness, measurement methodology, and accuracy of the models and Linked Open Data can help connect these media assets in a sensible and useful way.

The community of scholars, students, and the wider public should be involved, and we must endeavor to incorporate their understanding, feedback, and participation (in line with relevant charters, policies, and useful, succinct manifestos). Community involvement is necessary for scholars as well, and ideally, they dynamically link to journals and refereed conference papers and to the list of tools and methods that were used.

A robust feedback system could help continually improve the system. Other shareholder issues, such as varying levels of learning skills and knowledge required or cultural knowledge that needs to be hidden (privacy and ownership issues), should also be incorporated into the project.

The success of virtual place projects for communication and as a preservation medium depends on community involvement; this community includes schol- ars, students, the wider public as well as the original shareholders and owners of the content simulated. Shared understanding requires clear aims, methods, and terms, but above all, it requires a comprehensive methodology.

Notes

1. For more details see Champion (2017).

2. *Activeworlds* (previously *Active Worlds*) was originally *AlphaWorld* (Damer 2008) and is unusual in the array of free virtual world applications for being available on Mac OS, Windows, and Linux.

References

Alexander, Leigh, and Iain Chambers. 2017. "How Natural Language Tech Is Changing Interactive Gaming: Tech Podcast." *The Guardian*. Last Modified June 14, 2017. Accessed August 2, 2017. https://www.theguardian.com/technology/audio/2017/jun/09/natural-language-tech-changing-interactive-gaming-tech-podcast.

Ardito, Carmelo, Paolo Buono, Maria Francesca Costabile, Rosa Lanzilotti, and Antonio Piccinno. 2009. "Enabling Interactive Exploration of Cultural Heritage: An Experience of Designing Systems for Mobile Devices." *Knowledge, Technology & Policy* 22 (1): 79–86. https://doi.org/10.1007/s12130-009-9079-7.

Ardito, Carmelo, Giuseppe Desolda, and Rosa Lanzilotti. 2013. "Playing on Large Displays to Foster Children's Interest in Archaeology." In *Proceedings of International Conference on Distributed Multimedia Systems (Dms '13)*, edited by Paolo Nesi and Kia Ng, 79–84. Brighton, UK: Knowledge Systems Institute Graduate School.

Azuma, Ronald. 2004. "Overview of Augmented Reality." ACM SIGGRAPH 2004 Course Notes, Los Angeles, CA. http://doi.acm.org/10.1145/1103900.1103926.

Bajarin, Ben. 2013. "Microsoft and the Rise of Hardware Walled Gardens." *Time*. Last Modified July 31, 2017. Accessed July 31, 2017. http://techland.time.com/2013/11/25/microsoft-and-the-rise-of-hardware-walled-gardens/.

Baldwin, Joan. 2017. "Saying What You Mean & Getting Better at What You Do." *Leadership Matters: Thoughts on 21st Century Museum Leadership by Anne Ackerson and Joan Baldwin* (blog), June 13, 2017. Accessed April 30, 2021. https://leadershipmatters1213.wordpress.com/2017/06/12/saying-what-you-mean-getting-better-at-what-you-do/.

Barfield, Woodrow. 2015. *Fundamentals of Wearable Computers and Augmented Reality*. Boca Raton, FL: CRC Press.

Betts, Ben W., Jay Bal, and Alan W. Betts. 2013. "Gamification as a Tool for Increasing the Depth of Student Understanding Using a Collaborative e-Learning Environment." *International Journal of Continuing Engineering Education and Life Long Learning* 23 (3): 213–28.

Billinghurst, Mark, Adrian Clark, and Gun Lee. 2015. "A Survey of Augmented Reality." *Foundations and Trends® in Human-Computer Interaction* 8 (2–3): 73–272.

Bogost, Ian. 2011. "Gamification Is Bullshit." *Atlantic.* Last Modified December 15, 2014. Accessed July 21, 2017. http://www.theatlantic.com/technology/archive/2011/08 /gamification-is-bullshit/243338/.

Bonus, James Alex, Alanna Peebles, Marie-Louise Mares, and Irene G. Sarmiento. 2017. "Look on the Bright Side (of Media Effects): Pokémon Go as a Catalyst for Positive Life Experiences." *Media Psychology* 21 (2): 263–87. https://doi.org/10.1080/15213269.2017 .1305280.

Bostanci, Erkan, Nadia Kanwal, and Adrian F Clark. 2015. "Augmented Reality Applications for Cultural Heritage Using Kinect." *Human-Centric Computing and Information Sciences* 5 (1): 20.

Carroll, Cindy. 2012. "News Brief: Carnegie Mellon Awarded Grant to Preserve Executable Content." Carnegie Mellon University News. Last Modified October 4, 2012. Accessed January 31, 2017. http://www.cmu.edu/news/stories/archives/2012/october/oct4 _executablecontent.html.

Chalmers, Alan. 2014. "Level of Realism: Feel, Smell, and Taste in Virtual Environments." In *The Oxford Handbook of Virtuality,* edited by Mark Grimshaw, 602–14. Oxford: Oxford University Press.

Champion, Erik M. 2008. "Explorative Shadow Realms of Uncertain Histories." In *New Heritage: New Media and Cultural Heritage,* edited by Yehuda Kalay, Thomas Kvan, and Janice Affleck, 185–206. London: Routledge.

———. 2014. "Researchers as Infrastructure." Proceedings of the Digital Humanities Congress 2012, Studies in the Digital Humanities, Sheffield, UK, September 6–8, 2012.

———. 2017. "The Role of 3D Models in Virtual Heritage Infrastructures." In *Cultural Heritage Digital Tools and Infrastructures,* edited by Agiatis Benardou, Erik Champion, Costis Dallas, and Lorna Hughes, 15–35. Abingdon, UK: Routledge.

Champion, Erik M., and H. Rahaman. 2019. "3D Digital Heritage Models as Sustainable Scholarly Resources." *Sustainability* 11 (8): 2425. http://www.mdpi.com/2071-1050/11/8 /2425.

Chapman, Glenn. 2016. "Augmented Reality Looks to Future Where Screens Vanish." Phys .org. Last Modified July 27, 2017. Accessed January 29 2020. https://phys.org/news /2016-02-augmented-reality-future-screens.html#jCp.

Chung, Namho, Heejeong Han, and Youhee Joun. 2015. "Tourists' Intention to Visit a Destination: The Role of Augmented Reality (AR) Application for a Heritage Site." *Computers in Human Behavior* 50:588–99.

Conley, Tara. 2013. "Book Review Convergence Culture: Where Old and New Media Collide." *HASTAC* (blog), October 4, 2014. Accessed April 30, 2021. http://www .hastac.org/blogs/tara-l-conley/2013/11/01/book-review-convergence-culture-where -old-and-new-media-collide.

Damer, Bruce. 2008. "Meeting in the Ether: A Brief History of Virtual Worlds as a Medium for User-Created Events." *Artifact* 2 (2): 94–107.

Davies, Hugh. 2017. "Towards an Ethics of Alternate Reality Games." *Digital Studies/Le Champ Numérique.* Last Modified February 5, 2017. Accessed January 29, 2020. https:// www.digitalstudies.org/ojs/index.php/digital_studies/article/view/328.

De Sola, Pool Ithiel. 1983. *Technologies of Freedom.* Cambridge, MA: Harvard University Press.

Deterding, Sebastian, Dan Dixon, Rilla Khaled, and Lennart Nacke. 2011. "From Game Design Elements to Gamefulness: Defining Gamification." In *Proceedings of the 15th International Academic Mindtrek Conference: Envisioning Future Media Environments*, 9–15. Tampere, FIN: ACM.

Di Benedetto, Marco, Federico Ponchio, Luigi Malomo, Marco Callieri, Matteo Dellepiane, Paolo Cignoni, and Roberto Scopigno. 2014. "Web and Mobile Visualization for Cultural Heritage." In *3D Research Challenges in Cultural Heritage: A Roadmap in Digital Heritage Preservation*, edited by Marinos Ioannides and Ewald Quak, 18–35. Berlin: Springer.

Dingman, Hayden. 2014. "To Oculus and Beyond: Peering into the Future of Virtual Reality at GDC 2014." PCWorld, March 21, 2014. Accessed April 30, 2021. http://www.pcworld.com/article/2110427/to-oculus-and-beyond-peering-into-the-future-of-virtual-reality-at-gdc-2014.html.

Dredge, Stuart. 2011. "What Is Mobile Augmented Reality For?" *The Guardian*. Last Modified February 18, 2011. Accessed January 29, 2020. https://www.theguardian.com/technology/appsblog/2011/feb/17/augmented-reality-mobile-apps.

———. 2017. "Virtual Reality: Is This Really How We Will All Watch TV in Years to Come?". The Observer, *The Guardian*. Last Modified April 9, 2017. Accessed January 29, 2020. https://www.theguardian.com/technology/2017/apr/09/virtual-reality-is-it-the-future-of-television?CMP=share_btn_tw.

Edmond, Jennifer, and Vicky Garnett. 2015. "APIs and Researchers: The Emperor's New Clothes?" *International Journal of Digital Curation* 10 (1): 287–97.

Europeana Network Association Members Council. 2019. "3D Content in Europeana." Europeana Foundation, January 28, 2019. Last Modified March 26, 2020. Accessed April 30, 2021. https://pro.europeana.eu/project/3d-content-in-europeana.

Eve, Stuart. 2017. "The Embodied GIS. Using Mixed Reality to Explore Multi-Sensory Archaeological Landscapes." *Internet Archaeology* 44. https://doi.org/10.11141/ia.44.3.

Friedman, Doron. 2017. "Brain-Computer Interfacing and Virtual Reality." In *Handbook of Digital Games and Entertainment Technologies*, edited by Ryohei Nakatsu, Matthias Rauterberg, and Paolo Ciancarini, 151–71. Singapore: Springer.

Fullerton, Tracy. 2014. *Game Design Workshop: A Playcentric Approach to Creating Innovative Games*. Boca Raton, FL: CRC Press.

Gaines Lewis, Jordan. 2015. "Smells Ring Bells: How Smell Triggers Memories and Emotions." *Psychology Today*, January 12, 2015. Accessed July 31, 2017. https://www.psychologytoday.com/blog/brain-babble/201501/smells-ring-bells-how-smell-triggers-memories-and-emotions.

Garcia, Rosanna, and Roger Calantone. 2002. "A Critical Look at Technological Innovation Typology and Innovativeness Terminology: A Literature Review." *Journal of Product Innovation Management* 19 (2): 110–32.

Garnett, Vicky, and Jennifer Edmond. 2014. "Building an API Is Not Enough! Investigating Reuse of Cultural Heritage Data." *Impact of Social Science* (blog), September 8, 2014. London School of Economics. Accessed April 30, 2021. http://blogs.lse.ac.uk/impactofsocialsciences/2014/09/08/investigating-reuse-of-cultural-heritage-data-europeana/.

Gartner. 2014. "Gartner Says Worldwide Traditional PC, Tablet, Ultramobile and Mobile Phone Shipments to Grow 4.2 Percent in 2014." Press release, July 7, 2014. Last Modified July 7, 2014. Accessed January 29, 2020. https://www.gartner.com/en

Place-Making Interfaces and Platforms

/newsroom/press-releases/2014-07-07-gartner-says-worldwide-traditional-pc-tablet
-ultramobile-and-mobile-phone-shipments-to-grow-4-percent-in-2014.

Gaudiosi, John. 2016. "7 Ways AR and VR Will Change Tech in 2016." *Fortune*. Last
Modified January 4, 2016. Accessed January 29, 2020. http://fortune.com/2016/01/04
/augmented-reality-vr-change-tech/.

Gerardi, Matt. 2012. "Extra Lives: Preserving the History of Video Games." *Rated J for Janky*
(blog), January 17, 2012. Accessed April 30, 2021. https://jforjanky.wordpress.com/2012
/01/17/extra-lives-preserving-the-history-of-video-games/#more-882.

Gilbert, Ben. 2015. "It's Going to Be at Least 5 Years before Virtual Reality Goes Mainstream."
Business Insider, August 19, 2015. Last Modified August 19, 2015. Accessed April 30, 2021.
http://www.businessinsider.com.au/virtual-reality-on-gartner-hype-cycle-2015-8.

Giridharadas, Anand. 2014. "Museums See Different Virtues in Virtual Worlds." *New York
Times*, August 7, 2014. Last Modified August 7, 2014. Accessed July 31, 2017. https://
www.nytimes.com/2014/08/08/arts/design/museums-see-different-virtues-in-virtual
-worlds.html.

Gitelman, Lisa, and Geoffrey B. Pingree. 2003. *New Media, 1740–1915*. Boston, MA: MIT Press.

Graham, Peter. 2020. "Apple CEO Tim Cook Expects AR: 'Will Pervade Our Entire Lives.'"
VRfocus. Last Modified January 21, 2020. Accessed April 30, 2021. https://www
.vrfocus.com/2020/01/apple-ceo-tim-cook-expects-ar-will-pervade-our-entire-lives/.

Gray, Kyle, Kyle Gabler, Shalin Shodhan, and Matt Kucic. 2005. "How to Prototype a Game
in Under 7 Days." Gamasutra, October 26, 2005. Accessed Janurary 29, 2020. https://
www.gamasutra.com/view/feature/130848/how_to_prototype_a_game_in_under
_7_.php.

Grayburn, Jennifer, Zack Lischer-Katz, Kristina Golubiewski-Davis, and Veronica
Ikeshoji-Orlati. 2019. *3D/VR in the Academic Library: Emerging Practices and Trends*.
CLIR Publication No. 176. February 2019. Arlington, VA: Council on Library and
Information Resources.

Greenop, Kelly, and Justin R. Barton. 2014. "Scan, Save, and Archive: How to Protect Our
Digital Cultural Heritage." The Conversation, February 11, 2014. Last Modified June 14,
2017. Accessed January 29, 2020. https://theconversation.com/scan-save-and-archive
-how-to-protect-our-digital-cultural-heritage-22160.

Greenspan, Brian. 2015. "Don't Make a Scene: Game Studies for an Uncertain World." *Digital
Studies/Le Champ Numérique*. Accessed January 29, 2020. https://doi.org/http://doi
.org/10.16995/dscn.35.

Grubb, Jeffrey. 2013. "Apple: 'Want to Criticize Religion? Write a Book'—Don't Make a
Game." Venturebeat. Last Modified January 15, 2013. Accessed July 31, 2017. https://
venturebeat.com/2013/01/15/apple-want-to-criticize-religion-write-a-book-dont-make
-a-game/.

Gurkok, Hayrettin, Anton Nijholt, and Mannes Poel. 2017. "Brain-Computer Interface
Games: Towards a Framework." In *Handbook of Digital Games and Entertainment
Technologies*, edited by Ryohei Nakatsu, Matthias Rauterberg, and Paolo Ciancarini,
133–50. Singapore: Springer.

Hamari, Juho, Jonna Koivisto, and Harri Sarsa. 2014. "Does Gamification Work?—A Literature
Review of Empirical Studies on Gamification." Paper presented at the Forty-Seventh
Hawaii International Conference on System Sciences (HICSS), January 6–9, 2014.

Havemann, Sven. 2012. "Intricacies and Potentials of Gathering Paradate in the 3D Modelling
Workflow." In *Parada and Transparency in Virtual Heritage*, edited by A. Bentkowska-
Kafel, H. Denard, and D. Baker, 146–60. London: Ashgate.

Higa, D. 2008. "Walled Gardens versus the Wild West." *Computer* 41 (10): 102–105. https://doi
.org/10.1109/MC.2008.439.

Hruska, Joel. 2014. "Smartphone Usage Surges While PCS Show Startling Decline in New
Worldwide Stud." ExtremeTech. Last Modified August 20, 2014. Accessed July 31, 2017.
http://www.extremetech.com/computing/188314-smartphone-usage-surges-while-pcs
-show-startling-decline-in-new-worldwide-study.

Jenkins, Henry. 2006. *Convergence Culture: Where Old and New Media Collide.* New York:
New York University Press.

———. 2013. "Rethinking 'Rethinking Convergence/Culture.'" *Cultural Studies* 28 (2):
267–97. https://doi.org/10.1080/09502386.2013.801579.

Johnson, Steven. 2005. *Everything Bad Is Good for You: How Popular Culture Is Making Us
Smarter.* London: Allen Lane.

Jung, Timothy, M. Claudia tom Dieck, Hyunae Lee, and Namho Chung. 2016. "Effects
of Virtual Reality and Augmented Reality on Visitor Experiences in Museum."
In *Information and Communication Technologies in Tourism 2016: Proceedings of
the International Conference in Bilbao, Spain, February 2–5, 2016,* 621–35. Cham:
Springer.

Koller, David, Bernard Frischer, and Greg Humphreys. 2009. "Research Challenges for
Digital Archives of 3D Cultural Heritage Models." *Journal on Computing and Cultural
Heritage* 2 (3): 7.

Kounavis, Chris D., Anna E. Kasimati, and Efpraxia D. Zamani. 2012. "Enhancing the
Tourism Experience through Mobile Augmented Reality: Challenges and Prospects."
International Journal of Engineering Business Management 4:10.

Kraemer, Harald, and Norbert Kanter. 2014. "Use and Re-use of Data How Collection
Management Systems, Transmedia and Augmented Reality Impact the Future of
Museum." Paper presented at the 2014 International Conference on Virtual Systems &
Multimedia (VSMM), Hong Kong, December 9–11, 2014.

Langergaard, Luise Li, and Anne Vorre Hansen. 2013. "Innovation: A One Size Fits All
Concept?" Paper presented at the Twenty-Fourth ISPIM Conference, Helsinki,
June 16–19, 2013. Accessed April 30, 2021. https://forskning.ruc.dk/en/publications
/innovation-a-one-size-fits-all-concept.

Leadbetter, Richard. 2011. "Valve: Games Will Detect Your Feelings." Eurogamer. Last
Modified February 22, 2011. Accessed June 14, 2017. http://www.eurogamer.net
/articles/digitalfoundry-valve-biometrics-blog-entry.

Lévy, Pierre. 1997. *Collective Intelligence: Mankind's Emerging World in Cyberspace.* Translated
from French by Robert Bononno. New York: Plenum Trade.

Lewis-Evans, Ben. 2012. "Introduction to Game Prototyping & Research." Slideshare. Last
Modified December 16, 2012. Accessed April 30, 2021. http://www.slideshare.net
/Gortag/game-prototyping-and-research.

Limp, W. F., Angelia Payne, Snow Winters, Adam Barnes, and Jackson Cothren. 2013.
"Approaching 3D Digital Heritage Data from a Multi-Technology, Lifecycle
Perspective." In *Proceedings of the 38th Annual International Conference on Computer
Applications and Quantitative Methods in Archaeology (Caa), Granada, Spain, 2010,*
edited by Francisco Contreras, Mercedes Farjas, and Francisco Javier Melero, 1–8.
Annual International Conference on Computer Applications and Quantitative
Methods in Archaeology (CAA). Oxford: Archaeopress.

Lunden, Ingrid. 2014a. "Gartner: Device Shipments Break 2.4B Units in 2014, Tablets to
Overtake PC Sales in 2015." Techcrunch. Last Modified July 7, 2014. Accessed January

20, 2020. http://techcrunch.com/2014/07/06/gartner-device-shipments-break-2-4b -units-in-2014-tablets-to-overtake-pc-sales-in-2015/.

———. 2014b. "Smartphone Usage Surges While PCs Show Startling Decline in New Worldwide Study." ExtremeTech. Last Modified September 28, 2014. Accessed January 29, 2020. http://www.extremetech.com/computing/188314-smartphone-usage-surges -while-pcs-show-startling-decline-in-new-worldwide-study.

Maher, Jimmy. n.d. "Convergence." *Digital Antiquarian* (blog). Accessed April 30, 2021. http://maher.filfre.net/writings/convergence.html.

Manker, Jon. 2012. "Designscape–A Suggested Game Design Prototyping Process Tool." *Eludamos: Journal for Computer Game Culture 6* (1): 85–98. http://www.eludamos.org /index.php/eludamos/article/viewDownloadInterstitial/vol6no1-8/6-1-8-pdf.

McHenry, Kenton, and Peter Bajcsy. 2008. "An Overview of 3D Data Content, File Formats and Viewers." Technical Report: isda08-002. Image Spatial Data Analysis Group, National Center for Supercomputing Applications, University of Illinois at Urbana-Champaign. https://www.archives.gov/files/applied-research/ncsa/8-an-overview-of -3d-data-content-file-formats-and-viewers.pdf.

Meisenzahl, Mary. 2019. "5 Failed Tech Predictions for the 2010s That Didn't Work Out." Business Insider, December 19, 2019. Accessed December 31, 2019. https://www .businessinsider.com.au/failed-tech-predictions-decade-2019-12?r=US&IR=T.

Mentz, Jan Cornelius. 1999. "Developing a Competence Audit for Technological Innovation." Master's diss., Faculty of Engineering, University of Pretoria. Accessed April 30, 2021. http://hdl.handle.net/2263/30490.

Merriam-Webster. n.d. "Innovation." Accessed July 31, 2017. https://www.merriam-webster .com/dictionary/innovation.

Miller, Jennifer. 2014. "Mind Reading Comes One Step Closer to Reality with the Glass Brain." Fast Company. Last Modified March 21, 2014. Accessed February 3, 2020. http://www.fastcocreate.com/3027904/mind-reading-comes-one-step-closer-to -reality-with-the-glass-brain.

Miller-Kipp, Gisela, and Josh Constine. 2015. "Apple Acquires Augmented Reality Company Metaio." Techcrunch. Last Modified May 28, 2015. Accessed February 3, 2020. https:// techcrunch.com/2015/05/28/apple-metaio/.

Moskowitz, Blaire. 2016. "Poké It Up: How to Catch Millennials with Pokémon GO at Your Museum." Museumhack. Last Modified November 12, 2020. Accessed April 30, 2021. https://museumhack.com/pokemongo-museums/.

Neil, Katharine. 2015. "Game Design Tools: Can They Improve Game Design Practice?" Master's thesis. Signal and Image Processing. Conservatoire national des arts et metiers (CNAM). Flinders University of South Australia. https://tel.archives-ouvertes .fr/tel-01344638/document.

———. 2016. "How We Design Games Now and Why." Gamasutra. Last Modified January 24, 2017. Accessed January 29, 2020. http://www.gamasutra.com/blogs/KatharineNeil /20161214/287515/How_we_design_games_now_and_why.php.

Noh, Zakiah, Mohd Shahrizal Sunar, and Zhigeng Pan. 2009. "A Review on Augmented Reality for Virtual Heritage System." In *Learning by Playing. Game-Based Education System Design and Development*, edited by Maiga Chang, Rita Kuo, Kinshuk, Gwo-Dong Chen and Michitaka Hirose, 50–61. Lecture Notes in Computer Science. Berlin: Springer.

Ogden, Henry. 2015. "Augmented Reality: Believe the Hype (Cycle)." Techcrunch. Last Modified January 30, 2017. Accessed February 3, 2020. https://techcrunch.com/2015/11 /01/augmented-reality-believe-the-hype-cycle/.

Parkin, Simon. 2014. "Virtual Reality Startups Look Back to the Future." *MIT Technology Review*. Last Modified March 7, 2014. Accessed April 30, 2021. https://www.technologyreview.com/2014/03/07/173756/virtual-reality-startups-look-back-to-the-future/.

Pene, Bruce. 2016. "5 Ways Virtual and Augmented Reality Is Changing Our Lives." *World Economic Forum*, July 5, 2016. Accessed April 30, 2021. https://www.weforum.org/agenda/2016/07/5-ways-virtual-and-augmented-reality-is-changing-our-lives.

Poole, Stephen. 2005. "What Zelda Did [Book Review]." *The Guardian*. Last Modified July 2, 2005. Accessed July 31, 2017. https://www.theguardian.com/books/2005/jul/02/highereducation.news.

Prindle, Drew. 2015. "New French Law Tells Consumers How Long New Appliances Will Last." Digitaltrends. Last Modified March 3, 2015. Accessed July 25, 2017. https://www.digitaltrends.com/home/france-planned-obsolescence-law/.

Rieland, Randy. 2016. "How Augmented Reality Will Change How You Buy Furniture." *Smithsonian Magazine*. Last Modified June 28, 2016. Accessed July 31, 2017. http://www.smithsonianmag.com/innovation/how-augmented-reality-will-change-how-you-buy-furniture-180959586/.

Sag, Anshel. 2017. "The Future of Virtual Reality: Mobile VR Platforms in a Battle." *Forbes*. Last Modified February 9, 2017. Accessed July 31, 2017. https://www.forbes.com/sites/moorinsights/2017/02/09/the-future-of-virtual-reality-mobile-vr-platforms-in-a-battle/#677ff1783c9d.

Sanjeev, Arvind. 2018. "Digitizing Human Emotions for Virtual Reality Applications." Last March 1, 2018. Accessed April 30, 2021. https://maker.pro/custom/tutorial/how-to-digitize-human-emotions-for-virtual-reality-applications.

Schermer, Victor L. 2014. *Meaning, Mind, and Self-Transformation: Psychoanalytic Interpretation and the Interpretation of Psychoanalysis*. London: Karnac Books.

Schoech, Dick, Javier F. Boyas, Beverly M. Black, and Nada Elias-Lambert. 2013. "Gamification for Behavior Change: Lessons from Developing a Social, Multiuser, Web-Tablet Based Prevention Game for Youths." *Journal of Technology in Human Services* 31 (3): 197–217. https://doi.org/10.1080/15228835.2013.812512.

Schreiber, Ian. 2009. "I Just Found This Blog, What Do I Do?" Game Design Concepts: An Experiment in Game Design and Teaching. Last Modified July 2, 2007. Accessed Februray 3, 2020. https://gamedesignconcepts.wordpress.com/2009/07/02/level-2-game-design-iteration-and-rapid-prototyping/.

Serino, Maeve, Kyla Cordrey, Laura McLaughlin, and Ruth L Milanaik. 2016. "Pokémon Go and Augmented Virtual Reality Games: A Cautionary Commentary for Parents and Pediatricians." *Current Opinion in Pediatrics* 28 (5): 673–77.

Sewell, Robin, Sarah Potvin, Pauline Melgoza, James Creel, Jeremy Huff, Gregory Bailey, John Bondurant, Sean Buckner, Lisa Furubotten, and Julie Mosbo Ballestro. 2019. "When a Repository Is Not Enough: Redesigning a Digital Ecosystem to Serve Scholarly Communication." *Journal of Librarianship and Scholarly Communication* 7 (1). https://doi.org/10.7710/2162-3309.2225.

Side, Wei, Ren Gang, and E. O'Neill. 2014. "Haptic and Audio Displays for Augmented Reality Tourism Applications." Paper presented at the 2014 IEEE Haptics Symposium (HAPTICS), Houston, TX. February 23–26, 2014.

Speiginer, Gheric, Blair MacIntyre, Jay Bolter, Hafez Rouzati, Amy Lambeth, Laura Levy, Laurie Baird, Maribeth Gandy, Matt Sanders, and Brian Davidson. 2015. "The Evolution of the Argon Web Framework through Its Use Creating Cultural Heritage and Community-Based Augmented Reality Applications." Paper presented at the International Conference on Human-Computer Interaction, Los Angeles, CA, August 2–7, 2015.

Stommel, Jesse. 2013. "The Digital Humanities Is about Breaking Stuff." *Digital Pedagogy Lab* (blog), September 2, 2013. Accessed April 30, 2021. https://hybridpedagogy.org/the-digital-humanities-is-about-breaking-stuff/.

Tripp, Mary. 2008. "Henry Jenkins, *Convergence Culture*." *Hyperrhiz: New Media Cultures* (5). Accessed February 3, 2020. http://hyperrhiz.io/hyperrhiz05/reviews/henry-jenkins-convergence-culture.html.

Unver, Ertu, and Andrew Taylor. 2012. "Virtual Stonehenge Reconstruction." In *Progress in Cultural Heritage Preservation: 4th International Conference, EuroMed 2012, Limassol, Cyprus, October 29–November 3, 2012, Proceedings*, edited by Marinos Ioannides, Dieter Fritsch, Johanna Leissner, Rob Davies, Fabio Remondino, and Rossella Caffo, 449–60. Berlin: Springer.

Uzwyshyn, Raymond. 2019. "Developing an Open Source Digital Scholarly Research Ecosystem: Local and Global Possibilities." Presented at the Coalition for Networked Information Fall Meeting, Washington, DC. Accessed 29 January, 2020. https://digital.library.txstate.edu/handle/10877/9081.

Vincent, James. 2018. "Hyped AR Startup Blippar Crashes into Financial Reality." The Verge, December 18, 2018. Accessed April 22, 2020. https://www.theverge.com/2018/12/18/18146069/blippar-augmented-reality-startup-administration-uk.

Wright, Holly, and Julian D. Richards. 2018. "Reflections on Collaborative Archaeology and Large-Scale Online Research Infrastructures." *Journal of Field Archaeology* 43 (suppl. 1): S60–S67.

Zarembsky, Ilya. 2013. "How Will Historians Study Video Games?" *Atlantic*. Last Modified November 29, 2013. Accessed July 31, 2017. https://www.theatlantic.com/entertainment/archive/2013/11/how-will-historians-study-video-games/281767/.

Conclusion

DWELLING, CULTURE, CARE

THE FIRST OVERALL AIM GUIDING THE WRITING OF THIS BOOK WAS TO PRO-vide reflections and observations on how to design virtual places without mind-lessly replicating actual, current, or past places. A second major aim was to reflect on those theories that offer or could be adapted to offer useful new strategic targets for the design of virtual places and to avoid common criticisms of virtual worlds: that they are lifeless and not worth revisiting. (See fig. 11.1.)

In chapter 1, "A Potted History of Virtual Reality," I suggest that most virtual reality (VR) examples (and the wider field of virtual environments) lack collabor-ative and feedback-rich place design. Virtual places have typically been designed for a single viewer, not to live within or move between, with few if any meaningful between spaces, and without a way of *platially* recording the experience.

As VR definitions have traditionally emphasized vision and head tracking, place experience was predominantly equipment and vision focused, accessed via clunky interfaces, but not creative and not additive. Rather than a universal focus on photo-realism (an important goal for many but not all virtual place simula-tions), I suggested *experiential realism*, defining categories based on an evocative experience aimed for and remembered, not on universal metrics measuring only equipment performance; there is already too much confusion of terms and cat-egories and emphasis on technical immersivity (which is very dangerous given the speed at which VR technology is changing).

Stylistically, VR is heavily indebted to science fiction with dystopic themes and settings, resistant to user interaction and personalization, and typically designed to look at a screen as a window, which has repercussions for place. Related innovations in virtual reality have been innovative but sporadic and hard, if not impossible, to maintain, preventing continual improvement, which has not been helped by indefinite market goals. VR still lacks a "killer app," but while the com-puter game industry is booming, games do not provide great examples of virtual places; they are secondary to the main purpose of creating directed, meaning-ful entertainment. The activities that "take place" in games are not permanently recorded by that place to any great degree, nor are they linked back to the culture

Figure 11.1 Copyright Eastshade Studios, http://eastshade.com/. By permission from Eastshade Studios.

associated with that place. Game achievements may change a place, but they don't mold and redefine it.

In chapter 2, "Dead, Dying, Failed Worlds," I suggest dead and dying virtual worlds may have failed for many different reasons, but one reason was that they were not cultural worlds. A lack of cultural dimensions, physical embodiment, and environmental context is readily apparent in the virtual environments most explicitly dedicated to culture: virtual museums. Why are museums so important? To educate, to peruse? To buy objects from the safety of our living rooms? To previsit? To view the development of the museum as an artifact?

Real-world museums are wonderful spectator spaces. Museums are not just static photo collections; they are ergodic and sited. We sacrifice time and effort to reach them and donate money to preserve them. They are marked by touches of inhabitation and cohabitation; they are part of the city, its memory and lifeblood. Yet most virtual museums provide no feedback of real-world presence or invisible history, no sign of care, and no sign of shared, collaborative information. If presence in VR is the sense of being there, in a virtual museum what is *being* and what is *there*?

In chapter 3, "Architecture: Places without People," I summarize famous architectural theories and argued that they were typically essentialist, difficult to merge with other theories, and usually avoided the question as to how architecture could be evaluated and by whom. Architectural theory has been straitjacketed by the silo-creating effect of essentialism. The inherent organic and communal development of architectural spaces and, by extension, urban places is far more evident in vernacular architecture, not commercial buildings. Why? Because architects cannot control the detailed changes of engaging places; they are too complex and dynamic. Place involves the directed and complicit behavior of multiple people, interacting with others in many spontaneous and unpredictable ways.

Architectural education does not typically prepare for the interaction design requirements for virtual place design. Sketches create the atmospheric equivalent of screenshots, while computer-aided design (CAD) digital models are abstractions and formal properties. CAD models are not lived in, CAD does not by itself create living places. Building information modeling (BIM) is an advancement over CAD in terms of the planning and design of buildings, but even with the recent development of historic BIM (BIM for history and heritage, deployed by organizations such as Historic England), such modeling records assets rather than the values and deeds of the people who will inhabit those assets.

What is the significance here for designers of virtual places? I believe we can be inspired by and learn from many different builders, homeowners, and architects, but the Nordic architects I mentioned, and the writings of Christopher Alexander and his colleagues, hold special relevance to the design of virtual places. They were motivated by the concern for psychologically stimulating responses to the dynamics of climate, landscape, and material. These relationships are typically missing from virtual places. We can learn from both their practical applications and, in particular, from their design philosophies: more a matrix of design principles than the rigid rule set of a specific ideology.

Architectural theory does not automatically transfer to virtual place design, and the theories I referred to can be described as old and redundant. One architectural historian also once told me that practically every architectural theory is essentialist. I suspect there is some truth to his claim, but I don't believe theories have to be so closed and static; after all, the virtual inspiration for virtual reality was allegedly an art historian and philosopher, Suzanne Langer, who was talking about artistic realms (Evenden 2016).

There is another concern here: Who designs virtual places? How do we blend and integrate real-world theories of place design to combat essentialism and prepare for changing situations, and how do we help train traditional designers of place to design for the interactive and immersive possibilities of virtual places? Architects could learn here from landscape design, concerned with changes over time, processes, and with synergies, but it is typically taught as a separate degree and less focused on sophisticated environmental design applications. A strongly related field is participatory design; we need to design not just for people but *with* people. Applied to virtual environments attempting to be engaging virtual places, we need more user-designed infill, with creative tools and a way of recording, sharing, and commemorating both their designs and their user experiences.

In chapter 4, "Theories of Place and Cyberspace," I argue that phenomenologists concentrated almost exclusively on describing the attributes of real-world places. Developing a framework for the interpretation of sensory data in virtual worlds is a task that still lies ahead of us. One could well counter that philosophers have indeed written about virtual places (and virtual worlds), but they are still in the minority (Champion 2018).

An important issue that philosophers raise again and again is that realism is needed, but VR is only a parasitical attempt at simulating the real world. I have argued strongly against this view, not because it is not (currently) true, but because it does not have to be the sole purpose of VR and, by extension, the sole purpose of virtual places. And where it is true, it also holds for real-world places: they are also parasitical, on other places.

In chapter 5, "Rats and Goosebumps: Mind, Body, and Embodiment," I suggest that the role of the mind and the body are still not fully explored in virtual place-making. Places teach us how they are used, what they signify, and how they are valued through how they are inhabited and performed inside of; how artifacts are collected, stored, and performed with inside and beside them; how they are eroded by use (or how their activities and construction erode, damage, or otherwise respond to their surroundings); and how they are demarcated in terms of the sacred and profane, informal and formal, private and public. In other words, we find out about place through people, objects, travel, environmental history, or writing and painting (cultural memory), in terms of what they *do*, how they are *organized,* and how they *affect others*, not just from their external appearance.

Virtual place design can also adopt and modify ideas from architecture in terms of embodiment. Our memory and our subconscious reactions exist precisely because we have a mind inside of a body, not despite them. Although navigation in virtual environments and keyboard interfaces have long been researched, biofeedback, body monitors, and haptics of place will be intriguing areas of development in the future.

In chapter 6, "Games Are Not Interactive Places," I outline issues in discussing interactivity and to what extent interactivity is a good or a bad goal when designing virtual places. The emphasis in this chapter is on mechanics, how they are badly understood in games, and how they could be applied to the virtual place-making and related place experiences. Game mechanics are highly relevant to the design of virtual places because they add structure, goals, variety, and meaning. However, I caution against gamification; it can diminish or underestimate the explorative joy, imaginative setting, and strategic rewards of games—plus, it does not sit well with the more contemplative features of virtual places.

In chapter 7, "Do Serious Gamers Learn from Place?," I suggest that although we learn from buildings, from MMORPG places, from games, and online social worlds, it is still not clear how we learn *through virtual places*. We learn from interacting with the overall environment, objects (artifacts), erosion through use and nearness, or from the separation and ritualization of space. This requires more study on the processes of habitation and inhabitation, with help from environmental psychology. Virtual worlds lack elastic mutability, entropic memorialization, and ergodic impactful role-play. They also develop their character in the way, as worlds, they integrate and separate distinctive places. We could further improve the richness of collaborative meaning-making in these spaces.

Chapter 7 also builds on premises developed in the preceding chapters. Virtual museums have suffered from a lack of imagination due in part to insufficient understanding of how cultural frameworks are embodied, challenging, and contested. A schema separating types of interaction, starting with virtual environments, would be helpful to designers. Discussing interactive virtual places is difficult enough, but it can be approached by discussing how we learn, in particular, the modes of interaction that help us learn *about* places, *through* places, and *from* places, culturally (and not just socially) as well as, above all, how we learn *from* each other. How do we incorporate this need and this potential into virtual places?

Gamification is dangerous here, and so too is procedural rhetoric. Neither of these concepts fully encompass the importance of sharing and collaborative learning and collective action. This world is built not only by individuals but also by society. The current weakness of virtual places to afford, include, and preserve collective learning is a serious problem.

Chapter 8, "Cultural Places," outlines traditional, new, and emerging devices, displays, and peripherals that may change, threaten, or improve the way we experience, understand, and move through space and place as well as whether the technology could have long-term cognitive, physical, and social effects. My motivation is to determine if I can communicate why I believe that culture and place are entwined concepts and why both are predicated on a concept of care. Most virtual environments lack a sense of care, a sense of dwelling, and the ability to host the collaborative creativity of human visitors.

Partly the answer to this lack is a question of time, duration, legacy, and dwelling. I see culture as what is accumulated beyond me and you. Place is also a collection and compression of diaries, made from life's contact with concrete and plaster, mud and stone. So many people are now urbanized, living apart and unaware of the land that nourishes, clothes and shelters them. We are increasingly likely to forget the ties between human culture (intangible and tangible) and place (both individually encoded spatial experiences and culturally framed realms and territories), as intimately connected.

Culture forms from the land but it also helps us frame the land, demarcate the limits of our knowledge and the impact of our endeavors, to ourselves, others, and our descendants. Yet today's knowledge is based not on our interactions with our surroundings but on the external cognitive artifacts we carry around with us: our mobile phones and their data, saved remotely to an unknown server we convince ourselves is universal, impartial, and fail-safe (called, mysteriously, given the dynamics of weather, "the cloud").

Place is in a way both nourishment and framework for culture. Culture, in turn, allows us to view and respond to how a culture preserves and evokes place.

The four-millennia-old Mesopotamian *Epic of Gilgamesh* (Keys 1998) reminds us of the connection between land and cultural knowledge:

> He who saw all, who was the foundation of the land,
> Who knew (everything), was wise in all matters.
> Gilgamesh, who saw all, who was the foundation of the land,
> Who knew (everything), was wise in all matters.

To know the land was to know in general. Culture allowed the importance and achievement of this knowledge to be passed down from generation to generation as well as to feed generations so they had the time and the resources to record their success, values, and dreams. The meaning behind the word *culture* is complex: a value, a promise, a framework, an identity (distinguishes subjects), a knowing (object), and a doing (verb). For example, and I have mentioned before, the philosopher G. W. F. Hegel said that only humans create, wear, and value medals as objects of appreciation by others, to be appreciated by others (Champion 2015). Culture not only enables this sort of complex social relationship and expression but also provides a framework by which it is both preserved and learned again, and again, and again. Many years ago, I proposed cultural presence was a way forward for evaluating virtual places designed to convey cultural knowledge, but in chapter 8, I question my theory.

Chapter 9, "Evaluating Sense of Place, Virtual Places, and Virtual Worlds," summarizes pertinent human-computer interface guidelines, and heuristics for the design of usable, useful, and meaningful virtual places. However, the evaluation of virtual places is problematic not only because of the diffuse and sometimes ephemeral nature of places, and the restricted or fantastical way they are designed and experienced as virtual places, but also due to the wide variety of intentions and expected uses of the general public.

I suggested that evaluation (and results learned from that evaluation) should be built back into the experience of the virtual place itself. Why evaluate and learn from the evaluation but not make what is learned available to the participants through that experience?

My challenge to evaluators of virtual places is this: to what extent have your evaluations and observations contributed directly to the design of virtual worlds and virtual places themselves? If I could suggest one takeaway for this chapter, it would be to build the evaluation and the feedback from that evaluation into the virtual place itself and the learning of the people who visit and inhabit it. This world is made up of testing, results, and feedback. Virtual places typically lack these features. Most critically, who judges whether the virtual place was successful?

In chapter 10, "Place-Making Interfaces and Platforms," I suggest that augmented reality will increasingly dominate VR, and while overly convergent (as in, walled garden) software platforms will still be a problem, consumer component–based VR technology shows great promise; however, we need to further improve the reusability and reconfiguration of components so that they run on standard and extendible software and a wider range of devices, with dynamic Linked Open Data tying them to the real world. VR is too closed.

Current computer hardware and software are limited, expensive, and in some ways too crude to fully and richly simulate the complexities and details of a place. I agree, but I stress the way we remember and respond to place can be evoked by certain expressive (even dramatic) stimuli, not just by the level of detail or by overpowering technical complexity, but also in the way we can *share* our experiences of place, in that place. Place stores memories and experiences, but it is also shaped by how it stores those memories and experiences. And the development of place requires time and the expression *of* time. We continually forget how we observe changes in the world around us and how we can tell they occurred. Conveying time as the process and measure of change in virtual places is not as simple as it might seem.

Virtual places require a sacrifice of time, diversion of care, and attention away from real people and real places, but a focus on abstractions may eventually numb us to the subtlety of the real world or install in us default responses out of step with our complex society and ever-changing world. Despite common portrayals of virtual places as an individual, revelatory experience, how we experience a place and *experience the experience of place* is far more social and collaborative than we might initially think. Our experience *of* place is shared *via* place and *with* others.

I have argued that dwelling, the passing on of knowledge across time and generations, and the ability to care are important elements of virtual places. We can turn these attributes into three simple questions to determine the *placeness* of a virtual place. In this virtual place, can we dwell? Does it help us sense, create, and convey uniquely situated cultural knowledge over large periods? Can this environment help us care for this cultural knowledge and express that care with others?

References

Champion, Erik. 2015. *Critical Gaming: Interactive History and Virtual Heritage.* Edited by Marilyn Deegan, Lorna Hughes, Andrew Prescott, and Harold Short. Digital Research in the Arts and Humanities, edited by Dymphna Evans. Surrey, UK: Ashgate.

———, ed. 2018. *The Phenomenology of Real and Virtual Places.* Routledge Studies in Contemporary Philosophy. New York: Routledge.

Evenden, Ian. 2016. "The History of Virtual Reality: Step Back in Time to See How Art Fused with Cutting-Edge VR Technology to Create Entire Worlds. . . ." *Science Focus* (blog), March 17, 2016. Accessed April 17, 2021. https://www.sciencefocus.com/future -technology/the-history-of-virtual-reality/.

Keys, David. 1998. "First Lines of Oldest Epic Poem Found." *Independent*, November 16, 1998. Accessed April 27, 2021. https://www.independent.co.uk/news/first-lines-of-oldest -epic-poem-found-1185270.html.

GLOSSARY

artificial intelligence (AI): "the ability of a computer or other machine to perform those activities that are normally thought to require intelligence" (American Heritage® Dictionary of the English Language 2021).

apophenia: the player's perception of meaning, events, or relationships in a computer game not intended by the game designer (after Tynan Sylvester).

augmented reality (AR): Brian Jackson (2015) explains AR as follows: "The computer uses sensors and algorithms to determine the position and orientation of a camera. AR technology then renders the 3D graphics as they would appear from the viewpoint of the camera, superimposing the computer-generated images over a user's view of the real world." I define it as a calculation of real-world data to superimpose a digital simulation onto a camera-screen or see-through display showing the real-world or a provision of nonvisual data to the participant based on their view or position in relation to the real world.

biofeedback: represents a real-time two-way feedback loop between the machine and the user. The user reacts to an action initiated by the system, and the system can then react based on the participants' physical/emotional reaction (and so forth).

causal mechanics: the game mechanics of a virtual world that appear to dictate cause and effect from the player's perspective or the designed mechanics that specify cause and effect from the designer's perspective.

computer game: an engaging challenge that offers up the possibility of temporary or permanent tactical resolution without harmful outcomes to the real-world situation of the participant.

CRPG: computer role-playing game.

cultural presence: a visitor's overall subjective impression when visiting a virtual environment that people with a different cultural perspective occupy or have occupied as a place. Such a definition suggests that cultural presence is not just a feeling of being there but also a sense of being in a foreign time or not-so-well understood place.

cultural significance: following the Burra Charter 2013 (Australia ICOMOS Incorporated 2013): "Cultural significance means aesthetic, historic, scientific, social or spiritual value for past, present or future generations. Cultural significance is embodied in the place itself, its fabric, setting, use, associations, meanings, records, related places and related objects."

cyberplace: coined by Barry Wellman (2001), cyberplace is cyberspace but with community ties (participants feel a strong interpersonal sense of belonging in virtual communities).

cyberspace: various definitions are summarized in this book, but it sometimes is equated with hyperspace and with digital places available via the internet. Or, more broadly, it is used to describe the entire internet.

digital history: can be described as the visualization of historical resources using digital technology.

Dungeons & Dragons (D&D): fantasy tabletop role-playing game, published in 1974 by Tactical Studies Rules, Incorporated. Players create their character, explore dungeons, fight dragons and other creatures, and pick up loot. Apart from the board game, there were simple online games and "Choose Your Own Adventure" interactive fiction books (the reader selects an option and goes to that page) using this *D&D* theme.

encultured physicality: spatial demarcations of roles, statuses, rituals, laws of physics, constraints of climate and geography, and so on.

fMRI (functional magnetic resonance imaging): a safe, noninvasive way of mapping brain activity by detecting changes associated with blood flow.

game-based historical learning: the focused use of real-time rendering engines, game editors, game platforms, game peripherals, and/or game-style interaction metaphors to help the public enhance their awareness of historical issues and heritage sites. Generally, the term implies that the virtual environment experience is best achieved by playing, but that what is learned through such game play is designed to be perceived as being culturally or scientifically significant and authentic. This technology may also help scientists communicate, collaborate with other players, or otherwise evaluate various hypotheses on the validity, construction, significance, use, maintenance, or disappearance of historical and heritage-based sites, artifacts, and cultural beliefs.

gamification: applying game design principles and elements to non-game-orientated material. Note: More definitions are covered in this book.

head-mounted display (HMD): a dual-digital display that sits on the head; typically the display changes according to the movement of the user's head, and the display generally supports stereoscopic imagery (affording an illusion of spatial depth). Some HMD displays are see-through, therefore providing augmented reality.

hermeneutic richness: the depth of interpretation available to understanding oneself or others through artifacts and other cultural remains. As a defining feature of a virtual world, it refers to the rich support or fecundity of the virtual world for interpretation and creativity (see also worldfilledness).

human-computer interaction (HCI): a field studying the interaction between humans and computing devices.

intangible heritage: UNESCO (2003) defines this as follows: "The 'intangible cultural heritage' means the practices, representations, expressions, knowledge, skills—as well as the instruments, objects, artefacts [artifacts] and cultural spaces associated therewith—that communities, groups and, in some cases, individuals recognize as part of their cultural heritage."

interactive history: a shortened form of the more unwieldy phrase "interactive digital history," it can be seen as the development of digital resources that teaches historical learning through interactive media.

intercorporeality: stresses the role of social actors who understand each other through observing their body language and other physical expressions.

machinima: the practice or technique of producing animated films by using computer game engines.

mimesis: the representation or portrayal of action and behavior that together form a dramatic enactment.

mixed reality (MR): Paul Milgram and Fumio Kishino (1994) define it as "a particular subclass of VR related technologies that involve the merging of real and virtual worlds."

MMORPG: an online real-time role-playing game that is played by a very large number of people. Also known as massively multiplayer online role-playing games.

mod: many computer games now come with editors that allow users to modify the game or import their "levels," three-dimensional assets, characters, or scripts. These new or modified game levels are called mods.

multimodality (and here we can distinguish between how something is learned, not what the learning content is made of): several modes of expression combined to communicate.

narrative: a succession of events meaningfully experienced, told, or recalled.

NPC: a character in games not controlled by a player—usually an acronym for nonplaying character or nonplayable character.

place: place and virtual place are given various definitions in this book and are too nuanced to define in one sentence.

platial richness: the virtual world contains an engaging collection and intersection of places full of interactive possibilities (see also worldfulness).

procedural rhetoric: Ian Bogost (2007): "a practice of using processes persuasively."

serious games: serious games are games designed to train or educate users. Related terms are game-based learning, edutainment, and eduventures.

sociability: visitation, uniqueness, enculturation and acculturation, inhabitation, creativity, memetic output (how words, images, gestures, and concepts are spread and contaminate discourse and behavior, and how they are diffused and integrated into social activities and cultures), and alterity (encountering others with differing forms of behaviors, desires, and intentions).

social embeddedness: the extent to which a virtual world provides for influential, identity-forming, but potentially flexible social roles (see also worldliness).

taskscape: following Tim Ingold (1993), how landscapes and places emerge through the activities of people who dwell there.

virtual environment: according to John Wann and Mark Mon-Williams (1996, 833), "a Virtual Environment (VE) is a representation that capitalizes upon natural aspects of human perception by extending visual information in three spatial dimensions."

virtual heritage: the attempt to convey not just the appearance but also the meaning and significance of cultural artifacts and the associated social agency that designed and used them through the use of interactive and immersive digital media.

virtual reality (VR): according to Henry E. Lowood (2018), "the use of computer modeling and simulation that enables a person to interact with an artificial three-dimensional (3-D) visual or another sensory environment. VR applications immerse the user in a computer-generated environment that simulates reality through the use of interactive devices, which send and receive information and are worn as goggles, headsets, gloves, or body suits."

visualization: the process of representing information visually and nonvisually, with the aid of computer technologies.

Wi-Fi: a family of wireless networking technologies.

worldfilledness: the digital environment allows for different ways of *doing* a multitude of things; it is interactively rich and layered.

worldfulness: the hermeneutical extent to which the virtual environment or game can store, display, and retrieve information on the encounters of people in places

worldliness: the range of strategies available to players for choosing social roles to improve their standing and success in a virtual world.

References

American Heritage® Dictionary of the English Language. 2021. "Artificial Intelligence." Accessed April 15, 2021. https://www.thefreedictionary.com/Artificial+intelligences.

Australia ICOMOS Incorporated International Council on Monuments and Sites. 2013. *The Burra Charter: The Australia Icomos Charter for Places of Cultural Significance (2013)*. ICOMOS. Accessed May 20, 2021. http://australia.icomos.org/wp-content/uploads /The-Burra-Charter-2013-Adopted-31.10.2013.pdf.

Bogost, Ian. 2007. *Persuasive Games: The Expressive Power of Videogames*. Cambridge, MA: MIT Press.

Ingold, Tim. 1993. "The Temporality of the Landscape." *World Archaeology* 25 (2): 152–74. https://doi.org/10.1080/00438243.1993.9980235.

Jackson, Brian. 2015. "What Is Virtual Reality? [Definition and Examples]." *AR Blog: Augmented Reality Marketing Resources, Trends, Videos and Case Studies*. *MARXENT*, June 24, 2015. Accessed May 20, 2021. http://www.marxentlabs.com /what-is-virtual-reality-definition-and-examples/.

Lowood, Henry E. 2018. "Virtual Reality." *Encyclopædia Britannic*. Last Modified November 16, 2018. Accessed November 20. https://www.britannica.com/technology /virtual-reality.

Milgram, Paul, and Fumio Kishino. 1994. "A Taxonomy of Mixed Reality Visual Displays." *IEICE TRANSACTIONS on Information and Systems* 77 (12): 1321–29.

UNESCO. 2003. *Convention for the Safeguarding of the Intangible Cultural Heritage*. Paris: UNESCO.

Wann, John, and Mark Mon-Williams. 1996. "What Does Virtual Reality NEED?: Human Factors Issues in the Design of Three-Dimensional Computer Environments." *International Journal of Human-Computer Studies* 44 (6): 829–47.

Wellman, Barry. 2001. "Physical Place and Cyberplace: The Rise of Personalized Networking." *International Journal of Urban and Regional Research* 25 (2): 227–52.

INDEX

ERIK MALCOLM CHAMPION is Honorary Professor at the Centre for Digital Humanities Research at Australian National University, Canberra; Honorary Research Fellow at the University of Western Australia; and Emeritus Professor, Curtin University. He is author of *Organic Design in Twentieth-Century Nordic Architecture*; *Critical Gaming: Interactive History and Virtual Heritage*; and *Playing with the Past*. He is editor of *The Phenomenology of Real and Virtual Places*; *Game Mods: Design, Theory and Criticism*; and (with Agiatis Benardou, Costis Dallas, and Lorna Hughes) *Cultural Heritage Infrastructures in Digital Humanities*.

Lightning Source UK Ltd.
Milton Keynes UK
UKHW011036291021
393031UK00001B/5

9 780253 058348